UNWELCOME

Sexual Harassment, Sexual Discrimination,
Sexual Assault, and Rape in the Canadian Forces

Captain Dawn Ottman

UNWELCOME

Sexual Harassment, Sexual Discrimination,
Sexual Assault, and Rape in the Canadian Forces

Captain Dawn Ottman

CITI OF
BOOKS

CITIOFBOOKS, INC.
3736 Eubank NE Suite A1
Albuquerque, NM 87111-3579
www.citiofbooks.com
Hotline: 1 (877) 389-2759
Fax: 1 (505) 930-7244

Ordering Information:

Quantity sales. Special discounts are available on quantity purchases by corporations, associations, and others. For details, contact the publisher at the address above.

Printed in the United States of America.

ISBN-13:   Paperback   979-8-89391-751-2
                eBook   979-8-89391-752-9

Library of Congress Control Number: 2025912265

TO MY HUSBAND, Bill; my son Adam, my daughter Tracy, and my much missed best friend, Mimi. Thank you all for your love and unwavering support.

To Benz my PTSD dog, and best friend: the special bond between a service dog and a handler is so very unique. What a blessing he is in my life.

To my dear military buddies: Karen, Jayne, Alice, Ann, and Natalie, and the many other gal pals that I served with. You will always be a special part of who I am. None of you fully understands the difference you've made in my life.

Contents

Cabbage Town
Toronto, Ontario (1967)

Struggle is defined by many means and I am no stranger to adversity. As a child growing up in Toronto's Regent Park district – often dubbed 'Cabbage Town' and comparable to "the Projects" in the Bronx of New York City – I thought that I knew what it meant to suffer. Yet, I can only laugh when I reflect on that time fraught with abject poverty and abuse on the streets; what would have been a nightmare for many was just the starting gate of my life.

We all had to learn the way of the street lest others took advantage of us, and there was always an abundance of punks willing to gut you out of pride or simply out of boredom. As it was with my most memorable adversary of the time was Berta Torres* – a sixteen-year-old girl who found enjoyment from beating on younger children.

I was only nine when Berta and her posse were at their worst, and my lesser age only made me more of a target. Returning from school was sometimes a game of cat and mouse. I would need to decide whether it was a day to run or a day to stay and fight. Whenever my younger sister was with me, it was always a day to stand up to the bunch while she skirted for home.

I learned how to run – and run fast – at a young age. The 'Projects'-like community where I grew up was a dog-eat-dog community and I was beaten up more times than I can remember. I also returned many of these beatings. When we finally moved out of Regent Park, my mother said one thing to me…"Dede, stop fighting!"

Most of these encounters ended with me being bloody and bruised, but it preoccupied them from hitting my sister. My mother implored me never to fight, but I have always been prideful, maybe too much so, and there was my conscience to deal with as I would never have forgiven myself if another was hurt from a lack of action on my part. I took the beatings in stride, often giving as good as I got, and wore my bruises as a rite of passage.

My efforts paid off in time as those who I had protected eventually grew stronger and soon had my back (or what I later in the military called my "six"). When my younger sister was one of those, I knew that I was in good hands. This was proven on a troublesome day when Berta and her gang snuck up on my sister and I – blocking off any hope of us dashing away. As was the norm, they went for me, and I deflected their shoves and punches. However, amidst the turmoil, my sister snuck back from the scrap and – with the entirety of her might – kicked Berta in her rear!

An uncharacteristic yelp rose from Berta. As quickly as she had struck, my sister disappeared from the scene – running for home. Berta's pack was left dumbfounded, and unable to stop myself, I laughed out loud. Naturally, she and her friends exacted revenge, but as I took the beating from that gang, I was unable to remove the smirk from my face.

As my day-to-day was a struggle, I often dreamed of a life other than the one I had… My mother was a single parent and did not have the means to afford even furniture. Every week, we'd retrieve cardboard boxes from the back of a grocery store, use them as make-shift tables for our daily meal of Kraft Dinner. These were the days before lunches or breakfasts were provided at school. We would then unfold the boxes to make beds to insulate us from the floor at night.

To counter my dreary surroundings, I would visit the local library and loan Harlequin romance novels – allowing me to read of perfect and romantic worlds far apart from my own. I became a dreamer and longed for a life where anything was a possibility. I excelled in school – Mathematics being my forte – but I quickly grew bored with the curriculum.

In high school, I worked part-time at a bakery and the 4am morning and low pay were hardly inspiring. So, when I was given the chance to enter the workforce to financially help my mother, I jumped at the chance to make some "real money!" I left school at the end of the eleventh grade and I began work as a clerk. Within six months, my family's financial situation grew better and that's when I moved out.

I was seventeen.

Preface

This is the story of my career in the Canadian Forces. A career that spanned 20 years. It is the story of the obstacles to career success for women who serve Canada.

I joined the Canadian Armed Forces as a Private in 1978 and retired as a Captain in 1995. During my military service of almost 20 years, I would serve for eight years in the ranks before attending Canada's military academy, Royal Military College. In 1995, I retired under the Force Reduction Plan.

These were challenging times for a woman in uniform and I had many varied experiences as a woman in a man's military. My career in the military had its good times and its tough times. There were wonderful and fun times, which I am grateful for, but there was also gender discrimination and I am justifiable angry at the shameful way I was treated.

As one of the first females in the technical trades, gender discrimination was painful and it toughened me up. As an instructor in command of men, I was given the nickname, "the Dragon Lady." As one of the first women at a Royal Military College (RMC), I faced challenges and moral dilemmas not faced by my male counterparts. And, after graduation while in a leadership role as a woman Air Force engineering Officer I faced my most severe gender-based discrimination.

At a July 30, 2000 Press Conference held by my last Commanding Officer who was suing the Department of National Defence for three million dollars, a reporter asked the question, "So, you're saying that she's [that would be me] made charges of sexual harassment against somebody high up in the military who's now being protected?"

To which my ex-CO answered, "Correct, correct."

Then asked, "Aren't you trying to tell us, without giving any names or saying it directly, that you think that somebody who stepped in and stopped your complaint from being properly dealt with, that that person was somehow mixed up in what happened previously with Captain Lavigne...."

To which, my ex-CO replied, "Absolutely, absolutely." My last Commanding Officer was saying that the military was protecting something and he was right. They were trying to keep secret the facts regarding a case of sexual misconduct that involved me.

Although I remember many happy times in my military career, I also remember how I often felt unwelcome as a technician, at Royal Military College, as an engineer in the Communications & Electronics Branch and especially as an Officer. I have used many people's real names, but where I have used a pseudonym –for privacy or legal reasons – I have indicated that with an asterisk.

In 1995, I was raped by one of my fellow officers. Soon afterwards, I got the heck out of Dodge (spelt "C A N A D A"). I moved to the USA seeking sanctuary and that's exactly what I found. I was diagnosed with a stress disorder, anxiety, depression, etc. I have been treated via group therapy (at a Rape Crises Center), individual therapy, medication, and EMDR. And, although I have not let this criminal event in my military life define me, I acknowledge the crimes against me.

As a result of attending a VTP in 2014, I feel less ashamed of my demons and I have learned that my struggles with them have earned me respect and admiration. It was not what I expected. Now, after decades of hiding the events that cause my nightmares, I have come to realize that in order to right these wrongs, I must speak up.

I only recently found my voice but the results have been worth it. In an August, 2015, VAC decision, the Veteran's Affairs Canada granted me benefits based on the following ruling: "Post Traumatic Stress Disorder brought on by sexual harassment and assaults during military service."

To this day, I feel the effects. I continues to have trust issues and challenges with interpersonal relationships, I am quick to anger and I still have some pretty disturbing nightmares. From that day until this, I feel panic as I cross the 49th Parallel into Canada and that makes it difficult to visit my family back home. I learned this and now expect this feeling. I have crossed the 49th Parallel a few times: mostly to attend Remembrance Ceremonies each November 11th and once I returned to RMC to attend a Reunion.

I have made a good life for myself in the USA and I am blessed to have a loving husband, son and daughter who have stood by me through my challenges with mental illness. I will be eternally grateful. Without their support, I would be a statistic: another suicide caused because of PTSD.

Prologue
TO SERVE CANADA

Women who join the Canadian Forces do so to serve their country and I was one of these women. I love Canada. I love her so much. And I am idealistic: I was willing to give my life for her.

Women who serve in the Canadian Forces are heroes! We intended to serve and not to be served up. This book is filled with the memories of a woman soldier who served the Canadian military for almost 20 years.

Filled with determination, I ventured down a path that would have made a real-life hero out of me. Women soldiers are courageous femmes who are part of a world where the odds are stacked against them.

I knew I was entering a world dominated by men and in the Canadian Forces, there is a strong push for everyone to conform and we women soldiers conformed as well. We wanted to be part of this wonderful military family. Some of us wanted this feeling so badly that we conformed to much as we struggled to be "one of the guys" and in so doing, we lost ourselves.

In the military, the ratio of women to men can be attractive to some. "Like shooting fish in a barrel," my sister once said to me. Yet, I viewed the guys the same as if I was not in the military. In fact, I didn't think about the guys at all…..they were soldiers just like us.

Not surprisingly, all soldiers needed to be fit. When visiting Royal Military College for my graduation, my sister was mesmerized and exclaimed, "I can't believe how many nice asses there are around here." Until that moment, I hadn't noticed.

I'm sure that the advantage of the ratio difference between men and women soldiers was a benefit in that there were more men to choose from and in that you really got to know a person's character when you train with them. It was clear to me that if my sister had joined the Canadian Forces, it would have been to have a good time! She would have been one of the few women who join but never seems to last long when the real work began. For the rest of us, this ratio of men to women was not enough of a reason to put our lives on the line in service to our country.

Life is not fair! And, it is unfair that our brothers-in-arms only have one enemy when we have two: the second being those family members: that is, our brothers-in-arms. Sexual assault is ugly and yet it is acceptable in the military. On Civie Street, it is illegal yet in the Canadian Forces, it is swept under the carpet as a blind eye is turned away. Yet, we women did not join the military to be assaulted and raped. We joined to serve our country and NOT to be served up!

Why is that so hard to understand?

The indignity of such assaults is overwhelming. Yet, where do we turn for help when we are assaulted? There is nowhere to turn. To add insult to grievous injury, we knew that if we reported an assault, we would be perceived as "the problem" and not our attacker.

So, I kept quiet. My spirit was continually beaten and bruised, and I was brought to the lowest levels of my life when I should have been soaring. To write about these events has taken courage and it is not my intent to push others aside, but to claim my place on my own terms. I knew it was not acceptable to keep quiet but I had nowhere to turn. So, today, I have written this book to regain my personal dignity and restore my sense of self….that is, my self-esteem.

In 1978, I joined the Canadian Forces as a Private and quickly rose to the officer ranks. I am Canada's first female space scientist – a title I achieved by attending one of Canada's most prestigious institutes, the Royal Military College of Canada, after proving my merit and worth throughout eight years in the Ranks of the Canadian Forces.

Yet, it was difficult to feel proud of my achievements during this time as I was berated with harassment that would only grow fiercer as time passed. These personal attacks – based on a factor as uncontrollable as my gender – eventually chased me from my dreams and even my own country.

I resigned that my experiences with sexual misconduct in the Canadian Forces was little more than a series of unfortunate encounters, but I have since realized the situation did not end with me; it remains an issue that runs rampant through one of Canada's proudest entities. It was at the moment of this realization that I returned to my memories and catalogued them with the aim of giving solidarity to the females of the Canadian military and letting the world know of the crimes made against us yearly.

During my reflection, I remembered that my experiences were not always troubling ones and that I enjoyed the life of the military and I was good at what I did. I was elevated to the officer ranks based on my abilities and demonstrated them time and time again when I was in charge. Those in my ranks respected me. I could have travelled that path to military stardom, yet, the crushing, negative memories continually remind me of why I could no longer do that, and any semblance of pride in these achievements washes away.

For me, Canada was no longer safe and what allies I believed I had, I no longer trusted. I felt forced to leave my home and remember that I am unwelcome even in my own country because of my gender. I wish that I could say this was the worst that I had to endure, but this situation that drove me from the home I fought tirelessly to protect is just one of the many that plague my thoughts and dreams to this day. It has a title: PTSD.

Each memory brews a fiercer anger in my core – boiling me to near fury – until my mind stumbles upon the suppressed memory that makes me feel little more than emptiness: The day I was a victim of friendly fire… The day I was raped by a fellow officer in the Canadian Forces. I have made the most of my life and celebrate countless achievements, but there is no mistaking this blight on my soul.

Rape does strange things to one's psych. It makes the victim feel guilty and it is this feeling of guilt that kept me quiet so very long. But I have found my voice and I will no longer live in the shadow of fear. I hope my memories will assure other women affected by resentment, cruelty, and bigotry that they are not alone – that together, we can bring these wrongs to light.

So it is that I have written about my military career. I have written the truth because sexual misconduct in the Canadian Forces has not changed since I left. As proof, I offer Madame Deschamps' Report on

Sexual Misconduct in the Canadian Forces. For me, it was like reading the Bible: filled with many truths! Madame Deschamps, a former Supreme Court Justice, was asked by DND to investigate sexual misconduct in the Canadian Forces after DND publicly denied that a problem existed.

In her report, Madame Deschamps courageously brings the injustices faced by our women soldiers to light. Today, I have emerged from the shadows....the shadows of secrecy and the perception that if I said anything to anybody, I was simply being disloyal. Disloyal to my country, disloyal to the Canadian Forces, and disloyal to my C&E Branch.

When I first found my voice, I made an application for veteran's benefits based on the disabling effects of PTSD. In August of 2015, Veteran's Affairs Canada (VAC) awarded me disability benefits based on "PTSD induced by sexual harassment and assaults during my military service."

This is a precedent setting decision according to the Canadian Legion. Again, I have achieved another first. Within a week of the decision, and even before I'd received the paperwork from the VAC, a representative of the Canadian Legion contacted me and asked my permission to use the decision in my VAC case to help other pending VAC applications by Canadian Forces service women (past and present) claiming sexual misconduct.

The Legion was concerned for me that if my VAC case was used that the details of my case would become public but as I listened I learned that there were many pending cases and so I agreed. I will no longer hide what happened.

I did not deserve to be raped.....
No one does!

I did not deserve to be sexually assaulted.....
No one does!

I did not deserve to be sexually harassed......
No one does!

The fact that senior officers in the Canadian Forces believe this is okay haunts me as it should haunt every Canadian. If we cannot get the Canadian Forces to see the wrong in this, then the male soldiers of our military will continue to behave in this way.

I decided to help more than simply saying yes to the Legion to use my case for other active and previously serving military women. After studying Madame Deschamps report, I took action. Although in its infancy, a new organization has sprung up. This new organization is called CanMW (Canadian Military Women) and it is independent of DND yet it supports women soldiers victimized by sexual misconduct in the Canadian Forces. In addition, it is mandated to work towards killing the cancer of sexual misconduct in the military. At a time for the Canadian Forces and the Department of National Defence to act differently, it is an organization whose time has come. The past methods used by the CF and DND in dealing with rape of their woman soldiers by their brothers-in-arms is not acceptable. And, I can, and will, do something about it.

For starters, I will no longer keep quiet to protect the reputation of the Canadian Forces. I feel capable of writing and that's exactly what I am doing.

Why?

Because I have a duty to do so.

My goal is to help military women by telling my story and in that way, guide them. I hope and pray it will help other women soldiers deal with sexual harassment, sexual discrimination, sexual assault and rape in the military. For them, I want to let them know that they are not alone. For me, keeping quiet has not helped and sadly, mine was not an isolated incident.

PART ONE: As an Officer

Chapter One: Royal Military College
KINGSTON, ONTARIO (1987-1991)

I loved going to RMC! It made me feel like I was a part of something greater than myself. It is because I loved being in uniform that when I was accepted into the UTPM program and asked to pick three universities I'd like to attend, my choices were: RMC, RMC, and RMC!

With my application for UTPM, I was required to submit acceptances to three civilian universities but my heart's desire was to go to RMC. In so many ways, RMC is unlike civilian universities. For instance, they do not provide conditional acceptances....you're either in or not!

I had to wait. But, once accepted into the UTPM program, and although advised against making the three choices I did, I knew where I wanted to study. I was in the military and in the military I wanted to stay. So, I could see no other choice. Still, when I heard that RMC had accepted me, I was over the top overjoyed.

In my first year, as in the three following years, I worked hard at my academics. By the end of the year, I learned that I had won an academic prize: "Top Student in 1st Year Chemistry." Ironic, I thought!

It didn't bother me much when I heard the story of how a previous RMC Commandant had called the student body to a meeting and in his speech, he'd explained to them that women were coming to RMC and although he didn't like it, he couldn't stop them. He spoke about how his hand was being forced by Ottawa.

Great! Such "leadership!" His behaviour would be adopted by these young impressionable cadets and I wonder if he knew just how tough he was making it for us. It was obvious that he didn't think we women were good enough.

Still, I wasn't overly worried. I'd made it as a technician when these trades were first opened up to women. How hard could this be, I asked myself. I was foolishly idealistic when I figured that change is always difficult but that we women would prove our worth and there would be no problem.

Years later, one of the cadets at that meeting would be my Commanding Officer and he would drive me out of the Canadian Forces, but not before attempting to ruin my military record. He hated women and he blamed me personally for ruining his college. I've heard RMC referred to as an "asshole amplifier" but didn't truly know anyone that fit that description until this guy.

Otter Squadron (the UTPMs) was a large squadron and I was the only woman in the squadron who was doing engineering. I believe this made me a target because one day, after receiving the results of a Math quiz, a fellow squadron member became so enraged that I had done better than him, that he grabbed my arm and dragged down the hallway and back to the classroom. It was humiliating as I struggled unsuccessfully to free myself from his grip on my arm and as the young Cadets watched the shenanigans.

Once back at the classroom, my fellow squadron member pulled me down a series of steps to the front of the class and placed me in front of the professor. He was much stronger physically than me (but, obviously, not mentally!) and I had been unable to break his grip on my arm. When the Professor confirmed my mark on the quiz, this fellow told the Professor that I MUST have cheated if I got a better mark than him! He was so angry that he was yelling at the Professor.

Two things happened after that. First, the Professor told this UTPM that I couldn't have cheated as I had gotten the highest mark on the quiz. With this information, he released me and stomped up the stairs and away....with the other UTPMs following closely behind him. What a jerk, I thought as the Professor and I just looked at each other dumbfounded.

The second thing that happened was that right after I left the classroom, I headed straight for the Physics Department and approached one of our Physics professors who also happened to be the RMC Karate Team instructor. I had taken Karate before as a civie but obviously not for long enough as I hadn't been able to release myself from this UTPMs strong grip on my arm.

My intent was to ask the Karate Team instructor how I could have broken the hold on my arm. It had been humiliating to be dragged down a hallway in front of the young RMC cadets in such a blatant caveman fashion. The professor said he'd show me if I'd join the RMC Karate Team and so began my athletic team participation. I went on to win a gold medal in sparring and a silver medal in forms during a competition again our sister college, West Point Academy, but most important to me, I learned how to never again let anyone treat me the way this guy had.

At RMC, we had some quirky professors, from a Computer Science professor who used to scratch his balls on the edge of the table at the front of the class (yes, I am serious) to a professor who showed up in class with a baby squirrel in his shirt. We'd always thought he was a bit "squirrely" but now we was certain. It's hard to decide which incident was worse except that the short Computer Engineering Professor would do his dirty regularly and we would laugh heartily as he placed himself above the corner of the table at the front of the classroom and move his torso back and forth to scratch his itch. Gotta give it to him….he was ballsy!

My first summer was spent doing French language training as had all the other Anglophones at RMC. Being proficient in both of Canada's official languages was not only a want it was a necessity to graduating RMC. Without a proficiency in French, RMC would not allow us to graduate. Meanwhile, the Francophones went away to do a summer of on the job training at bases throughout Canada.

It is when these guys returned that I noticed a distinct change in their attitudes towards women cadets. A more pronounced effect happened early in my third year after the rest of the cadets had completed a summer of on the job training at a military base. The cadet cadre's attitude toward women cadets had clearly changed.

This shift in attitude was not a small change. It was huge! I now believe it was from being "integrated" into the dislike of women in uniform that is prevalent in the Canadian Forces.

When the cadets arrive at RMC right out of high school they were respectful of the women cadets, but after spending a summer in the field at military postings, their attitude was the opposite; that is they were not only disrespectful, they were very disrespectful.

This bothered me then as it does now. This wasn't just one or two of the cadets….this was so prevalent, it was tangible. Their attitudes towards women had changed…..sadly! When I first got to RMC, I was impressed with the comradery between the cadets and I thought this was the way it was in the Officer Corp but I was wrong. These kids coming from various high schools across the country all had a respect for one another and were gender unbiased. So, what changed them? I believe it was their exposure to the attitude towards military women prevalent in the Canadian Forces.

Other than academic and athletic classes, we also had drill classes. And it is from a drill class that I gained a special memory that always brings a smile to my face. One day, we were out on the parade square in front of the impressive administrative buildings of the college practicing for a major parade. RMC had nine squadrons and with these nine platoons on the parade square, more than 1,000 cadets were present and it was an impressive site! All nine squadrons were on the parade square that morning and I was in my 2nd year at RMC and a member of Otter Squadron (that is, No. 9 Platoon). Being tall, I was in the front row.

Not a lot of people know that on the parade square there is a faint line that stretches from one end of the square to the other. In charge of us that day was a long-in-the-tooth Sgt-Major. He marched straight and tall and tucked under his arm he carried a pace stick. His voice boomed out at us barking orders. This Sgt-Major reminds me of a television character: "Gibbs" on that TV show, NCIS.

On this particular day, while we were halted and dressing off, I became a source of frustration but also information for this long-in-the-tooth Sgt-Major. We'd just been marched around and we were dressing off. We were dressing off using this line across the parade square (that was not visible to spectators) but the student body knew was there. Only the front rank used this line as a reference, while the middle and rear ranks dressed off to us. I say "us" because I was in the front rank.

As the 4th "man" of Number 9 Platoon, I was expected to place my toes on the line when the command "Right Dress" was given. Once we had stopped shuffling about getting into position, the Sgt-Major who was out in front of the troops made a sharp turn and he marched down to the beginning of the line of the front rank where he wheeled into position. He halted and immediately began barking out orders to cadets to fix the line made up by the front rank into a straight line of cadets. I heard orders such as, "5th man, Number 3 Platoon….Move up" and "Number 8 man, 7 Platoon….Move back" but when I heard "Number 4 man, 9 Platoon…Toe the line" I knew he was speaking to me.

I shuffled forward and almost immediately heard his voice again. "Number 4 man, 9 Platoon ….TOE THE LINE!" Okay, I thought…. that didn't work…..so I shuffled back. Impatient with my unsuccessful efforts to dress off properly, the Sgt Major headed my way. With my head turned to the right in accordance with the Right Dress command, I saw him coming and my heart stopped as I watched him march purposefully past first 1 Platoon, and then 2 Platoon and 3 Platoon and 4 Platoon and 5 Platoon and 6 Platoon and 7 Platoon. As he got closer I could hear his hard footfalls. He marched past 8 Platoon and then he marched right up to 9 Platoon and wheeled to face me. With a sharp halt he stopped directly in front of me. He was pissed.

With his face just inches from mine, he shouted, "What is your problem? I said, TOE THE LINE!" I was still in the Right Dress pose of looking sideways when I averted my eyes and looked down at my chest and painfully explained, "I can't see it."

Without turning my head back forward and then bending forward to look past my boobs, I could not see the line! I was not that well-endowed but this was a problem faced by every woman in uniform. The Sgt-Major's face reddened like a cooked lobster and without another word, he turned and marched away.

The following week, I bumped into the Sgt-Major in the hallways of Mackenzie Hall and he stopped me. He then told me that I got him! With over 30 years in the military, he'd never been speechless on a parade square until that day. It was a first for him, he told me and I still can't help but smile whenever I remember it. It was just one of those things. We women are built differently.....differences that men usually appreciate....but not in this case!

While at RMC, I was working hard and studying hard. Classes took all my days and study reigned the night. One day in class, a cadet that I didn't know well, tell me that my father is great. I was surprised. How did this cadet know my father? That's when he tells me how he was riding his motorcycle to Toronto to see his parents for the weekend, when it broke down. Standing on the side of the 401 highway, a rig pulls off ahead of  him. The man gets out and comes back to talk to him. Then the guy loads up his motorcycle into his rig and drives the young man to his parent's house where he offloads the motorcycle. The rig driver was my father who later told me that he say the kid's "RMC" jacket and just had to stop and help. At my father's funeral, I shared this story with my family.

Most of my memories from my time at RMC are good and fun times. Some of these memories are just plain funny. We were a proud squadron and our spouses wore that same pride.

Yet, when the cadets had been scheduled to watch STD films after an outbreak in the cadet wing, we UTPMs had also been forced to attend these briefings and see these films. Most of us UTPMs were married and being married to her UTPM husband, this wife was angry that her faithful husband had been forced to watch such ugly films. Like the time at a UTPM Mess Dinner when a wife of one of our UTPM Cadets angrily pokes the Director of Cadets in the chest in response to her husband having been forced to watch a video on sexually transmitted diseases.

Wives of UTPM cadets were invited to attend certain mess dinners and it was a big affair for them much like going to a Prom or a Ball. It allowed them to go shopping for just the right gown and shoes for the event. My fellow cadets joked about how they had to take care of the kids while their wives were getting their hair and makeup done for the affair. Dressed to the nines in a beautiful ball gown, this angry wife was standing up to the Director of Cadets (DCdts). She personally blamed him for her husband having been forced to watch the STD films.

We were all in awe of her as she demanded to know, "What kind of values are you teaching here?" and she said this while poking her finger just above the medals on the Lieutenant-Colonel's uniform. The Director of Cadets simply didn't know what to say and wisely said nothing!

Academically, one has choices....right! Not me. I did four years at university and I didn't have a single choice of subjects. Welcome to military college! And, if you want to feel like a token, and you are a woman, then military college is for you. I was the only UTPM woman in EE when I first got to RMC and although there were a few women in my classes, they were part of the cadet wing and ten years younger than me. Often I'd pull all-nighters studying at either at the college in one of our Otter Squadron study rooms or at a 24 hour all-night restaurant at the top of Princess Street in Kingston. The restaurant staff got to know me so well that I even had my own table there!

I was so focused on studying. At first I tried studying at home, but I often disturbed my family and it was so very difficult to work when everyone in the house was sleeping. I had to be quiet and tiptoe about. So, I often headed back to the college or when the empty hallways got to me, I'd head to the restaurant.

 I did my first two years at RMC in electrical engineering. Well, almost! It was more like 1 ¾ years as one day after returning home from RMC to change into my karate guy and run to the SAM Center to join my karate team for practice, my daughter hit me. I was squat down in front of her at the front door of my PMQ to say goodbye, when she raised her fist and angrily brought it down on my shoulder. "Don't go!" She'd yelled at me.

I knew she was upset, so in order to calm her, I tried to explain that I had to go and again she said, "NO!" She had started to cry and through her tears, she again raised her small fist and hit me on the shoulder. She

9

wouldn't stop then and hit me again and again. After she had hit me five or six times she stopped and I sat there in my squat dumbfounded. I think I broke both our hearts that evening as I had to leave. I couldn't simply stay home without getting into some serious trouble. Still, I remained in a state of shock. Leaving her that night was one of the most difficult things I would ever do. The memory of her tears stayed with me throughout my practice, that evening, and through the night. It bothered me so much that I was affecting her in this way.

When I got to RMC the next morning, I asked for a meeting with my Squadron Commander and in that meeting, I asked him to transfer me out of my present academic program and into one that would be less time demanding. I had always dreamed of being an electrical engineer, but my family came first. I had heard how a fellow UTPM had asked to transfer academic programs and he'd been denied and so I was concerned.

Yet, I need not have been as my Squadron Commander didn't even flinch as he changed me out of an electrical engineering academic program and into an applied science degree program. Now, I would have more time for my family. I was relieved but also curious so I asked him why he'd approved my request so quickly. He told me that he knew I wouldn't have asked for it without good reason, "That's just the type of person you are," he said to me.

I was still concerned about my family and in order to give my family the time they needed, I had to make sacrifices. So, I quit the Karate Team. It was wonderful except that I now had too much time to myself and I often found myself without anything to do. A few weeks later, a classmate of mine asked me if I was interested in becoming a member of the Debating Team. With my experience in teaching, I was curious about public speaking and so I joined.

Some really sad stuff happened while I was at RMC and one of these things that happened was a suicide that took place on campus. It still amazes me the power of RMC to keep something out of the press. I knew this young fellow but not well. He was in his 4th year at RMC when he decided to punch out while I was only a 2nd year Cadet. Yet, it was shocking to learn how he was able to break into the weapons lockup and takes a bridge block and some ammunition. With his own

FNC1, he headed out to the Martello tower on campus, sat down and swallowed a bullet. The next morning, a security guard doing his rounds found him. We all knew about his suicide, but it never got in the newspapers nor did anyone on Base Kingston ask me about it. RMC knew how to keep its secrets.

As a UTPM at a RMC, we were expected to set a good example. We had already served for multiple years in the Canadian Forces and we knew how lucky we were to be at RMC. You'd always find us in class sitting near the front and working really, really hard on our academics. We knew what a privilege we'd been afforded and we were not about to screw it up. We UTPMs called the cadets of the Cadet Corp, the "kids" and they called us "UTs." It was difficult to bridge the gap between us due to the many differences in our ages and experiences.

For me, the young women cadets in my classes were single and had no children so we didn't have a lot in common. Nevertheless, while I was in electrical engineering (and yes, as a UT, I sat near the front of the class) I managed to get into a fair amount of trouble because of my friendship with the kids. Unlike most of the UTs, I was a member of an athletic team and I didn't distance myself from the student body, but like a good UT, I sat at the front of most of my classes and work seriously on my academics. I was fairly popular and the kids began to refer to me as their "pet UT" which although cute at first, didn't end up being a good thing.

As an example, one day as I quietly sat waiting for class to begin, I was hit by a paper airplane. I turned around but everyone behind me had a stupidly innocent look on their face and it was impossible to figure out who had thrown the paper airplane. So, I turned back to face the front. Yet, again I was hit by another paper airplane. This time I quickly turned around but I was still unable to identify the culprit but there were a lot of smiling faces back there! As I turned back to face forward, I was hit by more than a dozen paper airplanes all at once. That was it, I quickly I jumped up but not before grabbing one of the offensive paper airplanes and I pitched it back at them. And, that's when the camera went off! The next version of the RMC cadet wing newspaper's front page story showed the picture taken that day and the caption read, "UT Sets the Example!" I was called to the office of the

Director of Cadets to explain myself. My Squadron Commander was there as well and both of them were looking to me for an explanation. I said, "What can I say….they got me."

The cadets and I remained on friendly terms throughout my four years at the college and they sometimes had good advice. Once when I followed their advice, I ended up in academic hell! I was studying mostly math and sciences (you know "important" subjects for an engineering student) and for these course I was spot on in my efforts. But when it came time to exhibit the same effort in my arts classes (English, History, Psych, French, etc.), I was a bit slack academically. For example, while I was preparing for the history midterm, a fellow cadet told me I should "spot studying." She advised me that I should forget about studying all twelve topics taught during the term by the History Professor and instead only study half that many

We'd already been told the format of the midterm exam, which was to consist of five essay questions. Of which we had to pick three and write three essays. I didn't have a lot of time to study for my History midterm as I spent all my study time on the important course like math and science. So, I took her advice and spot studied and crammed on only six of the twelve topics. Imagine my surprise when I turned over the midterm paper in class and read the first two questions and they were NOT the topics I had studied. I had not studied those topics. Bugger! I felt panic rising up….so I turned the test paper back over and sat there. Okay, I told myself….what am I going to do if the next question is a topic I didn't study? I decided that if I didn't get really lucky with the next three questions, then I was going to write, "I don't know anything about the Russian Revolution, but let me tell you all about……." After all, I reasoned (mostly with myself) wasn't the purpose of teaching for us to learn something! Yeah, right! I turned my test paper back over and I knew the next two questions. The 5th question was a bit tricky…..not exactly what I had studied, but I felt I could swing it. Whew! I got an 87% on the midterm and I learned a valuable lesson about NOT spot studying. It just wasn't worth the panic. I'd rather pull an all-nighters than deal with that stress-filled moment in class ever again!

The cadets were great jokesters and it was during my second year at RMC, that a cadet friend of mine told me just how far they would go to pull a joke. The cadets loved playing practical jokes on one another and they were very inventive. For instance, this friend of mine had video tapped the 649 Lottery drawing one week and replayed it the following week. Of course, he and his buddies were always pitching in to buy group tickets. That particular week, my friend was tasked with buying the tickets and what he did was cruel and heartless and as funny as heck! Having watched (and taped) the previous week's 649 drawing, he selected the numbers that had won the previous week for this week's 649 Lottery ticket. Then, before everyone settled in the common room to watch the drawing live, he put the video tape in and started it.

There they were watching their numbers come up....one at a time and they truly thought they had won. One of the cadets told the rest that he was going to go see the Commandant and tell him off, while another cadet grabbed his car keys and said he was going to drive his old jalopy off the pier. Before either of them could take action on their plans, my friend got up from the couch and moved towards the door (as he knew he would need to make a quick escape) and from there, he rewound the video and set it to play again. He later heard that it only took a few seconds of blank stares before someone got it but by then he had disappeared!

Revenge had to be exercised and they did get him back. One of the cadets was of Indian decent and everyone loved the food he brought back from his weekends at home. One Friday evening, before heading downtown to one of the clubs, this fellow served his friends Indian meatballs he said his mother had made. Everyone chowed down on them.....except for one of his friends who spit it out and looked at him with hate in his eyes. Still, this fellow didn't say anything to the other guys as they ate one meatball after the other. It wasn't long before all the meatballs were gone. And, that's when one of the other cadets asked him if he had anymore, he said, sure and reached into his dresser for a large can of Alpo. No one caught up with him as he ran for his life!

Most of my friends at Milcol (Military College) were in my squadron as was my best friend, Natalie Payette. Natalie was a UTPM who had been an aircraft technician in CFB Summerside, PEI before she'd come to RMC the year after I did. She was married and during her second year at the college, she got unexpectedly pregnant. It was the first time that RMC had ever to deal with a situation like this. At first, they weren't sure how to deal with this situation as in the past, if a female cadet got pregnant, she would simply be asked to leave the college.

Natalie was a different situation because she was both a UTPM and married. She wasn't pregnant out of marriage and RMC could not claim that she had behaved immorally. So, what to do....what to do? The college decided that Natalie should be allowed to continue at RMC and a special uniform was provided for her. Those were the days when we'd see her proudly carrying a pillow from class to class to help her aching back. She was normally very fit so it wasn't a concern for the college when she was excused the physical fitness tests during her pregnancy, although she was expected to return to these demands upon her return from maternity leave. Her academics went on as scheduled and Natalie held her own. She carried her daughter to term and even shortened her maternity leave to accommodate RMC's and the Canadian Force's demands on her time. She was amazing!

An amazing person that Natalie and I got to know was a fellow UTPM and a dear friend of ours, Real LaBelle who got sick with cancer while at RMC. He had leukemia. In his former life (before RMC), Real had been a Radar Technician and he was married with young children. His disease progressed rapidly and although he struggled to continue at RMC, it was not to be. Natalie and I visited him at the hospital both in Kingston and later in Ottawa.

Becoming an officer was important to me because I felt the need to support my troops. I'd had one spectacular Commanding Officer, a few good ones, and I'd also seen officers who were ineffective leaders. Being an officer, comes with power and what one does with that power defines them.

So it was that after I graduated RMC, I used that power to help Real's family. At first, the CFB Ottawa officer in charge of housing at CFB Uplands refused my request for Real's family to get a PMQ there but I pulled in every favor I'd had owed to me and was able to get him to allow Real's wife and children to move up to Ottawa and as a result they were able to spend a great deal of time with him during his last few months. Before then, she'd been travelling from Kingston to Ottawa and their toddlers never got to see their father. Real hadn't seen the children he loved so dearly in months. After Real passed, I was made the Assisting Officer to his family. The practicality of a death had never crossed my mind before then, but as I helped his wife shop: first for funeral clothes for his children and then for a coffin for Real, it hit home. I was proud of the way I had been able to help and I believe that this is how a good officer should provide for the needs of her troops.

Two months after I had transferred out of electrical engineering, the Department of National Defence informed the students at RMC that a new degree program was about to be offered in Space Science. And although it was not be offered to the students in Applied Science, I asked to be considered. It was going to be an academically demanding program but not as demanding as the electrical engineering degree program had been, yet it would not be as easy as the applied science program had been. I was academically dying in AppleSci and found each day tougher than the day before. I needed more of a challenge.

When the Space Science degree program was first announced, almost 200 cadets volunteered for the program but when they were told that only a 3rd year had been approved by DND, most of them backed out. Although it looked good that the 4th year of Space Science would be approved, we were told it may not happen and that if it did not, then we would have to do an additional year of academics at RMC and in our previous degree program. That is, we'd have to go back a year; complete our 3rd year in our original degree program; and then do the 4th year in that program.

It was a serious risk and not a lot of cadets were willing to take it and in the end only 10 cadets remained in the Space Science degree program. Maybe this is why they accepted me into the

program or maybe their decision was based on my strong academics in the electrical engineering program, I don't know and I don't care. I was glad to be there and so it was that I began my journey into space! I'd been accepted into Canada's first ever Space Science degree program and being the only woman, I made history by being the first woman space scientist in Canadian history. It wasn't planned......it just happened. We were extremely grateful when DND approved the 4th year of study and now Space Science is an entrenched degree program at RMC.

Without the on-site resources to fully establish all aspects of the Space Science degree program, RMC hired and borrowed resources from other university. We learned astronomy from a Queen's professor and we even started an Astronomy Club at RMC. Actually, I started it. I had always been interested in astronomy and was a member of the RASC (Royal Astronomical Society of Canada), Kingston Branch. The Club bought an impressive 10" Meade telescope and a pair of 12" long binoculars; from which I clearly saw the Andromeda Galaxy one fall evening. It was amazing and it was an amazing time.

I remained a serious student and surprisingly, I paid a price for being so. In my military career, I'd learned the price that could be paid if something went wrong and that the price was paid in human lives. This made me careful to properly understand what I was learning. In my 4th year of study, I had a serious problem arise with one of my professors who claimed that I had cheated on an exam. This happened because I was so conscientious. As with all my courses, I visited my professor after a test to find out what I had missed or to better understand something I had not understood on that exam. On this day, after the exam, I'd gone to professor's office to ask about a question on the practical part of a math exam where we were using the computer to execute mathematical principals in the practical application of satellite imagery.

After he'd explained to me the correct way to do a question on the exam, I headed back to the computer lab to test it out. It was no surprise that what the professor had instructed me to do had worked and I'd wished I'd thought of it sooner. Still, I'd not forget now. I saved my work and headed out of the lab. And, that ended up being the problem.

The professor had not security blocked the exam files and when I saved my rework it copied over the original exam file. In this case, my dedication to understanding would bite me in the ass when the professor claimed that I had cheated on one of his exams. Even though I believed then and still believe that the professor knew I had not done this intentionally, he still went forward with the accusation.

Besides being honest, I was a good student and I was doing well academically in his class and all my classes. This was a serious matter as at RMC cheating means only one thing....being expelled. The impact for me would be compounded and would result in a court martial and probably a dishonorable discharge from the Canadian Forces.

So, the question is: why did he do this? I have only one explanation. It was probably because I was avoiding his advances. Even within my squadron it was well known that this particular professor would try to see me. His visits to try and see me were so well known, and my unwillingness to let him see me, that whenever he approached the squadron someone would race to me and warn me so I could hide. This professor was more than a little squirrely.

I was not going to let him ruin my military career because I wouldn't have a relationship with him. So I contacted a lawyer friend whose business was in Kingston. He had known me for about a dozen years and he also knew what kind of person I am. He prepared a letter to RMC's Commandant on my behalf and in it, he informed the Commandant that I was prepared to take a polygraph test to prove my innocence. In addition, he offered the professor the opportunity to directly ask me questions while I was being tested. In a rather smart move, he also asked that in return for this, the professor be given a polygraph test where I could ask him three questions. He explained that I was willing to pay for both tests but this never took place as the matter was quickly dropped.

Most of the wrong things that happened at the college I got over but there is one that still haunts me. It happened when I was in my 4th year at RMC, a classmate and friend of mine was involved in the gang rape of a 1st year female cadet. I feel very confident about speaking about this because he admitted it directly to me when I told him about some pretty bad rumours circulating the college about his involvement in the gang rape. He got away with it.

This 4th year cadet was very smart and in my Classical Mechanics class, he was topping the course. He was also very personable and we got along well. In fact, I admired him for his smarts and I thought him a good person. I would never have believed the stories about him except that I heard it from the horse's mouth. He just didn't seem like the sort of person capable of this. Yet, as we were leaving class one day, I raised the subject to him and he said to me, "What can I say, I was drunk!"

I was devastated. Obviously my judgement of him was all wrong. He was allowed to graduate while the other two 4th year cadets involved in the gang rape were both expelled and the 1st year female Cadet also left RMC. I was told she was asked to leave the college and she gratefully left. Who could blame her! Part of the reason why I didn't believe my friend was involved was that he was still at the college. After hearing directly from him, I've come to believe that RMC allowed him to graduate for two reasons: 1. he had a NSERC Scholarship and RMC did not want to explain to the NSERC Board why he wouldn't be accepting it; and 2. he had a powerful daddy.

We had a special visitor in my final year at RMC when Prime Minister Brian Mulroney's helicopter landed on our parade square one cold February day. At the time, it was very controversial for the PM to visit RMC and we had lots of protestors show up. In fact, the student body of cadets stood side by side to create a human blockade to protect the PM and the college but this is not why I'll never forget his visit. What I remember about that day were the three protestors who tried to block my path as I walked home.

Most days I walked to and from RMC and my PMQ on Base Kingston. That day, I was in my formal dress uniform due to the PM's visit, so instead of taking the shortcut across the fields and up the hill to my PMQ, I used the sidewalks on campus and then walked up the sidewalk beside Highway 2.

We were dismissed after the Prime Minister left the college and I began my walk home along the sidewalk on campus when these three protestors walked up to me. As they approached me, they were staring angrily at me and whispering among themselves. It made me feel very uncomfortable. When they were only a foot in front of me, one of them hocked and prepared to spit at me.

Very quickly, I got very angry and I clenched my fist while I marched purposefully toward them staring directly into the eyes of the guy who had hocked. I was proud to be in the military and my uniform was a representation of that and no one....but no one was going to spit on my uniform. It was one of those moments when I was prepared to do what I had to do to defend my uniform....and my country. I was not about to let anyone get away with dishonoring either. The fellow swallowed his spit and the three of them walked passed me without incident.

Another significant event that took place during those four years it that my grandpa died. Such a loss is a sad occurrence in life, but for me, it took on a whole new meaning because at the time, I was at a military college. The day started disturbingly for me. I woke up with this awful feeling that I couldn't shake and over the next few hours it took a more defined shape. I discovered it was about my grandfather so I telephoned my aunt as my grandpa had been living with her since my grandma had died yet she told me that he was fine.

Still I couldn't shake the feeling of dread that assailed me. On this premonition, I went to my Squadron Commander and asked for permission to visit my grandfather even though it was the middle of the week. I didn't expect him to say yes, and he didn't, but I had to try. I headed to my next class still unable to shake the powerful feeling of dread that I had and its intensity was overwhelmingly. When next I was between classes, I again called my aunt and checked on grandpa. She again said that he was fine although she must have wondered what was up.

Unable to concentrate, I excused myself from class and headed for home. I could no longer ignore this feeling. Once there, I packed a bag and headed for the train station where I got on the train and headed for Toronto. My aunt's home was about an hour's drive north of Toronto. While on the train, I used their phone to call my father and I pleaded with him to go see grandpa (his father). He reassured me that all was fine and he'd see grandpa on the weekend.

19

Next I telephone my sister at work. As a nurse at a hospital, she had a shift to work so she couldn't come with me but when I asked her if I could borrow her car and she agreed and said she'd meet me at the train station. When I got to the train station in Toronto, my sister did meet me but she had her overnight bag with her. She'd taken a few days off work and had packed a bag and she was going with me. At first, she didn't ask about the fact that I should be at the college and in class, but she eventually got around to it. I didn't know what to say so I told her that I just had to go see grandpa although I didn't know why.

It was a wonderful visit. Grandpa, my sister and I watched a Toronto Maple Leaf's hockey game on the TV and when they lost, as they often do, Grandpa exclaimed, "Last God-damned game I'm ever going to see, the least they could have done was win!" Once he had nodded off, the rest of us headed for bed.

Early the next morning it was snowing hard and my aunt didn't want us to get on the road, but I had to get back to the college. I knew what I had done and I knew I was AWOL but if I could get back early enough, my absence may not be noticed. Foolishly, I had confidence in my timing of my classes and on the train to Toronto, I mapped out that if things worked out right, they might not even notice my absence as I'd only miss a few classes.

Yet, Mother Nature conspired against me and my plan as the falling snow turned into a full blown blizzard. I did the drive to Toronto with my bundle of nerves sister beside me. When we got to Toronto, my sister expressed her eternal gratitude for my having done the driving. "You have nerves of steel," she told me and I smiled. I sure hoped so because I would need then when I got back to RMC.

When I got back to Kingston, I was told to change into my formal uniform and that the Squadron Commander wanted to see me and that he was pissed. When I showed up at his office, the Squadron Commander didn't even say a word to me but his disappointment was tangible: gone was the kind face I'd often seen. I was marched down the hall to the RMC Commandant's office where we waited outside his office for a few minutes, although it felt like hours to me.

Both of us marched into the Commandant's Office and after we saluted him, he launched into a lecture directed at me. He looked me directly in the eye and told me how disappointed he was in me and how I should have known better and asked how the heck I'd ever gotten into the UTPM program with an obvious disrespect of military protocol.

I was getting it with both barrels and I could see the Squadron Commander was eating it up. The Commandant was obviously saying all the things that he had obviously wanted to say to me. During this deserved dressing down, a knock came at the Commandant's Office door. He bellowed, "Come In." and the door opened although his secretary's voice could be heard, I did not hear any footfalls.

She said, "Sir, can I talk with you?" and the Commandant bellowed, "NOT NOW!"

She paused and then said, "I'm sorry Sir, but I think you need to hear this right away." It was obviously important and he waved her in. I stood stock still hoping to impress him with my military bearing. Kind of late in the game, but I was desperate. She walked around his big oak desk and then bent down and whispered something into his ear.

The Commandant went from looking straight ahead to bending his head and looking at his desk. He thanked her as his secretary turned to leave the office quietly closing the door behind her. The Squadron Commander stood erectly to attention and I copied him throughout this interruption. After the door closed, the Commandant looked up at me and said, "Cadet Lavigne, I'm sorry to be the one to tell you this but your grandfather died this morning." I didn't move. It was surreal. The room was so very quiet. Next the Commandant said, "I think we're done here," then added, "Never lose those instincts of yours," he said, "They're going to save someone's life one day!"

The next year when I graduated from RMC, I was honoured by the Commandant at our Commencement Ceremony. We lined up to receive our Diplomas and our Commissioning Scroll. Individually, we moved towards our seated Commandant and as I moved up the line of cadets, I heard the Commandant say to each of them, "Congratulations." Yet when my turn came and I had stepped forward, saluted him and then knelt before his chair, the

Commandant smiled at me and as he handed me my commissioning scroll, he said to me, "I'm proud to be the one to give this to you." I will always remember his words and that moment because from that day on, I was a real Officer!

Chapter Two: Becoming a CELE Officer

A SQN, CFSCE, KINGSTON, ONTARIO (1991)

The Communications & Electronics Branch was my home. I had been a part of the C&E Branch throughout my military career so far and now I was going to be an officer in my home branch. My radio technician trade was a C&E Branch trade and when I was accepted into the UTPM program, I opted to stay with my Branch. I would become an officer in that branch and that meant I would be a CELE (Communications and ELectrical Engineering) Officer. After four tough years of academics at Royal Military College, I was looking forward to some "real" work and my first posting as an officer.

So, after graduating, I was sent to do two officer training courses: the CELE Common Course and then the CELE Air Officer's Course. Both of these training courses were held in Kingston, Ontario at the CFSCE School and in Alpha Squadron. The training at A Sqn was fun for me. I had come from the C&E Branch and even spent two years as an instructor at the CFSCE school so I had a bit of an academic edge on most of the other students because part of my job as an instructor was to give a two week course to the incoming CELE Officers.

23

Yet there was a lot of training I was unfamiliar with such as the Survival Training, the Search and Rescue Training (although I'd learnt some of this in Gander, Newfoundland), and the Escape and Evasion Training. I have fond memories from the training exercises we did.

For instance, during Survival Training, we were "dropped" into a secluded area of Algonquin Park given the bare necessities and simply told to survive. We had received some training beforehand from the Canadian Airborne Troopers who taught how to use the parts and pieces of our parachute to build a shelter. make snares to trap food (they called it "fuel"), build a signal fire, build a safe campfire (which we were not allowed to light since the training accident the year before where a CELE student had started a forest fire that burned many acres of parkland before being brought under control).

We wore a flight suit and we were given a parachute before being dropped off in the middle of nowhere. We were paired off and another female CELE officer in training and I were paired up. 2Lt Mary Pisser* was from northern Saskatchewan and her parents ran a campground there. Perfect, I thought! Mary and I immediately set to work and fell a couple of rotting trees. We used the strings on our parachute to tie one of them horizontally to healthy trees and then draped the parachute over it. As the ground we were on was fairly steep (having an angle of near 45 degrees), we needed to level out the "floor" that we would sleep on. We had both listened carefully to our airborne instructors and set to work to get this done using pine branches.

We had been dropped off at dusk and we had worked through the thick mosquitos and flies early on and we were grateful when they had settled down as it got later. We didn't put much effort into the signal fire since we couldn't even light it and the same went for the campfire. Due to the forest fire caused last year, we weren't allowed to light a campfire, so we kind of built one although it was a miniature model about a tenth the size recommended.

Exhausted, we hit the hay. Mary had hidden in her pocket some mosquito coils and after we were safely seconded away under the net of the parachute, she showed them to me and we lit one and killed any remaining mosquitos in our sleeping quarters. What an awesome hootchie mate, I thought just before falling soundly to sleep.

The Directing Staff (DS....our instructors) visited us each day to check on us but the only time we got into serious trouble was that first morning. That day, we were rudely awaken by a DS: an Air Force Captain with a horribly thick French accent. At first he tried knocking on one of the trees holding up our shelter and then he started shaking it as he bellowed, "What do you think this is...the fucking Holiday Inn?"

Mary and I had adopted a head to foot sleeping format and at his question, she raised her head and whispered to me, "I don't think so..... we didn't get our wake-up call!" I had to cover my mouth to stop from laughing out loud. The DS was rightfully upset at our immensely small campfire (a round of stones with some twigs in a teepee format at the center and measuring about 8" in diameter) and he was too mad to even comment on our too small signal fire. He was outraged!

Other training exercises that I enjoyed and have fond memories of was our Search & Rescue and Escape & Invasion training. Both were something I was familiar with, having received similar training before. Even today as I clean up my front yard of dog poop (from the way too many dogs that are walked by my home and do their business), I still look left to right just as we were taught in Search & Rescue training. It was explained to us that when we read, we look left to right and looking right to left forces our minds to slow down and we end up looking more carefully. I'd never imagined I'd be using it to clean up dog shit!

C'est la vie!

During the seven months of CELE officer training, I went to the CELE Officer's Mess on Base Kingston each Friday for TGIF. This was required of all officers but especially those on training. The purpose was not to drink as you were allowed to but it did foster an acceptance of consuming alcohol. I didn't have a problem with it as I was a light weight and couldn't consume too much. I either nursed a few draft beer or I drank pop.

After a C&E Mess Dinner, when most of us were sloshed, someone came up with the bright idea that we should go skinny dipping. The Mess was up on a hill from the St. Lawrence River and has a magnificent view over its manicured lawns that sloped downwards the St. Lawrence River behind the Officer's Mess. I am a prude! I had never skinny dipped and wasn't about to now. Still, these were my friends....drunk friends.....that I felt the need to protect. There was eight of us and I was one of the three women who headed down to the water's edge that night. And although I went down to the water's edge with them, I did not take off my clothes nor did I go in for a swim.....instead, I guarded their clothes....their mess kits as I sat on a bench and listening to them laugh and frolic in the water. The bench I sat on was on a trail that I was familiar with. At this point in the trail, it followed the edge of the water. I'd often used to do my morning runs. It is both a beautiful run, with the morning sun peeking through the tree canopy overhead, and a tough run, fraught with zig-zags as it winds through the woods. It was great for athletic as it was always a challenging run.

My C&E Branch had two main types of officers: Air Force CELE officers and Army Signals Officers. At Base Kingston, there is an Army Division: 4 Division where some of the Signals officers were posted. I had a run-in with a junior Signals officer during TGIF at the Base Kingston Officer's Mess. This young officer was not drunk but he was full of himself and had a chip on his shoulder. Rudely, he asks me, "What are you doing at my mess?" I was shocked because he is was so young and yet, he'd already developed this prejudice towards women officers. When he confronted me, I was at the bar buying a jug of draft beer for my friends and I. I offer to buy him a beer and he accepts and after delivering the jug of beer to my friends, the two of us sit down at a nearby table and talk.

I want to ask him why he feels this way and address his discrimination towards women officers in the C&E Branch. He is so young and already hates women in the military and I am curious to know why. He tells me that we (women) don't belong as we can't do his job at 4 Division and so I ask him what he does. In an ill-conceived attempt to be fair, he says I can do the office work of his job, but I can't lead the men and when I ask why, he tells me of the morning runs and workout they do and how I just don't have what it takes to do that. When I ask him what the morning fitness runs consist of, he breaks it down for me and tells me how they do a three mile run. I tell him that I do a three mile run each morning and I've always gotten excellent on my PT tests (at RMC we had to complete PT tests three times a year) so I have a pretty good pace.

Not discouraged by this, he explains that during the run, they do sit-ups and push-ups and so I ask him how many. When he tells me, I me there is three times that they stop their run to do these and they do 25 of each, I share with him that I weight train and do 200 sit-ups to warm up. He concedes that I may be able to do the sit-ups but not the push-ups because they are guy push-ups (from the toes) and not women push-ups (from the knees) but I have him here as well as I only do guy-pushups and have since joining the RMC Karate Team. Unwilling to concede, he tells me they do 15 chin-ups and that's when I concede. I tell him that chin-ups are my downfall and I struggle to do 10 of them. Happy at his victory, he puffs up his chest and says, "See, you can't do my job!" And, that when I agree to disagree. I tell him, "You're right, I can't do your job but not for the reason you think. I can't do your job because from the moment you receive my posting message into your unit, you've already decided I can't and you will never give me the chance to do so" and I get up from the table and walk back to my friends. I don't know if I've scored a point or changed his point of view, but I've had my say and I was okay with that.

C'est la vie!

Our training had its fun and validating moments and I smile as I remember when we were dropped off to execute an Escape & Invasion exercise. We had been placed in groups of eight with one DS assigned to each group: he wasn't allowed to help us as his job was to evaluate us. Still, he was expected to toe the line with respect to doing what the leader commanded. We were blindfolded and put into a bus and each group was dropped off one at a time. The blind-folds did not come off until the bus was well out of site.

I was assigned to be the leader and I had a great group of eight. I was the only woman assigned to be a leader so the pressure was on. It was after dark when we were dropped off in the middle of nowhere. We had compasses and a topographical map and the only information we were given was the coordinates of the location where we were to get to. I was sure that this Rendezvous (RV) point was miles away and we'd have to move to it through the dark of night while avoiding the enemy (that is, the searchers....other DS) who would be looking for us. If we got caught, we would be relocated to another drop off spot.

I wasn't going to let that happen. I took out the map and my compass and asked my crew who had experience in this sort of exercise. Two of the guys came forward and I sent the rest of the guys to sit down and keep quiet. First, I had to figure out where we were and there were visual clues as on the horizon, I saw some red lights which I knew must be a communications tower. I had worked on one of these isolated towers as a technician at 764 Comm Sqn. On the map, I located two possible towers yet because it was so dark, we couldn't tell which one it was. I had to choose one of them and I got lucky. I had a backup plan if I had chosen the wrong tower, so we were good either way.

The map showed that there was a railway track not far from the tower and therefore, not far from us. If I'd chosen the wrong tower, we would soon know. As the radio was heavy to carry, I assigned three guys to share that task; switching up when it got heavy. Although the radio was a necessity it was also difficult to lug and even though we were on radio silence, it would be invaluable if anyone got hurt. If that happened, we'd give up our position so that medical help could arrive. Luckily, we didn't have to deal with that.

We started to move and one of the guys with experience took the lead and acted as our scout. As we moved, I sent him off ahead of the group to look for the railway track which he found and then led us to. Twice we saw the DS jeep looking for us and we squatted down in bushes and kept quiet. The jeeps had only the cat's eyes headlights and they were difficult to see but we could hear the engine as they approached. We would follow the railway track path for a few miles, then we would have to sneak through a small town, and after that we would have to follow a roadway.

When we first got to the railway tracks, I discovered there were no actual railway tracks. They had been lifted and instead we had a very nice walking path. Thank you Lord! Four times we crossed a roadway and each time, we stopped and I let the scout go ahead and check for DS. One of these times, he got across the street when a DS jeep showed up.

From the bushes, we watched as he flatted himself on the ground not 30 feet from where they pulled the jeep in. The DS sat there for about 20 minutes and for that 20 minutes, we stayed stock still in the bushes. It was obvious that the DS were looking for us. Most of us were even controlling our breathing to be quieter. As we watched, our scout didn't move a muscle especially when the DS jumped out of the jeep and pulled out the UV binoculars to look about.

UV detects movement and as long as we didn't move, we were set. These days, they have IR binoculars which detect heat signatures and if the DS had them then, we would have been caught as each of our heat signatures would have lit up the bush we were hiding in like a Christmas tree.

Not seeing anything, the DS moved off and as they did I heard each one of us catch a breath of relief. We all were smiling. Our scout soon returned and was shaking with excitement. He told us how one of the DS that had gotten out of the jeep and walked within five feet of him and still not spotted him. He was so pleased with himself and I was as proud of him as I could have been.

The moon was nearly full and provided us with a fair amount of light during our march. We crossed that road and continued on our way and the only other excitement we had on the railroad path was barking dogs at a nearby farm that we passed. At first we stopped but once we assessed the situation, we moved quickly and quietly away from them.

Our next bit of excitement came when we had to cross a town. The guys were amazing as in groups of two, we ran from one moon shadows to another. The buildings were giving off shadows in the moonlight. We gathered at each point along the way before moving to the next point and we got through the town even though we spotted one DS jeep.

Lucky for us, they were just driving through the town although slowly and with the UV binoculars to the face of the DS in the passenger seat. When we heard a vehicle, we crouched down low beside the outside wall of a house and didn't move. Still, we were in plain sight but we got lucky when the DS didn't look that way. On the other side of the town, we followed the roadway to the RV point and at 3am we marched into it.

We were the first to make it in and for the next few hours we were provided with refreshments and we were allowed to rest. We were told to make as little noise as possible and we watched as other groups came in: some voluntarily and others with the DS who had found them. They were blindfolded and taken back out while we were fed and allowed to sleep.

We were kept at the RV point until 11am and then we were transported back to Base Kingston. There were still two groups unaccounted for but the DS knew where they were. We had instructions that if we had not reached the RV point by 10am, that we were to break radio silence. Both of the groups had done that but they were so far away (having headed in the wrong direction), that the DS decided to wait for them to reach the RV point. They would wait most of the rest of that day. I suspect that they were the two groups that had been caught and had been taken back out to a different drop off point.

While we were relaxing at the RV point, the DS that travelled with us shared with us that the instructor staff had a bet going and the winner of the bet got a case of beer. The winner was the DS accompanying the first group to reach the RV point. Our DS guy was especially happy as he was to get two cases of beer as no one thought that the woman led group would be the first group in. Huh, go figure! I felt especially proud....showed them, eh!

During the final phase of this training, the Colonel in charge of satellite engineering at NDHQ arranged for me to be posted to the SATCOM Group, DEEM. He had strongly supported the Space Science degree program taught at RMC and I was personally selected to work at DEEM by him. Although grateful for being wanted, I had my sights set on heading to US Air Space Command at Cheyenne Mountain in Colorado Springs.

Traditionally, the officer on the CELE Air Course who completes the course as the top student gets their choice of posting and I was aiming to be first. Already, I was topping the course so I had a very real chance to be posted to Colorado Springs and work at US Space Command and I could not imagine a more perfect fit for my newly acquired degree in Space Science.

It was not to be. Although determined to top the course, this Colonel had other ideas and wanted me in Ottawa and that was that. Long before the course was done, I was notified that my posting message had already come in and I was heading to DEEM at NDHQ in Ottawa.

It was November, 1991, I completed the Air Force CELE Officer training. I was a bit disappointed, but also grateful. It didn't take me long to get over my disappointment about the posting to Space Command and now I was full of hope and dreamt of a future filled with satellite engineering and leadership. Finally I was an Air Force officer in my home C&E Branch.

Our C&E Branch was mostly Army "Signals" officers and Air Force officers, but there were one or two who wore the Navy uniform. I was proud to have been selected to work in Satcom engineering at DEEM. This would be my first posting as an officer and as I looked to the future, I saw my dream about to be realized. It was what I had worked for all these years and I was looking forward to using the academics learned and the leadership skills I had been taught. I was chomping at the bit to turn these academic lessons into practice!

The year was 1991 and Canada had its first group of space scientists and I wanted to show the DEEM Colonel that his support was well placed. There was no civilian degree nor a military degree in space science before this and having been the only woman in the graduating class, I have the distinction of being Canada's First Woman Space Scientist. I enjoy letting people know that space science students at the military academy were called "space cadets!"

Chapter Three: Working at Satcom Engineering, NDHQ
OTTAWA, ONTARIO (1991-1994)

My first day on the job was November 11th. I was to report to the DEEM Colonel on that day yet that morning, I had been on a Remembrance Day Parade at CFSCE in Kingston. Kingston is an hour and a half's drive from Ottawa so after I got off parade, I headed home and changed into some civies. After a quick goodbye to my family, I got into the car and headed for Ottawa. The night before, I had packed up my car so that I would be ready for the drive to Ottawa. I would need to look neat and sharp when I arrived so I prepared a 2nd dress uniform for my first appearance before the Colonel at NDHQ.

I arrived in Ottawa about a half hour before my scheduled meeting with the Colonel late that afternoon and I found my way to the Canadian Building and a parking lot nearby. In the car, I changed into my neatly pressed uniform and put my hair up in a bun. When the reflections in the car window and rear view mirror confirmed that I looked good enough to present myself, I left the parking lot and headed for the Colonel's office and my new job. I was thrilled.

When I first arrived at DEEM, I was a Second-Lieutenant (2Lt) and my immediate boss was a Major. DEEM was part of DCEEM and that was part of National Defence Headquarters in Ottawa. My posting to Ottawa was difficult because at first I'd be separated from my family who were being left behind in Kingston as the children's school year couldn't be disrupted and besides, there were no PMQs (Personal Married Quarters) available in Ottawa at the time.

My job was located in the Canadian Building on Laurier Street and at the head of Space Systems Engineering Group was DEEM; a C&E Branch officer of Colonel rank. The subgroup of DEEM where I worked was known as the SATCOM (Satellite Communications) Engineering Group. Here I was a new space science graduate of RMC and DEEM himself had wanted me working for him in satellite engineering. Wow!

The first project assigned to me was a seven million dollar DND project with Telesat Canada and related to Telesat's Anik E communications satellites which the CF used. This project was expected to cost us $11.2M but it was brought it in at $7.8M. It was amazing work and I loved it. As my next assignment, I was made the junior project officer on SBWAS, a $47 million dollar space-based surveillance project where Canada was developing seven niche space technologies such as inter-satellite link antennas. This technology was amazing and new and simply a geek's dream. I was on top of the world.

On the SBWAS (Space Based Wide Area Surveillance) project, I worked more closely with my new boss. I was proud to be a small part of something so special and being done by Canada. One of our subcontractors, ComDev developed one of these truly Canadian technologies: the inter-satellite link antennas. I would stand a bit taller when I saw them selected to be used on the Iridium satellites that I would work on years later. My heart was cheering, "GO CANADA!"

At NDHQ I was geeking out and loving it as this space stuff was my world. I loved the work and I was working hard. I had a great boss who was a pleasure to work for and I felt very lucky indeed. My boss was a cool dude with a strong work ethic and high moral standards, he was a top-notch officer. In fact, in my estimation, he was the perfect officer. On top of it all, I had a wonderful feeling of contributing to my country's effort. I was so proud of my country.

I had a life outside of work. I was married and I had two young children even though they weren't with me. In my spare time, I learned to downhill ski at the small (and manageable) Ottawa area ski hills of Gatineau Park. I was able to learn after work as many of these small hills had night skiing and I became addicted to the sport.

When I became a competent skier, I taught my children how to downhill ski and it became a special family time as we all would go together to the ski slopes. Both of my children, like their mom, learned to love skiing but it was my son who would often skip eating supper at the lodge in favor of time on the slopes.

Camp Fortune was a small mountain where we often skied and where I, with clenched teeth, watched my son barreled down the slopes as fast as he could go. My daughter was a different type of skier, preferring style over speed. She loved to do the jumps. There would be times when I lose track of both of them as my daughter headed for the trees and glade skiing and my son, impatient waiting for us at the lift line, would head up without us. Still, I didn't worry much about him as I knew he was safe. He preferred to ski with some kids his own age.... all of which barreled down the slopes!

Although I had a good salary, my husband didn't work so we were tight for money and skiing is an expensive sport. It was because renting ski gear was so expensive, that I found and bought my children second hand ski gear, which they promptly grew out of each year. The cost was worth it as I loved to ski with my children and it was awesome family time.

One of my funniest memories from this time was also one of my most embarrassing moments on the slopes. As my daughter and I rode

a chair lift over the slopes, my son skied underneath us and spotting us, he yelled to me, "MOM....I PEED MY PANTS!" I wasn't surprised that he hadn't even stopped to go pee although I had warned him more than once. On this occasion, he would learn that it was important to listen to his mom, as he did not ski the rest of that night. Instead, he would sit in the lodge in his mother's spare pink ski pants and sulk while his sister mom continued to enjoy the slopes.

I also liked to challenge myself on the slopes and skiing with the kids didn't allow me to do this. So I made a concerted effort to join the Wednesday ski day with the Forces Ottawa Ski Club (FOSC). During the winter, I often put in a leave pass for a Wednesday so that I could go skiing and I became known for ditching my ski buddies to go off and ski alone. I'd rejoin them for the après-ski and some socializing.

Downhill skiing is a social sport and in the lift lines and on the ski lifts, my friends and I would joke and laugh but skiing is also a physically challenging sport and I loved it. Some people drink, others smoke, and still others gambled.....I skied! And, my friends forgave me my addition!

Although there was a lot to be grateful for in my life, I also had to deal with some serious sexual harassment at work. Today, they call it sexual misconduct and I like that term because it is based on conduct unbecoming an officer and that simply fit especially when describing the LCol I worked for. Although my immediate boss was a major, my Major's boss was a Lieutenant Colonel (LCol). Being short, fat and balding, the LCol was physically unattractive, yet he must have been narcissistic as he pranced around like he was the cat's meow.

In contrast, I had a runner's body and was shapely in all the right places. My mother had told me that I was "killer good looking in uniform." I was way out of his league. Besides, I was married and had two beautiful children and although the LCol was married as well, it didn't seem to matter to him. His married status did it stop him from making overt and public passes at me and it made me cringe whenever he would tiptoe and whisper that I he wanted "a piece of me" in my ear. I still shudder at the memory.

To say I was so uncomfortable would be making light of the situation. Each day I felt as if I was holding my breath from the moment I got to work until I left and I would not properly exhale until I was safely away from him. That was when my mind finally felt free but it is also when it would replay the events of the day and even though it upset me, I couldn't stop the memories of the day from rerunning in my mind.

My LCol should never have behaved the way he did and the stress it caused me was horrendous. I bottled my feelings up inside as I didn't know how to deal with the harassment but you can only do that for a time before it bubble over on you. For me, the bubbling in my tummy often caused me to throw up. The LCol was making my life a living hell and I just didn't know how to get him to quit. Every day it got worse until I was throwing up daily. I was in a bad situation.

After a year of this, my stomach was a mess. The daily harassment spilled over one day on my way home from work when I was forced to quickly get off a city bus before I threw up. I ended up throwing up in the garbage can beside the bus stop. There I was….puking in public in my uniform. It was humiliating! After I'd finished throwing up, I lifted my head and that's when I saw the people. People had stopped to stare at the military officer throwing up in the public. Even the bus driver was watching. And, although sympathetic, I could also see the look of shock on his face. He was kind and was holding up the bus up for me. He asked me if I was okay and I just wanted to die of embarrassment.

I felt the heat of embarrassment on my face and didn't even look at him as I told him to go ahead and leave. I was ashamed and felt as if I had disgraced the uniform. I couldn't get back on that bus nor any other bus for the rest of my posting in Ottawa. Instead, I walked. That day, I walked the few miles to my home on the Rockcliffe Base and after that day, I started to walk to and from work. It was about a five mile trek each way but I felt that I would die if anyone ever approached me and asked me how I was today. So, instead of taking the bus, I walked because I didn't want to ever face any of those people again. I did not want to be recognized on the bus or by the people who'd gotten off the bus that day when I had or the people who had been waiting for this rush-hour bus. I didn't even want to be recognized by anyone who'd been walking by that day. I've often wondered what they must have thought and suspect they probably thought I had been drinking! Bugger!

I made this decision because I didn't want someone to see and recognize me. I was always proud of my uniform and I wanted to wear it around….but….I was too embarrassed after that so when I walked to and from work, I wore civies. For the next year, I walked to and from NDHQ from my home on CFB Rockcliffe. It was only five miles. Right!

I developed a schedule where I prepared my uniforms and drove them into work on the weekends and left them in my office so that when I arrived at work, I could change into my uniform in the ladies bathroom before starting my day's work. Then, at the end of the day, I would change back into my civies for my walk home.

This was toughest in the winter but I wore my ski suit when I walked. It kept me warm most days. Although there was that day when the temperature dropped to -25 degrees Celsius. That day, I stopped into stores and even gas stations and anyplace I could to warm up for a few minutes before continuing on my way. Dang, it was cold that day!

The harassment at work was so bad that I didn't think it could possibly get worse. Yet, when it was finally clear to the LCol that I was unreceptive to his advances, he made it well known that he didn't think I was a good engineer. And even though he spread the word that I was incompetent, it was me he selected to be a technical advisor to the President of the Canadian Space Agency on a TD to NORAD's satellite tracking facility in Colorado Springs. I was asked to go as someone competent was needed to explain to Mr. Dorian the space and satellite technology and I had the skill set required for the job.

We flew to Montreal and met up with the CSA President and boarded a military aircraft bound for Colorado Springs. We had three days of meetings with the US Air Force Space Command and the Army Space Command. It was all very impressive. Lunches were served in a board room at the USAF Space Command building. Also in this building were the administrative offices for the base hospital. I learned this because I ended up in the hospital.

I had a number of interesting assignments during my time working at DEEM. As a Project Officer for the C&E Branch's involvement in R&D of new space-based technologies, I often went to meetings at DREO and DREV which are the Defence Research Establishments in Ottawa and at Valcartier (in Quebec). Canada was developing five niche space-based technologies at the time and during my time at DEEM, I was assigned to ensuring that I followed what was happening and reported on these.

In 1992, I was asked to be the technical advisor to the President of the Canadian Space Agency (CSA) who was heading to US Space Command in Cheyenne Mountain. I had a strong understanding of the job of their space-based assets as well as the supporting ground-based communications technology used. I was to answer any questions Mr. Dore asked.

We flew from Ottawa to Montreal to meet up with Mr. Dore before boarding the military plane that would take us to Colorado Springs. Mr. Dore was personable and very kind when I was medically unavailable to assist him. We were served a lunch of shrimp salad one day in a conference room of Air Force Space Command. I am allergic to shellfish and it had been prearranged that I would be served a salad without the shrimp but that is not what happened. When the plate was put in front of me, the Captain responsible for making the arrangements for the lunch, asked them to take it away and bring me a "clean" salad.

I was fearful that they would simply scoop the shrimp off and reserve the salad to me and that is exactly what they did. Because I was concerned, I asked the server to confirm for me that this was indeed a "clean" salad and she said it was. But, it was not. My allergy is severe enough that I had an epipen needle with me. Unfortunately, it was in my briefcase on the bus that had been touring us around.

My reaction was almost immediate and I explained to the Captain what was happening and exited the room. There were not a lot of people there.....perhaps 15 or so. He followed me out of the room and I headed down the stairs next to the room. On the steps I saw a US lady officer and I quickly explained what was up and asked her for help.

She took me to an office where they called an ambulance for me. Breathing was becoming difficult but the ambulance was there within a few minutes and loaded me up. The Captain headed back to the conference room knowing that I was in good hands. The EMTs immediately put me on oxygen and tilted my head back as far as they could to ensure my airway was as open as it could be. We got to the hospital on base within a few minutes. Honestly, I don't remember as I was struggling to breath and focused all my energy on staying calm.

I was raced into an emergency room where five doctors and nurses were running around my stretcher. They immediately injected me with epinephrine followed by a shot of Benadryl. I started to recover and within a few minutes and was soon able to breathe on my own again. Still, the hospital staff kept me there for a few hours and during that time they shared with me that they thought the call for an ambulance to the Air Force Space Command building was a drill because the call had come from the base hospital's Director, who had his offices in that building. They told me that they did NOT expect to see me there and it was a total surprise to them.

It's not every day that one gets to be a technical advisor to the President of the CSA and I felt a deep sense of responsibility for the job I was assigned to do. As soon as they let me go, I left the hospital and returned to our meetings. Mr. Dore was sympathetic regarding my absence and even told me that he also had a severe allergy but that his reaction was to break out in hives. We joked about which was worse and then the matter was dropped.

In early 1993, I became desperate to get out of my bad work environment. I felt as if I had put up with the sexual harassment and discrimination at DEEM for too long already. Yet, on average, a postings to NDHQ lasted four years so I looked for alternatives. I figured, when the going gets tough, the tough get going!

First I applied for a Master's degree in the United States at the US Air Force Academy, but my efforts and application required approval by my Colonel and I was denied. Next, I applied to study overseas in Canberra, Australia at the Australian Military Academy but again, I was denied approval by my Colonel. Then when the Canadian Space Agency put out a call for astronauts, I applied. This time I did not need my Colonel's consent but ultimately I was denied. It wasn't DND's fault, the CSA didn't accept me and so I framed my rejection letter and looked for another way out.

The sexual harassment at DEEM were overwhelming at times and I desperately looked for a way out as early as a few months after I got there. The harassment started right away and early on I started to look for a way out. One of the things I did was apply to become an astronaut with the Canadian Space Agency. It was a dream, but I had to

Agence spatiale   Canadian Space
canadienne   Agency

March 19, 1992

1382E
Ms Dawn E.M. Lavigne
39 Brock Crescent
Kingston, Ontario
K7K 5K7

Dear Ms Lavigne,

This is to acknowledge receipt of your application for the position of Astronaut which you recently sent to the Canadian Space Agency.

As anticipated, interest in the Astronaut recruitment campaign has been very high and the Agency has had the challenging task of selecting a relatively small number of candidates from among the many diverse and interesting applications received.

Your submission was carefully considered, but we are unfortunately unable to offer you employment. However, your application form will be kept on file for a period of six months. Should a suitable position become available within this period, we will be pleased to communicate with you again.

Your interest in the Canadian Space Program is much appreciated and we wish you success in your endeavours.

Yours sincerely,

William J. Moroz
Deputy Program Manager
Canadian Astronaut Recruitment Program

WJM/cs

Canada

try even though I knew I was not qualified, and not surprisingly, I was not accepted. Still, I have framed my rejection letter!

I believe in trying. One does not always succeed, but one must try. I guess that's why I'm a fan of what Michelangelo once said, *"The greater danger for most of us is not that our aim is too high and we miss it, but that it is too low and we hit it."*

Believing in education as I do, my next attempt to get out of DEEM was in touching base with colleagues with higher education. From these people, I learned of and then sought to do an overseas Master's degree. I first applied to the US Air Force Academy for the Master's degree in Space and then to the Australian military college in Canberra, Australia.

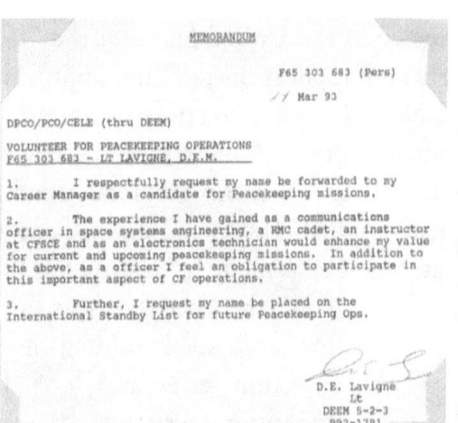

I'd continued my personal studies at night both at Carleton University where I did a course on the *Principles of Digital Communications* and at the University of Ottawa, where I studied *Digital Communications by Satellite.* I found both of these courses very rewarding.

Time dragged on and my situation at work kept getting worse and when neither of these educational options panned out, I became even more desperate and volunteered for peacekeeping missions. That didn't pan out either.

Late in 1993, the head of Britain's Military Avionics, Weapons and Information Systems, Dr. Mabberley visited Canada to see what we were up to. This fellow was the civilian head of the British military's communications and electronics engineering branch. I was assigned to be his technical advisor and also arranged his visits to our subcontractors including SPAR Aerospace, ComDev and Raytheon.

If I was as incompetent as my LCol portrayed me as, why was I assigned to oversee Dr. Mabberley visit from Great Britain and why was I put out in the public like this? It is because I was competent. We took him to SPAR Aerospace and ComDev and Raytheon Canada and showed off the niche technologies they were developing in accordance with DND's $47M project for space based surveillance.

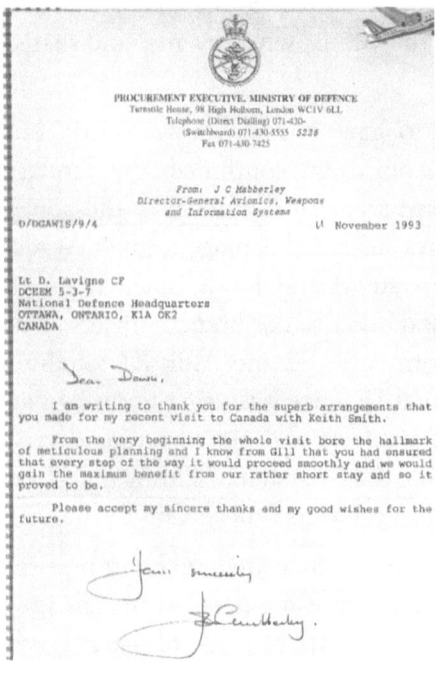

We met him at the Montreal airport and headed straight for SPAR Aerospace but it was when we returned to the airport to fly to Toronto and head to ComDev that we had a chance to sit down and visit. Our group consisted of Canadian C&E Officers and DREO civilian engineers, a US Signals Officer, and Mr. Mabberley. While we waited for our delayed flight, we sat and enjoyed a beer and the conversation turned to the rules regarding gifts from subcontractors and what Mr. Mabberley would do with the gift given to him by SPAR. I learned that the rules we lived, which were strict, were not near as strict as those of the United States military. The British military fell somewhere in between.

Mr. Mabberley explained that as long as the gift was below a certain value, they were allowed to keep it and as an example, he pointed out his tie. He explained that it had been a gift from a subcontractor of his but he had been allowed to keep it because its value was below the allowed limit set by the British military. With one too many beers in me (that would be one beer in my case....I'm such a light weight!), I said something rather insulting like, "What surprises me is that you actually wear it!" A hearty laugh went around the table and I was excused me inappropriate remark. We went on to see the inter-satellite link antennas that ComDev had developed before visiting Raytheon Canada. It was an interesting trip and I felt privileged to be privy to this technological research.

After doing well on both of these tasks, I was asked to be a liaison officer for the visit of the Australian Ambassador although that task required no technical know-how as I accompanied the CDS's wife and the wife of the Aussie Ambassador to various "wives' events" and shared lunch with the two women.

At DEEM, the LCol crusade to have it well known within our branch that he considered me incompetent continued. On January 20, 1994 when a solar storm caused a partial shutdown of the power grid in Canada, the Anik E satellites sustained damage to their AOCS (Attitude and Orbit Control Subsystem) and I was called upon to report on this event to DCEEM and other senior branch officers. This major solar event knocked out both Anik E2 and Anik E1 satellite's AOCS. The Department of National Defence was using these civilian communication satellites and had paid for and placed onboard each satellite, a Command Link Security (CLS) system. Within the C&E Branch, I was responsible for this project as its Project Officer.

Knowing the Anik E AOCS's job better than anyone in our branch, combined with my space background, gave me detailed insight into the damage sustained. Knowing the characteristics of near Earth environment particle physics, I grasped the problem quickly and I was easily able to bring the Branch senior staff up to speed by clearly explaining it to the General. My grasp of the technical challenge that we would face resulting from the effects of the solar storm on the Anik E satellites was presented to DCEEM at a meeting in his conference room. The ability to give a detailed account of the problems caused to the AOCS by the solar storm and what Telesat was doing to handle the problem was critical. Also important to DND was the impact on our onboard Command Link Security System

It was my job to analyze the situation and brief DCEEM so he could make decisions on how DND was to move forward. My LCol took this opportunity to publicly discredit me. In the middle of my briefing, the LCol spoke up and told the senior military staff that I didn't know what I was talking about and then went so far as to ask me what I was doing there! Yet, that was my job and it was I who was called upon to brief these senior officers on the status of the satellites and what Telesat was doing to try and save them. My LCol's dislike of me was on display with everyone in that conference room as well as the spectators in the room: the other engineering officers who I worked with.

I just about died from humiliation! I was shocked that he would go this far. The one thing I did have was my confidence in my knowledge. I was the satellite expert and the Anik E Command Link Security System was my project! I knew what I was talking about but that ended up not mattering. You see, in the military you don't say anything to an LCol.....you just don't....and I didn't.

The LCol ordered me to leave and as I packed my papers into my briefcase, I knew that the LCol had just ruined my professional reputation with this group of officers. Sadly, it wasn't just me that was impacted by the LCol's behaviour: he had callously hurt the C&E Branch and even the Department of National Defence. In his need to extract a pound of my flesh, he'd discredited the Branch. I shook my head as I realized the extent he was willing to go to. He'd not only hurt my career, but the C&E Branch's reputation. Yet, he didn't seem to care.

That same year, someone proposed that DEEM have an "Adventure Training." Adventure training was designed to provide members with a military-like outdoors experience and help to develop esprit de corps. While at DEEM, there were two Adventure Trainings that I participated in. The first one was to the west coast of Vancouver Island, the West Coast Trail and the second one was the Sawback Trail; a mountainous hike between Banff and Lake Louise.

The West Coast Trail (WCT) has the reputation of being one of the most grueling treks in North America as it is physically challenging and potentially hazardous. It was over 70 km long and you travel between Port Renfrew and Bamfield in mostly isolated areas of the west coast of Vancouver Island in British Columbia. There were water crossing that could only be traversed using cable cars, ladders, foot suspension bridges, or by wading in surge canals. The WCT is accurately reputed to be dangerous and it was an exhausting test of endurance. I just couldn't wait to try it.

I signed up right away and would not be swayed to cancel out of it even when I was told that I was the only English speaking person and the only woman who had signed up. I naively thought that this would be a great way to form bonds of friendship. Instead, I found myself "outside" the group and was often forced to hike alone. Placed at the back, I intentionally fell back from the group as every effort I made to engage them in conversation was ignored. More often than was comfortable, I could not even see the group.

Undaunted, I made the best of a bad situation as I hiked on. By the way, this is NOT recommended as the WCT can be treacherous. Still, I had little choice in the matter. There was a strong and pervasive environment in the group of my being unwelcome. It didn't matter to me as the WCT was beautiful and peaceful and I loved it.

Yet, not being close to the guys proved to be dangerous for me. On our first day out, we were hiking along some steep edges of a cliff which fell away to the ocean some 150 feet below. It was on this narrow path that I stumbled and fell and I started to slide off the edge of the cliff. As my legs slid over the edge, my heavy backpack was making it impossible for me to swing my body back onto the trail and I was inching over the edge. As I was being pulled over the edge by the weight of my backpack, I got very, very scared.

If you don't believe in God or miracles, then, for you, there would be no explanation for what happened next. When my legs were fully dangling over the edge and my torso was dragging me closer and closer towards the steep drop to the ocean, the only thing I could think to do was pray. It was while I was fervently praying that I saw IT! Like a gift from God, a root shaped like a handle was sticking out of the ground.

I hadn't seen it before but there it was. I grabbed for it for dear life and using it I was able to pull my legs back from over the cliff and back onto solid ground. I laid there for a few seconds catching my breath and looking up at the sky and yes, saying a prayer of thanks. When I stood up, I looked over the edge of the cliff and shuddered before breaking into a heavily laden jog to catch up with the guys.

When I reached them, I was really breathing hard and for the rest of the trek, I stayed as close to them as possible. I no longer cared if they were uncomfortable having me so close. It wasn't my problem! There ended up being a huge advantage for me as I listened to them speak French 24/7, my understanding of the language deepened. I didn't talk much but I listened a lot. In situations like this, strangers became brothers and over the next few days, I felt as if we had become members of the same family.

Still, when we got back to Ottawa, it was business as usual. The harassment continued and these guys (my "brothers") turned a blind eye to it. It was during this tough time for me that I learned that Captain Kyle Thorne* was a pig. Kyle worked on the 14th Floor of the Canadian Building….two floors above me for the Colonel that dealt with NORAD projects including NORAD satellite technology. Kyle often made his way down to the 12th floor to where I worked to pick my brain. Without a background in satellite technology, and too lazy to learn, he would stop by my desk and ask for my help. I would help him as best I could.

I've had other officers make passes at me but not set out to humiliate me the way Kyle did at a C&E Branch Mess Dinner held in Ottawa. At this 1993 Mess Dinner, Kyle (who was one of the C&E Branch's few Naval CELE Officers) looked sharp dressed in his Navy whites. He was a runner and was fit and the mess kit fit him well.

The mess dinner was held at a very old museum in Ottawa. It was an icon of a place and impressively huge. Inside the main entrance was a spiral staircase right out of "Gone with the Wind." The bannisters were thick wood bannisters as were the railings off the 2nd level which the staircase led up to and where the Mess Dinner was served. From the 2nd level one could look down over the big open space of the foyer.

I walked to the museum as it was only ten blocks from the Canadian Building and I was used to walking much further. The weekend before, when I'd brought my uniforms to work, I'd also brought my Mess Kit to work and stored it in my office. I usually walked the five miles from the Rockcliffe Base to the Canadian Building in downtown Ottawa and I was in the habit of driving my pressed uniforms and shone shoes and boots in on the weekend. The weekend before the C&E Mess Dinner, I'd also prepared my mess kit and taken it into work. A lady officer's mess kit is a formal dress uniform consisting of a floor length skirt, a white turtleneck blouse, and a short jacket with the rank on the sleeve.

The C&E Mess Dinner was on a Thursday night and on that Thursday, I had worked until it was time to get ready for the Mess Dinner. Dressed in my Mess Kit, I felt beautiful. I was sharply dressed and there wasn't a wrinkle or a smug in sight! Keeping fit was important to me and the walking to work was a great way to keep fit. With a touch of makeup and a dab of perfume, I felt on top of the world.

We met and mingled in the foyer and were piped into dinner. The meal was delicious and the traditional port was used to do the toasts. After the meal was over we congregated downstairs in the big foyer hall for drinks and conversation. It was a time to talk and catch up with friends. I loved it and was enjoying myself until I walked past Kyle and he reached out and with his finger, he gitchy, gitchy goo'ed my ass!

If all Navy officers were like him then it is no wonder that my Uncle Norm (who had served 30 years as an NCM in the Canadian Navy) had such a bad opinion of officers. I remember when my uncle heard that I had been selected for UTPM, he called me to offer his condolences!

When Kyle did this to me, I was shocked and then just as quickly I became pissed off. Yet as I turned to confront him, with the plan of telling him off, I saw a whole line of Army Signals officers standing in a row looking at me. Each of them had a big stupid and silly grin on his face and some of them were outright laughing.

Kyle had set me up. He had intentionally embarrassed and humiliated me.

Why? And, what was wrong with those Army officers who all thought that what Kyle did was okay. I was angry and I'm sure I looked it but it took only a second before I felt my face redden as humiliation spread over me. I looked at Kyle and he was smiling widely but he wasn't looking at me, he was looking at the Army officers. To him, and to them, it was all a big joke.

I wasn't smiling then nor was I able to let it slide. I felt awful. There was a moment when I thought of revenge: Kyle had a glass of red wine in his hand and I thought wouldn't that look nice on his white mess kit. But I didn't do that. In fact, I didn't know exactly how to react. I felt so lost and I didn't know what to do or say.

Deciding it was best to do nothing and to say nothing, I took a deep breath and turned away. It wouldn't have done any good to yell at Kyle or the group of Army officers. It would have made me more of a joke. Needing to escape the humiliation, I headed for the cloak room and grabbed my coat.

As I exited the mess dinner, I had to walk through the large gathering of senior C&E Officers and I knew I was breaking protocol but I didn't care. Despite the humiliation I felt, I held my head high and looked straight ahead as I walked briskly through the group and out the front door. I was in escape mode.

Overwhelmed, I walked the five miles home in my patent leather high heels. I was unable to think clearly as the hurt waves rolled over me. I had thought I was a good officer, a good engineer, and now it felt like I had gone to university for four years to become a plaything for my fellow officers. I didn't know how to ease the pain so I walked.

Not even thinking to stop at the Canadian Building and change my clothes, I wore my Mess Kit home. It was cold outside as it was autumn. The five mile walk home was a dark, cold, miserable hike. The sidewalks were alternatingly slushy or icy making it treacherous to walk in my high heels but I didn't care.

I wasn't thinking clearly at the time and it wasn't until the next morning as I headed to work that I remembered that I had broken protocol and walked out of a Mess Dinner. I knew I would have to explain that and I wondered what to say. Before a junior officer leaves a Mess Dinner, she/he is supposed to ask permission to leave.

Not surprisingly, when I got to work, I found out I was in trouble. I was called into my Major's office and he formally asked what happened. I told him the truth about what had happened and he said, "Oh, no.... you're kidding!"

The meeting ended and forty minutes later, he came into my office to talk to me. He'd checked around and Kyle's boss was a Major who knew and more importantly, he knew what type of person I was. He told my boss that he respected me and then he also told my boss that he knew me from church and had known me for years. This did not bode well for Kyle but I didn't really care about him right then.

Major Pinkney told his boss what had happened at the C&E Mess Dinner the night before and then the two Majors, without my knowledge, hatched a plan to teach Kyle a lesson. In addition, Maj Pinkney visited our Colonel and gave him a heads up about what had happened. Kyle's boss was pissed off at him and told him that I was pressing harassment charges on Monday and suggested that he spend the weekend thinking about that. For me, the rest of that Friday was uneventful and I gratefully headed home at 4:30 to spend a weekend with my family.

Kyle didn't have such a relaxing weekend. You see, his boss' little talk with him had scared the bee gees out of him. His boss told my Major that he was shocked at Kyle's behavior. I later learned that he told Kyle that there was a very good chance that I was going to press harassment charges against him on Monday. I had no such plans and didn't know about it being threatened to him. It was said to Kyle to scare him and it did. His Major suggested that he write me a letter of apology and he also suggested that he make it very to make it very sincere and then maybe....just maybe.....I'd not press charges.

On Monday morning, my Major handed me Kyle's two page handwritten letter of apology (copied below) saying he didn't know what came over him and he shouldn't have treated me with such disrespect.

> 22 April 93
>
> Lt Lavigne,
>
> This note is written to you to express my misgivings with regards to the incident that occurred at the mess dinner.
>
> In an ill-conceived act of camaraderie, I abused your rights and violated your dignity as a human being. No person has the right to do that to a fellow human being. Even more, no officer should ever exhibit the lack of discretion that I have displayed. The disrespect that I have shown you is inexcuseable and I take it to heart the injurious nature of my actions. I have failed to act both professionally to you as a fellow officer and courteously to you as an equal.
>
> There was no malice, intent of flirtation, or attempt at causing you harm in what I mistakenly believed to be an innocent act. I was wrong in what I did and cannot express enough my deep regret at having made you feel to be less than anything other that the fine person that you are. Please accept my deepest and most sincere apology.
>
> If you feel compelled to carry forth with further action I am prepared to accept the consequences of my actions. I will bear you no ill will for any action you feel is appropriate in bringing this matter to a close. I had no right to expect any other reaction other than what you have shown at the inappropriateness of my behaviour.
>
> ½

...I have the highest regard for you as both a military professional and as a person and it is my hope that we may carry on working in this Division without allowing this incident to colour any future dealings that we may have on a professional level.

Once again, I express to you my most profound apology for what I have done.

Most sincerely,

I was surprised to get it until my boss, Major Pinkney told me how he and Kyle's Major had cooked this up to scare Kyle with the threat of harassment charges. I couldn't help smiling. Serves him right, I thought! I continued to think it was funny until my next posting! What goes around comes around! Soon after I was posted to the NATO Satellite Ground Terminal at Carp, Ontario, Kyle arrived. I ended up having to work with him. And to make matters worse, he was the senior Captain of the two of us and had authority over me. It was a bad situation.

At NDHQ, this was not the only time I had to deal with an officer that doesn't like women in the military. One of these fellows was a high ranking officer….a General, in fact. And he made it very clear to everyone that he did not like me because I am a woman. At first I took his dislike personally, then I learned it wasn't me, it was something I could do nothing about: my gender.

For years, he had shot me down whenever he got the chance and although I stood my ground, I had not directly responded in deference to his rank. He was the General in my branch and I was a junior officer, so, I shut up and put up with his bullshit. Yet this is only so much a person can take of this type of public embarrassment and humiliation and so it happened that one day I'd had enough and spoke up.

This event took place when I was a junior officer. I was nearing the end of my term as a 2nd Lieutenant when I attended a meeting where a Lieutenant-Colonel from our C&E Branch was giving a briefing. He had just returned from a tour where he was the communications officer at the Korean DMZ (Demilitarized Zone) and he was giving us some details about what his role and responsibilities had been as well as some information about what it was like to in Korea.

The presentation was given in the upstairs meeting room of the RCAF Officer's Mess in Ottawa. The chairs were set up in two columns or groups of about five rows of five chairs in each column leaving a walking aisle between the columns. About 40 CELE Officers attended the presentation, yet I was the only woman CELE officer there. This was not unusual. Still, I was looking forward to the meeting although my enthusiasm didn't matter as all junior C&E officers were expected to attend.

When I arrived with a few of my fellow officers from the Canadian Building, there was mingling going on as the presentation wasn't due to start for about ten minutes. A small crowd of junior officers crowded around and were brown-nosing to my less than favorite C&E General, who was also in attendance.

This Senior Branch officer had made it clear that he didn't appreciate his C&E Branch being polluted with women and on this day when the General saw me enter the room, he sneered at me. I was familiar with his sentiments and ignored it as it was something he often did. No worries, I thought! The effect though was visible as my colleagues quickly moved away from me and left me standing alone. It was a hostile environment whenever he was there. My "friends" all sat together and left me to find my own chair.

I took a chair in the middle of the third row on the right side and the General took a chair in the middle of the third row on the left side. He was directly across from me on my left. I could feel his eyes on me, but I ignored it. The presentation was quite good and informative. It was good to learn how we C&E officers operate in unusual postings.

At the end of his presentation, the LCol opened up the floor for questions. A few posting related questions were asked as the LCol answered raised hands. Then the General spoke up and as he did, he turned to look directly at me instead of at the LCol while he addressed his question to him.

He asked the LCol if women in Korea still walked six paces behind the men. The room hushed to a dead silence. You could have heard a pin drop. The LCol looked so uncomfortably. He looked at me as he fished for an answer.

I was amused and proud of him when he responded, "That depends Sir," he said, "if we're going through a mine field we prefer them to walk in front of us!"

The room erupted in laughter. It was a great tension breaker. Unfortunately, the General was not satisfied and wouldn't let it go. Again and more firmly, he asked the same question and again he turned to look at me addressing his question to the LCol. He stared at me so intently that it was clear that he hated me.

The whole room went quiet again and I felt for the LCol whose feet were so obviously put to the fire. Backed into a corner, the LCol responded with a simple, "Yes, Sir." Then the General looked me in the eye and said, "Well, at least in Korea, women know where they belong!"

I got pissed but what could I do. How dare he, this C&E Branch General make it clearer to the group that he did not welcome women in the officer corps! I felt personally attacked and worse still was the knowledge that as leadership comes from the top, and this General was making it clear that it was okay to treat women in uniform disrespectfully, he was in effect telling all the other branch officers present that it was okay to treat me this way.

He way out of line and he had made his message clear....in his estimation, women do not belong in the military. Any officers ambitious enough to brown-nose to the General, and there was a room full of young and ambitious officers, now had a means to gain his favour. It was all they needed. His message was the mistreatment of women who dared to serve, was fine by him.....all that was required was to be ambitious enough to adopt a dislike of women in uniform to appease this General.

I felt my world falling away from me and because I am not passive by nature, I got angry....very angry! At first, I held it in as I knew that within the military, anything I said or did at this point would be considered insubordination, but I lost it. I was too angry and getting angrier and seeing more red as the seconds ticked away. I turned towards this jerk of a General and looking him square in the face, I said, "Yes Sir and dinosaurs belong in museums!"

Although it seemed impossible, the room got even quieter and once again, you could have heard a pin drop. With baited breath, it seemed as if everyone waited to see what the General would do or say. Yet, he didn't respond which made me wonder if I had caught him off guard by my forwardness. Later, back at work, I was worried that I would be charged with insubordination. Bugger! I should have kept my mouth shut!

It took a while for me to realize that I had the General over a barrel: in order for him to follow up with a charge of insubordination, he'd have to admit to sexual harassment. He wasn't about to do that so nothing happened.

At least not for a few years. If we fast-forward a few years later to a time after I became a Captain, we come to a day when my Major comes to my office and tells me that our Colonel wants to see me in his office RIGHT AWAY. When I get there, my Colonel asks me to take a seat before telling me that this same C&E General has called him and wants to see with me.

Me? I'm also told that the General won't tell the Colonel why he wants to see me. The DEEM Colonel asked me if I knew what this was about and I told him I had no idea. Oh boy, I think. The shit is about to hit the fan! I figure that I'm in trouble…..BIG TROUBLE! And, as I march myself over to the main NDHQ Building on Colonel-By Drive, all the time I am wondering what this is about. I was afraid of what was about to happen.

During my march over to his office, I rack my brain trying to figure out what was up but I come up empty and decide to simply let the cards fall where they may. Why, years later, did this General, who hated women in uniform, now wants to see me? I could not be good news!

Arriving at the General's office, his secretary announces me and leads me into his office where I stand to attention and salute him. The General returns my salute and this shocks me but not as much as when he kindly asks me to take a seat. Obviously, I'm not here to be charged. This just adds to my confusion.

So, I sit down and wait for the General to speak. At first, he clears his throat and with his eyes downcast, he tells me that he needs my help. "WHAT," my brains screams, "MY HELP?"

That's when he tells me that he has a daughter and that she has joined the military. This is all new news to me. I guess it is no big surprise that I was never interested in knowing anything about this General. As he continues, he tells me that she is at her first posting and has a problem with her supervisor. She says she's being given a hard time and has called Daddy to ask for his advice.

"You see," he says to me, "she's being sexually harassed by him." I damn near fell out of the chair! Unaware of my shock (or simply ignoring it), the General continues and tells me what she is dealing with and that he doesn't know what to advise her to do. Then he looks directly at me and asks me what I would do given these circumstances.

I guess what goes around does come around. Here was someone who had made my life hell by harassing me because of my gender asking me to help him help his daughter put into a situation much like he had put me in. Oh, I so wanted to tell him to go to hell.

What a wake-up call this must have been for him and as much as I didn't want to help HIM, it was his daughter who needed my help and it wasn't her fault that her father was a jackass. I hated him but I couldn't take it out on her. Still, I didn't immediately answer him. I made him wait while I wrapping my head around the whole unreal situation and to be honest, I was giving myself a little time to revel in the justice of the whole situation.

After enjoying the moment for a moment, I came back to the situation and asked a few probing questions wherein I gained a better understanding of her situation. He answered my questions while commenting that her supervisor's behaviour was totally inappropriate and, get this, un-officer-like! At that comment, I almost laughed out loud. Instead, I controlled myself and gave him the best advice I could.

He was very grateful and thanked me yet my unforgiving heart didn't want to hear any of it. I had done this for his daughter....not for him! He capped off the meeting by saying something that seriously pissed me off....he said that he knew that I'd know what to do because

I'd handled myself pretty good in dealing with sexual harassment in our branch.

All I could think was, "He should know.....he was the dealer!"

Before I left his office, the General told me that he didn't want this conversation to go any further than his office and I was to keep this conversation confidential. I wondered if he was embarrassed at needing my help or at having a daughter in the military. Nothing had changed!

I didn't realize the extent of what giving that promise meant until later. When I get back to work, I was called in to speak with my Colonel and his first question to me was what the General had wanted with me.

I didn't know what to say. Having promised to say nothing, I was unable to answer the Colonel's question so I said that it was personal. The Colonel's face turned into a sneer and he winked at me saying he "understood." It was obvious that he had come to the wrong conclusion and the conclusion he'd made caused me to feel totally grossed out. I wanted to scream at him that it amazed me that until this day he knew the General hated me and so how had he suddenly gone from thinking I was in trouble with a General to even conceiving that I was screwing the General! Friggin Amazing!

At the C&E Branch Mess Dinner at CFSCE's Officer's Mess in Kingston in 1992, I was horribly sexually harassed during the meal and then sexually assaulted by a drunken Base Commander during the socializing after the Mess Dinner while 200 of my fellow officers looked on and did NOTHING!

I'm a junior officer, now a Lieutenant, I was back in Kingston for the Annual C&E Branch Mess Dinner held each September. I was posted to Ottawa and my family had just moved to Ottawa the previous month and I wouldn't have attended except that I had signed up to attend the previous month while we were still living in Kingston.

My husband had already turned down three PMQs offered to us over the course of the 10 months since my posting to Ottawa, citing that they were not as nice as our PMQ in Kingston when his real reason was that he was having an affair in Kingston and his mistress couldn't make the move just yet. I didn't know this at the time and would not learn of it until years later. I missed my family greatly and had called in favour after favour to be offered a PMQ only to have my husband reject it.

While in Ottawa, I became lonely and I started to drink. It is a frustrating time for me. Although I loved my work, I had a LCol at work who, after rejecting his passes time after time, had decided to destroy my career. The work was great; fantastic even; but the work environment was toxic.

Travelling to and from Kingston for 10 months, had made me numb to the understanding that this was a long way to go to attend a Mess Dinner. Still, I'd already signed up for the event and made the arrangements to head to Kingston that Thursday to attend the C&E Branch Mess Dinner at the C&E Branch's home base in Kingston. My plan was to drive back to Ottawa early on that Friday morning.

The C&E Branch Mess Dinner was a grand affair with approximately 200 CELE officers attending and although vastly outnumbered (there was only three women there), I was not concerned. I'd now been in the Canadian Forces for more than a dozen years and I was very used to being outnumbered by the guys.

And, it was a nice break from the toxic work environment in Ottawa. Here, I felt safe and welcomed. My DEEM LCol was not going to be there so I didn't have him to deal with. Already, it was getting better. Maybe it was that feeling of being someplace safe that made what happened next so very surprising to me.

When I got to the C&E Officer's Mess that evening, I was dressed in my formal mess kit which I felt and looked sharp plus I was standing a little bit taller as I was wearing my new rank of Lieutenant proudly. After arriving I got myself a beer and headed over to the posted seating plan to find out where I was seated. Honestly, I felt myself swell with pride when I saw that I was seated at the head table. I figured it was because my C&E Branch was proud of me. Not only had I just graduated from RMC second in my class, but I had also graduated as Canada's 1st Woman Space Scientist and I had been an NCM, done the UTPM thing and here I was back with my branch as an officer.

During the dinner, I was seated beside the Base Commander, a Colonel who began laughing and joking with me. He was showing me a lot of attention and I was flirting back. I figured it was harmless, but I was wrong. Even today I wonder how many people there knew what he did to me. During the meal, he put his hand on my thigh and started rubbing his hand on my leg and moving it upwards toward my private parts.

I was shocked by his behaviour but I could not make a scene. It just wasn't done. So, I looked out over the 200+ dinner attendees and smiled as I reached below the table and took his hand off my leg and placed it on his leg. I shouldn't have flirted back with him and now I was paying the price. I did my best to not let anyone see what he was doing. I was afraid my face would give me away so I smiled as I leaned towards him and whispered to him to stop.

He didn't and time and time again, I would ask him to stop but he was drunk and obviously horny. I wanted to scream but did nothing other than continue to take his hand off my leg and put it back on his. I turned to the fellow to my other side and tried to engage him in conversation. He was also a Colonel and I'd seen him often as he also worked in Ottawa and at DCEEM.

Whenever at the RCAF Officer's Mess in Ottawa, he was being buddy-buddy with the LCol I was having a problem with in Ottawa. Dang, he was no help at all and I was sure that the LCol was going to get an earful from this guy. He could see my struggles, and I believe he knew what was happening, but he did nothing to help me. He had never been friendly towards me.

Probably another one of "those" I thought. One of the C&E officers who didn't like women in the branch. He had nothing to say to me and even turned away from me. At the head table he made sure I knew that he didn't like me. So, I was stuck with only the Base Commander for conversation and we all know how that was working out for me. Bugger!

The Base Commander didn't stop trying to manhandle me and it upset me but I couldn't....just couldn't make a scene. I felt intimidated by his rank and position and never even considered anything other than getting through the ordeal. Of course, if it had been anybody else, I would have stood up and then yelled at him to stop this shit! Then I would have marched out of there and to hell with protocol. But, I did not feel I had that option as that would have been insubordinate and I could have been charged if I had done so.

With 200 pairs of eyes on me, I just kept picking up his hand off my leg and placing it on his leg, smiling at him the whole time and numerous times whispering for him to stop. I was unable to eat and was so grateful when the Mess Dinner was over. And, although I wanted to leave the Mess, that was not an option for me.

At Mess Dinners, it is customary for the junior officers to stay behind in the dining room after the meal was done to finish off the Port wine (that is, the wine used for toasts during the meal). I was grateful for the reprieve and felt able to breath for the first time in hours. But what I found was that I couldn't relax. Some of my once friendly fellow officers were sneering at me. At the time, I discounted those reactions as jealousy. I'd never sat at the head table before but I remember enviously looking at the junior officer that was selected to sit there.

Maybe that was all it was. We all were ambitious young officers and we all wanted to get that next promotion and sitting at the head table gave one the advantage of having the ear of two senior branch officers seated next to you. My having been seated at the head table must have seemed like a huge advantage to them. And, it wasn't until much later that I wondered how it must have looked to my fellow junior officers as I laughed and flirted with the Base Commander.

Still I did relax a bit and after the port was finished off, we rejoined the rest of the C&E officers in the main hall of the Officer's Mess. As I exited the dining room door, the Base Commander was there at my side. And he was even drunker than during dinner. He placed his hand on my elbow and guided me out of the main hall saying he wanted to talk with me. I figured he wanted to apologize and I didn't put up a fuss. We went into a side room which we call the "Jimmy Room" and he closed the door. Then he came over to me and went to kiss me.

No way was I letting that happen. He was caught off guard when I shoved him away and being a little more than a little drunk, he swayed and I got away and headed back into the main hall. Unable to immediately face my peers, I headed for the bathroom. I had drank a bit too much port in trying to dial down what had happened during the dinner. I had to get my shit together.

Still I wasn't expecting him to have followed me to the bathroom. When I came outside the door, he was there. I ignored him and dang near marched into the main hall of the Mess. I paused in the doorway and that gave him the opportunity to come up next to me and before I knew what hit me, he had me pressed against a wall. He had actually grabbed my boob and with his large hand on my breast, he pinned me before planting a sloppy drunken kiss on my lips and I recoiled.

I should have slapped him in the face or kicked him in the balls but I did neither. And not because he was big and strong, but because he was a Colonel and the Base Commander. Instead, I put my hand on his chest and pushed him up and away from me and said to him, "NO SIR, I'm a good girl!"

He let me go then and I left the Officer's Mess feeling just awful. I was disgusted and heartbroken that my fellow officers were looking at me. There had been over 200 officers there and as sure as I am that many of them didn't see the assault, I know that some of them did and still, they did nothing. They stood there and watched and not one of them had the courage to step in and help me.

I walked to the barracks where I would spend the night and berated myself for having said something as inane as "NO SIR, I'm a good girl!" If I could, I would have kicked myself. I reasoned that I must have been intimated by both his rank and his position, yet I wondered if I still thought like a Corporal (where we regard a Base Commander almost as highly as we did God).

I also reflected on how everyone there...all those officers....must have seen some of what he did to me and I felt ashamed for them. Yes, the Base Commander's behaviour was inexcusable, but what about all those witnesses who stood by and did nothing. I was ashamed of them and it made me wonder why in the hell I ever wanted to become an officer!

I felt lost and confused to have been treated so disrespectfully. This fellow who'd just assaulted me was the same person who had nominated me to go to university and I had such a high opinion of him. And I had believed he had a high opinion of me. At the time, I did not know him to be like this but when I later asked around about him, I learned that it was his nature and I felt naïve for having been so stupid. I had been ill prepared to deal with this situation.

Later, as I questioned myself, I asked myself if I'd asked for this by flirting and I came to the conclusion that I didn't. I also asked myself how I could have prevented the assault and I didn't know how I could have stopped someone else from behaving badly. If I'd have known what the Colonel was like, I would never have flirted with him but that doesn't excuse him. And, I decided that I was not going to excuse his behaviour and blame myself for this assault.

Back in Ottawa the next day, I was at my desk, when my phone rang. It was the Base Commander. I was shocked. He apologized for his behaviour during the Mess Dinner saying that he had had too much to drink. He told me that he had heard that he was out of line but that he doesn't personally remember much of it. And, so on and so forth.

I was still reeling from even haven gotten the phone call. Still, I thought, "Whatever!" I hadn't slept much the night before and during my drive to Ottawa, I couldn't stop thinking about the events of the night before. I'd spent all that time going over what had happened… reviewing it and then reviewing it again and now I was angry.

I understood that I had been intimidated by him and during my review, I thought I should have done this or I should have done that. Things like knee him in the crotch and make a scene. All kinds of thought had ran though my head but, I hadn't done any of those things and I was disappointed in myself. Yet, here was the Colonel apologizing to me and asking how he could make it up to me and I didn't want to hear his voice.

I didn't want to talk to him and even considered hanging up but I didn't. Instead I listened as the Colonel insisted that he wanted to do something to make up for his behaviour. I told him, "No thank you, Sir."

I wanted to say more but I didn't because I was disgusted by him and more out of disgust and an unwillingness to be beholding to him for anything, I kept quiet. I no longer trusted him and my opinion of him was low. I was sure that any advantage he offered to make up for the embarrassment he had caused me at the Mess Dinner would only get the C&E Branch tongues wagging. So I simply said, "No thank you, Sir!"

He had done his research and I knew this when he mentioned that he knew I had wanted a posting to US Space Command in Colorado Springs and he said he could "make that happen for me." Again I said, "No, thank you, Sir." It must have been infuriating for him. I would not be bought. I would have loved to get that posting but not as a consolation prize for keeping my mouth shut about his behaviour at the Mess Dinner.

"If I'm going to get a posting to Colorado Springs, I'm going to earn it," I told him, "It was NOT going to be because you're apologizing for making sexual advances to me. It's going to happen because I've earned it." He paused then and next he said, "There's got to be something I can do for you."

Remember how I said I was angry....well, this conversation got me fired up and I saw red. Maybe it was the separation of the phone line that made me feel safe, I'm not sure but I lost my temper and I spoke out of turn. I said, "Yes, Sir there is one thing."

And he said, "What's that?" I took a deep breath and said, "Sir, you can stop drinking because it makes you stupid!" He must have been shocked at my forwardness as he paused and the line went quiet for a second on two before he said, "Thank you for your input Lieutenant. Goodbye" and he hung up.

This story does not end yet as a few months later when I was on course at a Life Cycle Material Management course at RMC, I went for TGIF at the C&E Officer's Mess on Base Kingston with a friend of mine. She was still posted to CFSCE and when I lived there, she had lived just a few doors down the street from me on the base. Then, we'd often walked together to attend TGIF at the Officer's Mess as it was only three miles away from our homes and it gave us time to catch up and enjoy girlfriend time.

Almost as soon as we walked into the Officer's Mess, the Base Commander approached me. We had joined a group of our fellow officers at a tall tables where we were had just ordered a round of beers when the Colonel walked over and ignoring everyone else's greetings, he turned and spoke to me. I was embarrassed and didn't like it the attention from him. What he had done at the Mess Dinner and our telephone conversation was still very fresh in my memory.

Over the four years while I was at RMC, I'd been invited many times to TGIF at the C&E Officer's Mess on Base Kingston. And on more than one occasion, the Colonel had come over to talk to my group. Making the rounds, I figured. Yet, to me, he'd come over to me and say stupid stuff like, "I can't talk right now, but in about 10 minutes come over and talk to me even if you have to interrupt me." I figured because he had recommended me for UTPM, he felt some sort of ownership and maybe he would be introducing me to others and wanted to show off the UTPM he'd recommended. I had felt honoured that he was interested even though when he had recommended me in 1987, he hadn't even known my name and I believe he only recommended me because Captain Key has been so persuasive.

Now, like a bull in a china shop, he paraded around the Officer's Mess stopping to talk to this group and that. He was so full of himself and was showing off by exerting his authority. At the time I thought that was all it was, but now I wonder how it must have looked but I can't change the past.

When he came over this time, he turned to me and said, "Let me buy you a beer." Geez-whiz, he has some gall. I wished he would just leave me alone and declined the offer, "No thank you Sir," I said. But then he insisted and firming up his voice, he said, "NO, LET ME GET YOU A BEER!" and putting his hand around my waist, he turned me and then guided me towards the bar.

When we got there, he asked me what I wanted and ordered a draft beer. Then the Base Commander surprised me when he said to the bartender, "I'll have my usual" and the bartender brought him an O'Doul's (a non-alcoholic beer).

I was speechless but the Colonel wasn't. "This is what I wanted to show you," he said to me, "since our phone conversation, I've had the Officer's Mess stock O'Doul's and that's all I've drink now."

It was so good to learn this news and although I don't know if he continued this lifestyle change as I've had no conversations with him since that day, I was impressed. As I returned to my friends, I contemplated what had just happened. It was a lot to take in so I may have stood quietly drinking my beer as I digested the ramifications of what had just happened.

There was a MWO working at DEEM whose family were still in Kingston and when we learned of one another's circumstance, we agreed to share the commute to and from Kingston each weekend. During the long commutes to and from Kingston, we developed a friendship and back in Ottawa, we became running partners.

Unfortunately, we became too familiar with one another, and the differences in our ranks was ignored by him. One day, at work, he showed disrespect towards me and then openly objected to taking orders from a woman.

I had to take the matter in hand right away and I did so. He had the responsibility to provide me with a report and he'd been late all week. By Friday, I still didn't have the report on my desk. That's when I started to drive to and from Kingston alone after ordering him to work the weekend and making it clear that the expected report had better be on my desk by zero eight hundred hours Monday morning.

With the office being an open area of cubicle offices, others had heard the exchange. One of those who had heard the exchange was a Major who was on a posting from the US Army Signal Corp. Major George Spriggs and I had become friends at work but our friendship had blossomed when a few of us from DEEM had taught him how to downhill ski.

It was a fun time and George was hilarious. The first time out, he wore a bright yellow pair of pants which was a good thing as it allowed us to find him in the snow! He was so funny to watch. He had come in from Georgia (yeah, George from Georgia) and skiing just did not come natural to him. We spent many hours teaching him how to get up after falling down (an important skill for a beginner) and the contrast of the white Canadian snow and the black officer's skin was a blessing. George is an African-American.

Near the end of that friday that I had the confrontation with the MWO, George walked with me to the Air Force Officer's Mess where the officers at DEEM were expected to be from 1600 to 1800 hours each Friday to "develop espirit de corp." It didn't matter if we were having a beer or a soda, we had to be there and although it always delayed my departure for Kingston, I had no choice.

As we walked to the Mess, George told me how difficult it was for him in the US Army as the guys simply didn't want to take orders from a black officer. Then he said, "But they would rather take orders from a black man than a white woman!" I was speechless and I hated that he was right!

At the DEEM Christmas Party in 1993, the LCol made a very obviously harassing statement to me and it was the straw that broke the camel's back. I was standing beside my boss, who raised his eyebrows when the LCol said that the only way I could go on a TD trip was if I stayed in his hotel room. Not long afterwards, I left the party as did my boss. When we got back to our desk areas, he told me that he was surprised that the LCol would go this far. Then he told me that he knew of some of the stuff that was going on and that he felt that I was handling it okay. But this latest incident was over the fence bad. Still, we were both at a loss about what to do now.

What ended up happening was Major Pinkney decided that this harassment of me had to stop and a few weeks later he advised me to go to JAG (the Judge Advocate General for the Canadian Forces). He must have looked into this after the Christmas Party incident as he seemed well informed about who to go to and even who I was to speak to if I did go to JAG. I will always be grateful to him for that.

So I went over and visited with the folks in the JAG office which was just across Laurier Street from the Canadian Building where I worked. Initially I spoke to Captain Cindy Allen who had me go in and speak with her LCol about what was going on at DEEM. I had not spoken to anyone in uniform about what was going on at work. The only other person who knew, besides my Major and anyone else who'd noticed at work, was my husband.

I found it difficult to talk about the matter but Cindy drew me out. She would become a dear friend and ally. The following week, she had me meet with her boss, an LCol, who told me that my C&E Branch was one of the worst branch in the Canadian Forces for sexual harassment. He was anxious for me to step up and press charges. He said, he wanted to "get them."

I was advised to write everything down about what had happened and was happening and so I did. It is from those notes that I have such clarity as I write this book. I also wrote about the strong sense of loyalty I felt for my branch and my hesitation to move forward. I didn't want to see my C&E Branch splashed in a bloody way all over the front page of tomorrow's newspaper!

Even to have their reputation brought down within the military seemed disloyal to me. I didn't know what to do. Sensing my hesitation, the JAG LCol advised me to go and speak to my Colonel about the matter. He said I needed to go over my LCol's head and I did that. That didn't work out so good for me as after I spoke with DEEM, I became distraught.

What an asshole he'd been! The Colonel had got angry and screamed at me that he didn't want "any black balls" in his organization. I was told that I was to keep my mouth shut and soldier on.

He went so far as to say, "I thought you would make a good officer, but I was wrong!" He tore my heart from my chest when he said that. Then as if adding salt to a wound, he added, "A good officer would know how to deal with this." Then he ordered me out of his office.

The disappointment in me that the Colonel expressed struck deep and tore me apart. This Colonel had been one of two colonels who had ceremoniously removed my Corporal Rank and replaced it with Officer Cadet Rank as I was welcomed into the C&E Officer Corp back in 1987. And here he was telling me I was no good as an officer. I felt like such as failure. I don't get to tears easily but he brought me to tears that day. Shamefaced, I left his office and walked blindly to the ladies room where I threw cold water on my face and breathed deeply in an effort calm myself.

When I got back to my desk, I called Cindy over at JAG. Major Pinkney was watching me worriedly and I could tangible feel his sense loss. He didn't know what to do. This was new territory for both of us. Cindy, hearing my voice, knew I was upset and suggested we meet downstairs in the Canadian Building restaurant.

It hadn't taken much more than that invitation for me to latch onto the opportunity to escape my work environment. As soon as I got off the phone, I headed straight for the elevators that would take me to the main floor of the building. The restaurant was on the main floor and I took the side door into the restaurant, found a booth and collapsed. I was exhausted.

Cindy showed up a few minutes later and we talked for about a half hour. I told her what had happened and she asked me to now move forward with harassment charges. She reaffirmed JAG's support yet I was still hesitant as I didn't want to hurt my branch.

When I thought of how my branch's name would get dragged through the mud, I cringed. My loyalty to my branch was strong and I didn't want this to happen to them and I told her so. She then asked me if there was a senior female officer in my branch that could help me and immediately I thought of Major Laurel Cook. I had known Laurel Cook for a few years and we had become friends years earlier. She was a smart cookie and had learned how to navigate her way through the sexual discrimination in our branch. I felt confident that she would know what to do. I knew she had recently been promoted to the rank of major making her the first woman in our C&E Branch to ever be promoted to this level and she worked in Ottawa. So, I called her.

Laurel met us at the restaurant and Cindy brought her up to speed about the situation. She remained calm as the details were explained to her and a few times she turned to me for confirmation, which I gave her. I felt as though she just wanted to hug me and say how sorry she was for this shit. Once she had heard the details, Laurel suggested a potential solution: she offered to talk to my Colonel (whom she knew). Our C&E world is a small one. Cindy made it clear to Laurel that on my behalf, she would need to confirm what I had said had happened for it to be invaluable to JAG.

After some discussion back and forth between Laurel and Cindy, we headed back up to DEEM and my Colonel's office. Laurel respectfully asked the Colonel if he would speak with her and me. He agreed and the three of us went into his office. Laurel took the reins for the conversation that ensued. She asked him for a summary of what had happened and the Colonel told Laurel the same thing she had just heard downstairs.

He shared with her how he was pissed off with me and like a spoiled, privileged child, he didn't sugar coated any of it. It was disheartening to know that he didn't think he had done anything wrong when he had yelled at me as he saw it as a disciplinary action. The Colonel boldly and self-righteously spoke up when he told Laurel what he had said to me.

Laurel then turned to me and asked me to leave. I did so and she walked outside his office with me and told me to head to the ladies bathroom and wait there until she got there. I waited for over a half hour before she joined me. When she came into the bathroom, she shared with me the conversation she had just had with the Colonel and how she had explained to him that not only was he professionally responsible for what he had said but that he was sexually harassing me and that his behaviour was an assault. She warned him that he would be held accountable in a personal financial way as well and that this was not good for him nor the C&E Branch. She shared with the Colonel what she expected the outcome to be and how his bullying of me was totally inappropriate. She told him that he was victimizing a victim.

When she told me that he wanted to speak to me, I was wary but the hope that this matter could be resolved at the lowest possible level was attractive to me. She prepared me to expect apologies: first from the Colonel and then from the LCol. I was told that the Colonel would now back me up 100% and had already spoken to the LCol. She then told me that he had explained to the LCol that I had gone to JAG and that I was no longer willing to be harassed.

Laurel then asked me what I wanted to do. My options were to proceed with charges against the LCol through JAG (and with the Colonel's support) or I could have a conversation with the LCol who now wanted to speak with me. Of course I wanted to speak to the LCol. This was my chance to clear the air: to let him know how I felt and how he was making me feel. I wanted to have my say and to tell him to just friggin stop it!

She made it clear to me that if I allowed it that this would not be the end of the matter. We would just listen to the LCol and go from there. Laurel and I headed back to the Colonel's office but when we got to his office, and I was face to face with the LCol, I found myself intimidated by his rank and I didn't feel it was appropriate for a Lieutenant to tell off a Lieutenant-Colonel.

I had spent over a dozen years in the Canadian Forces and you don't spend that much time in the military without such things as rank respect becoming ingrained in you. Although I felt justified in what I wanted to say, I felt a strong level of intimidation simply by his rank. When we first got to the Colonel's office, the LCol wasn't there. The Colonel made his apologies and voiced his support (just as Laurel had said he would).

Then the LCol was called into the Colonel's office and for the first time, he spoke respectfully with me. I had heard him to speak to my fellow officers in this way, but I had never been afforded the same level of respect until that moment. With the Colonel and Major Laurel Cook listening in, the two of us had a one on one conversation as best we could under the circumstances.

During our discussion, the LCol apologized for his behaviour and explained to me that he thought the way he was behaving was okay but now he knows that it was not okay. He said he was sorry and he then he asked for a consideration: he wanted six months to clean up his behaviour and it came with a promise.

He promised me that if I gave him this six months, he would prove to me that he was a different person. Then he said that if I didn't think he had done enough within that six months, then I could press harassment charges and he would not even argue them but instead he would plead guilty to them. When he promised me that he would not do anything to fight them, he sounded contrite and sincere fully admitting that I had not said anything that was untrue. He said, "I'm the person that has done the wrong and I want to make it right."

I was surprised by this admission as I had assumed that he would deny everything and he didn't. Instead, he fessed up and apologized and asked for leniency so that he could right his wrongs. My LCol at DEEM wasn't the sort of person to humble himself like this. He'd always been the sort of person who'd put on a front and wore it until it wore out.

I listened as he went on to tell me that he knew I was a good engineer, but now he knows that I am also a good officer. He apologized again for having treated me any other way than with the respect that I deserve. I hadn't expected this from him and his humble demeanor went a long way towards restoring my faith in the goodness of people. My nemesis had somehow renewed my faith at that very moment.

My attitude has always been to "fix" the problem at the lowest level possible and so I agreed to the six month hold rather than making this a public spectacle. I didn't want that. What I wanted was for the LCol to stop harassing me. That's what I wanted. I wanted it to stop permanently!

So, I gave him the six months he had asked for. There were no exceptions or special circumstances for me. Nothing like that. I didn't want any special treatment nor did I want a pat on the back for not following through on the sexual harassment charges or going public. Basically, I was simply wanted to be left alone to do my work.

The change I wanted, at first appeared as if I had got as the LCol changed his attitude and even became an advocate for women in our C&E Branch.

As the years passed, I heard through the grapevine how he stepped up to tell other officers that their behaviour was inappropriate and it made my heart swell. I was really impressed with him and I felt as if I had done the right thing in giving him that six months. It was a good outcome from a very bad situation, I thought. A few years ago, as a retired General, the once LCol told me that if I ever needed him to that he would step up to the plate and expose what he had done.

But, it didn't last long. A few months later, a Captain that worked upstairs would humiliate me at a Branch Mess Dinner and these same guys (these brothers) would look on and watch this humiliation and they would laugh at me. I felt a deep sense of betrayal then and a few years after that, one of these brothers in arms of mine would rape me.

Was my sudden posting out of DEEM and to NICS Carp part of a conspiracy? If so, I was set up to take a fall. I don't coddle conspiracy theories and I don't even want to go there as it seems so farfetched but the facts are the facts. I cannot ignore the evidence.

My harasser, the Lcol was best friends with a Colonel within DCEEM. The two of them always lunched together and were always seen having a drink together at the RCAF Mess. My new Commanding Officer (CO) at NICS Carp was a Major who had come from that Colonel's group. It was after I was posted to Carp, I learned that the out-going CO was surprised when he was unexpectedly asked to retire. This concerned me and my concern heightened as an overwhelming change of staff at the site was happening. The whole of the officer staff at a site was being cycled. As knowledge of how a site is run is maintained by the officer leadership, at least one of the officer staff traditionally stays put within any posting cycle and this was not happening. It disconcerted me and made the hairs on the back of my neck stand up.

Back in 1993, I was asked to be the Publicity Chair for the upcoming Canadian AFCEA (Armed Forces Communications & Electronics Association) Conference to be held in Ottawa in 1994. I had been a member of AFCEA for years and truly supported this international organization. In 1993, I'd attended the Washington, DC AFCEA Conference and every other year, we held an AFCEA Conference in Canada. In preparation for this big event, a board was appointed to handle the details. As the Publicity Chair, I was tasked with ensuring that we got a good turnout via properly publicizing the event and

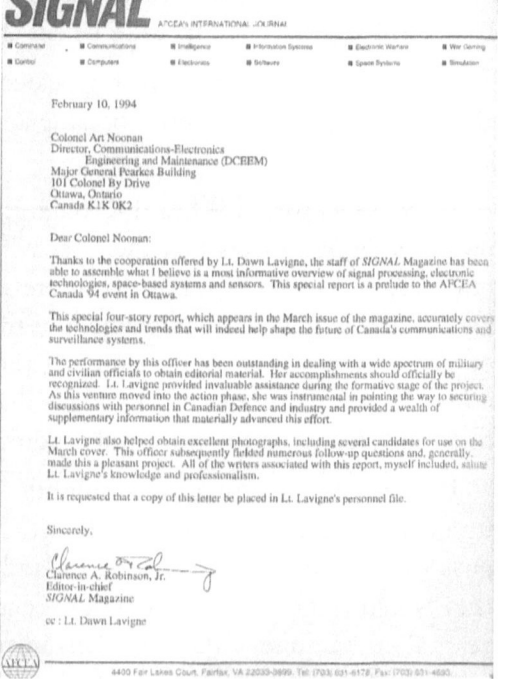

making sure that engineering professionals were made aware of why it was important for them to attend. I worked very hard to ensure that Canada got the exposure she deserved.

Wanting more to help others, in 1994, I was elected President of the Ottawa branch of WISE (Women In Science and Engineering). I had been a member for years and over time had stepped up to a position on the executive. My focus was on the promotion of education as it was discovered that most young women drop their courses in math and the sciences in high school. I made this my mission. WISE's objective was to spread the good news that science and engineering were work fields that young women should consider and we worked to promote STEM even before the acronym was coined.

It was during this time that I learned to downhill ski and fell in love with the sport. It was also a way to push the stress from work off me. The fresh air cleared my head and it was fun as well. I became so enamored with downhill skiing that each Wednesday over the winter, I would try to take a day's leave and head off with the FOSC (Forces Ottawa Ski Club) to ski on Mount Tremblant near Montreal. I was addicted to the sport! The Wednesday ski trip was not the only skiing I did. A week consisted of a few nights of skiing on local hills and one weekend day was spent on the slopes with my children.

During this difficult time, there was a bright spot in meeting Major

George Spriggs. While I was posted at DEEM, we had a US Army Signals Officer posted in. Major George Spriggs had come to us from the southern United States and to everyone's amazement (and amusement), he learned how to downhill ski. George is an African-American and at first, he was very clumsy (like any beginner skier) but his wardrobe was unlike anything we'd ever seen before. I still kid him about it. We had a fun time with him as a few of us at

DEEM taught him how to downhill ski. He was always good company and had a wonderful sense of humour. He easily was able to laugh at himself (which made us feel less alone in our amusement)! I also liked the way George was a deep thinker.

I'll never forget the day we walked together to the RCAF Officer's Mess one Friday for TGIF. On the way to the Officer's Mess, George shared with me some of the challenges he'd had in the US Army, where as a "black" man he'd often been disrespected by white soldiers. Then he said the thing I will never forget. He said, "A white man would rather take orders from a black man than a white woman!" I could have kicked his butt.....but, you know, he was right!

The cubicle format of our offices did not allow for private conversations so a lot of people had heard the exchange between a MWO and myself. The MWO was disrespectful of me and everyone knew it. It should never have been that way, but it was and for me it was frustrating and embarrassing as I donned my "dragon-lady" attitude and straightened him out.

Chapter Four: NATO Satellite Ground Terminal and LCWB

OTTAWA AREA, ONTARIO (1994-1995)

I was posted to NICS in 1994, just 2.5 years into a 4 year posting. I thought it was unusual to be posted out after only 2 ½ years but I was glad for posting out….at first. It didn't take long to figure out that I'd moved from the frying pan to the fire.

This posting was to the NATO Satellite Ground Terminal near Carp, Ontario, known as NICS Carp. At the NATO Integrated Communications Site (NICS) site, there was three officers yet the Commanding Officer at the site was retiring and a different Major was slotted to be posted in. I was posted into the vacancy left by the junior C&E officer and my job title was Chief Network Controller.

At the NICS site there were three officers' positions and all of these positions were filled with new people. Soon after I arrived as the junior Captain, the senior Captain received a surprise out of cycle posting message. Most postings are executed during the summer months to make the move to a new school by the member's children easier on the family.

To provide continuity of the executive of any military installation, one officer who knew how the site operated was supposed to be left in place during the posting cycle as knowledge of how a site is run is then maintained but, that's not what happened at NICS Carp that year. The legacy officer, a senior Captain told me that he wasn't supposed to be posted that year. I wondered if I was somehow being set up but not being big on conspiracy theory, I found it hard to accept. I was naïve.

In time the evidence would be too obvious to ignore. I knew I was in trouble when the CO made it clear that he didn't like women in the military and when the senior Captain was unexpectedly posted out and his job was taken by the very same captain who had harassed me at the C&E Mess Dinner a few years earlier.

Although we were not friends, the DCEEM Captain who got posted in and I spoke about his sudden posting and he told me that he didn't expect to get posted that year and he didn't know why he was at NICS as it hadn't been one of his choices of postings. Both of these officers came from the same DCEEM whose Colonel was best friends with the LCol who had harassed me.

Although commanded by three officers, the NICS site was operated by 30 plus NCMs, overseen by a Chief Warrant Officer and two Master Warrant Officers. The CWO was a long-in-the tooth Chief who simply hated women in the military and had no qualms about letting me know. He was a grumpy old guy who yielded a lot of power and influence over the troops under his command. He had arrived before I did and seemed to know the ropes so I defaulted to him while I learned my job.

Then, the MWO that worked directly for me suddenly retired. I liked this guy a lot especially when he came into my office the morning of his retirement party and asked me if I'd read the Montreal Gazette that morning. When I answered no, he put the newspaper in front of me and strongly suggested that I read the story about women and chocolate. He warned me that I would be asked about its validity later in the day.

I opened the newspaper and read how women in Montreal had been surveyed as to which they prefer: sex or chocolate. Chocolate won! A few hours later at my MWO's retirement luncheon, we were standing about in a circle waiting for everyone to arrive. I was the only woman there until my MWO arrived with his wife. While we were waiting, the MCpl from the Orderly Room asked me if I had read the Montreal Gazette that morning.

I played dumb and said no and asked why. He then explained to me that women were reported to prefer chocolate over sex and then he asked me what I think of that. Thank goodness, my MWO had prepared me for this. "Hmmmmm…" I said, "It's probably easier to get good chocolate!"

A round of laughter went up and that was the end of that! We had a delightful lunch although it was sad to see my MWO go. We got a new MWO into the job and although the new MWO appeared friendly, he was a real snake in the grass. I was naïve and believed this new MWO would be as protective of me as his predecessor had been. I was wrong.

The NICS site was a viper's nest and I quickly learned how difficult this posting was going to be when the new CO at NICS Carp made it clear that he hated women in his C&E Branch, women who'd gone to his college (RMC), and women in the military in general. When I arrived at the SGT, I found that I was the only woman there. I was at my new posting for only a few weeks when my new Commanding Officer unexpectedly asks me to come to his office to explain to me his position on my uselessness.

He spoke plainly as he tells me that women don't belong in the military and certainly not in his Branch or at "his" college. Like me, he was also a graduate of Royal Military College (RMC). Then he takes off his graduation ring and slams it on his desk in front of me and tells me to look at the inscription inside the ring. Where normally an inscription of a name and college number would be, his is inscribed with only four capital letters, "LCWB." He puffs up his chest and sits up straighter before explaining to me that LCWB stands for "Last Class With Balls!

I was shocked by his admission. He continued to inform me that women ruined his college's standards and tells me how he thinks they don't even belong in the Canadian Forces. Then he shares with me that as a graduate of the last class at RMC (that is, where there were no women graduates), he is very proud to be one of the LCWBs.

I wanted to get out of there but I couldn't so I sat and listened as he tells me that he was at RMC when women first got there; how "they" ruined "his" college; how the physical fitness standards were changed to accommodate "them" and how he was there when the first woman in our branch came to RMC. He describes her to me and says I probably know her and then he tells me that she was a waste of flesh.

I got the message loud and clear: He hates me. I can see it on his face. It wasn't like he was trying to hide it. To say that I felt sexually harassed would be putting it mildly. Actually, I felt nauseous and when allowed to leave his office, I went straight to the bathroom.

I looked at myself in the mirror and I could see how white I was. "Oh, my God," I thought, "out of the frying pan (at DEEM) and into the fire!" As my CO had made it abundantly clear that he hated me for nothing I could change.....my gender! He wasn't going to give me a chance to prove how good a worker I was or how good an officer I was. I was scared: scared for my person and scared about my military career. How in the heck was I going to navigate my way through the next two years? I didn't have a clue.

Now, as I look back, I realize that the LCWB must have been the year before he graduated! Not long after I was posted to the NICS site, a Tel Type Technician, MCpl Alice Gillis was posted in. Alice and I had been close friends years earlier, but she was no longer friendly. When I desperately needed a friend at work, she'd put such distance between us and I knew it had to be the new difference in our ranks (that is, her being an NCM and my being an officer). My long-time and dear friend, Alice was now wary of me. While I was at RMC, she had risen to the rank of MCpl in addition to having learned how to play the piano (which has always been a dream of mine). I was proud of her on multiple levels and I looked forward to working with her. Sadly, I believe she only saw my rank and not me. It saddened me to realize that she was not looking forward to working with me and to this day I miss her friendship.

While I was still at DEEM and before I started my job at NICS Carp, I'd sent a memo to the fellow that would be my new CO requesting permission to attend an Adventure Training exercise that I had signed up for months earlier. I'd signed up when I wasn't expecting to be posted for another two years and now I was committed to this exercise. The training was to take place a few weeks after my posting date and without the CO's permission, I wouldn't have been allowed to participate.

I knew very little about my CO except that he had been a silver spoon case with prominent military figures in his family. At the time, I wondered how he would get along with a kid from Regent Park and figured it might be like mixing oil and water. Still, I was pleased that he gave his permission for me to attend the Adventure Training in June and a few weeks after I was posted to NICS, I happily headed off to Alberta to backpack the Sawback Trail with six other DEEM officers. The Sawback Trail is a mountainous trail between Banff and

Lake Louise). This was my 3rd adventure training and my 2nd one with the DEEM group.

The year before, on another DEEM Adventure Training, I had backpacked the West Coast Trail with 11 of these guys and on this year's Adventure Training was similar to the one the year before in that I was the only woman on this exercise. What can I say, I loved the great outdoors and the physical challenge presented by Adventure Training suited me.

This year's Adventure Training would be much more difficult for me as I was barely recovering from the stress the harassment at DEEM has caused me and now I had just recently learned about the LCWB and overwhelmed, I was very worried about my future in the Canadian Forces.

I hoped that this Adventure Training's fresh air backpacking trip would help me clear my head and figure out how to deal with this hound on my back. Instead of the backpacking trip helping me, it hurt me as I did not know how badly this stress would play havoc with my concentration as it would weigh heavily on my mind. Being distracted on such a treacherous trail is not a good thing and as best as I could, I tried and failed to keep it off my mind. I didn't know how my career would survive the more recent assault at NICS and eventually it didn't.

Although my CO had made it obvious that he didn't like me, he thought I was competent in my job. Throughout my time at NICS, he continued to assign me serious tasks without any supervision. My first big assignment at my new posting happened when an underground fuel tank was discovered to be leaking into the Carp River. The CO assigned me to oversee the investigation and deal with the environmental issues.

I was aware that this could have been a public nightmare for the Department of National Defence and I was determined that that would not happen so I ensured that all matters related to this event were addressed promptly and properly. My handling of this event resulted in DND being perceived as being environmentally responsible.

After I had been on the job for a few months, the other Captain at the site was unexpectedly posted out. He tracks me down one day and tells me that he has been posted out. Although he had only been at the site for a year, he went as ordered to his new posting although he was unhappy and shocked about the sudden change in plans. It was strange and a bit scary to have a complete changeover of staff at the NICS site. When asked who was replacing him, the CO was evasive but a few weeks later, Captain Thorne is posted in.

At the end of the summer, in September of 1994, I was sent to do NATO job training to be a satellite ground terminal Chief Network Controller. The NATO training was held at an Italian Air Force Base in north-western Italy. When I was told that I would be heading to do the training, I was also asked to represent Canada in NATO's Partnership for Peace effort. The Partnership for Peace (or PFP) effort was a

consideration by NATO to include previous Warsaw Pact countries into the NATO alliance. I agreed to be a liaison communications engineering officer to a Lithuanian Military communications engineering officer. I was proud to represent Canada in this and I considered it an honour to be asked. This was my second big assignment at my new posting.

Unknown to me at the time, just before I left for Italy in the fall of 1994, my Commanding Officer contacted Colonel Stevens and tries to have me charged with "mutiny." Seriously! My CO was a man on a mission! This ridiculous effort didn't work out because his boss, the officer he contacted to make this accusation, advised him to contact the Military Police and have me arrested if what he said was true. The Colonel called my CO's bluff and he backed down.

By the way, the Colonel was Colonel Joe Stevens and he had been a Major and my CO when I was a Corporal. After I received a commendation from the Minister of National Defence, Major Stevens had hand delivered it to me and at that time I first heard about the UTPM program. He had been the one to first suggest to me the UTPM program and had told me that I had the qualities and ethics to become a good officer.

I'm sure that as soon as he heard my name from the NICS CO, he had an inkling that the accusation was bogus. Due to his previous working knowledge of me, he knew what type of person I am. I didn't even know about this when it happened but learned about it years later at a CF Hearing convened when this CO of mine attempted to sue DND.

During the summer, when my kids were on summer break, I moved my family from CFB Rockcliffe to CFB Uplands. The PMQ was much smaller than the one we had on Rockcliffe, but it was also less expensive while having two other advantages. First off, it allowed my children to walk to school and secondly, it helped me to have less time away from the NICS site by reducing my commute to the many meeting I was responsible to attend at the Uplands Base.

As part of my responsibilities at my job at NICS, I oversaw the support of the site administration which was carried out by the Uplands Base. Living on the Base, made it easier to get to these meetings as the representative of the NICS site.

I got along well with all of my new neighbours except one. Next door to me lived a woman who had made it clear that she didn't like me much. Her husband liked me well enough but not her. And, she had good reason. When I first moved in, her slime-ball of a husband made an overt pass at me in front of everyone at a neighbourhood BBQ.

Her husband was a pilot on base and he had a reputation for "roaming." I felt sorry for her and although I tried numerous times to be friendly towards her, she wouldn't even say hello to me. My mother described me as "killer good looking in my uniform" and I wore the uniform proudly each day and that just made matter worse. This was obviously a source of discomfort for my lady neighbour. No sane woman wants a single attractive single parent living next door especially when your husband has a roaming eye!

I was sorry that the relationship with my neighbour was so tense and wished things were different but I felt helpless to change her. I had thought the stares of dislike would be the extent of her expression of dislike toward me until the day my son brought a letter home from school. I was shocked when I read it as in the letter, I was accused of not taking care of the basic needs of my children.

When asking my son why his teacher felt this way, he said he'd never heard her say anything before but on this day our neighbour had been in his classroom and had dictated the letter to the teacher. If I had any doubt before, now I knew for sure that she blamed and hated me. The fact that my neighbour had my son's teacher at the school write a letter of reproach to me about my neglect of my children went too far and I had to stand up for myself. This was not true as I was overly protective of my children and she knew this.

I was shocked that my son's teacher would do this and it hurt that this woman whose class I had volunteered in and who knew me, would write such a letter. I was also shocked that my neighbour would take her dislike to this level. My son description of how he had been told to wait in the classroom while his teacher sat at her desk and our neighbour told her what to write was disturbing and I found that this was not something I could excuse.

The following morning was a work day but I called in to work and told them I would be in as soon as I could. Then I visited the school and spoke to the Principal who knew me as well. He had written a letter of appreciation to me for my having been a volunteer at the school. He said he would look into it.

Later that day, I received a telephone call from the Principal and he told me that although inappropriate, I had no proof that the letter was dictated by my neighbour (other than a little boy's word) and the teacher had told him that she had written the letter without any help. When I told him that the details of the letter proved otherwise, he told me he was sticking by his teacher. I was distressed and needed to know if he believed the content of the letter and he told me that he didn't.

I sat with this information for a few hours but could not settle it in my heart so I called the CFB Uplands Base Support Officer and explained the circumstances. He advised me to call the Base Commander and I made that phone call next. After I told the Base Commander's secretary why I was calling, she put me through to the Base Commander right away. I explained to him what had happened and I suspected that my neighbour's husband's bad reputation was known among the officers on Base.

I felt sure that the Base Commander knew of him. I provided the Base Commander with proof of the letter along with the letter of appreciation from the school and that was all it took for him to take the matter into his own hands. I knew he had called the school when a few hours later, the Principal telephoned me and apologized. He now said the teacher would be reprimanded and although I felt bad for her, I believed it was deserved as she had behaved inappropriately.

A little while later the Base Commander called and told me that he had spoken with my neighbour's husband's Commanding Officer about the whole matter. I was told that in the afternoon of that same day my neighbour's husband was called in for a little talk with his CO. I believe he was told of the situation and perhaps advised to tell his wife to "stand down!" Although my neighbour never spoke to me again, her maliciousness stopped. Sometimes, in life, it is hard to get justice but I believe if you stand up for what is right, things will work out.

As the CNC (Chief Network Controller), it was my job to coordinate the administrative aspect of the NICS site with two subordinate sites in Nova Scotia located at Debert and Folley Lake so I called them daily to get reports and deal with any problems that arose. One day, while I was working with the NICS site engineer in a small control room, the door to the room was suddenly opened and Captain Thorne looked at me and said, "Ah-hah, there you are" before slamming the door closed and leaving. Both the site engineer and I were dumbfounded and neither of us knew what that was all about. But, it wouldn't be long before our curiosity was satisfied as a few minutes later, the door opened again and my CO was standing there waving a collection of papers and saying, "We've caught you!"

It was comical how Captain Thorne, who was standing behind the CO, was grinning from ear to ear. Still, I didn't get why they were there and figured they were pulling a prank on me. I still didn't get it until the CO ordered me to his office where I was told that they had been watching my telephone usage.

I was responsible for the telephone control and the payment of the telephone bill yet I had not been privy to their investigation into what they called the misuse of the telephone and a larger than normal long-distance calls bill. It felt like a witch hunt!

I was told by the CO that I had been caught red-handed and that I would be charged. When I asked what for, I was told that my misuse of the telephone to make long-distance calls to my girlfriend in Halifax was now a matter of record and that he and Captain Thorne had been investigating this for months.

At first, I didn't know what to say or do. I just shook my head. I asked if they took into account my calls to our subunits at Debert, Nova Scotia and Folley Lake, Nova Scotia; both of which went through the Halifax exchange. The stupid looks on their faces was simply comical! What a couple of idiots, I thought!

The stress I felt at work was becoming overwhelming. The work environment was becoming more hostile every day and I felt as if I had a couple of hounds on my back. It shouldn't have been surprising for me when on my drive to work one day, I got strong chest pains. As I passed a nearby construction site, I considered getting off the Queensway and head to the site in the hope of finding medical help. I was in uniform and felt fairly confident that they would help a soldier, so I took the exit but then hesitated to approach a group of men.

Unsure what to do, I sat at the exit in my car and did some deep breathing before turning my car around and heading back towards Ottawa and to the military hospital. I went to the Emergency Department of the National Defence Medical Center (NDMC). I was scared that I was having a heart attack. A few years earlier, I had seen and helped a MWO who was having a heart attack and I was having those same symptoms.

I checked in at Emergency thinking I was having a heart attack but instead, it was stress/anxiety attack. I should have known. Still, when the same thing happened again a month later, I was again frightened by the intensity of the pain. And, again I headed to NDMC and again I was diagnosed with a panic attack. The fact that this was only happening on my way to work, made it clear to me where the root of the problem lied. I was scared to go to work. I didn't know from day to day what was going to happen that day but I was confident that something bad would happen.

When the Force Reduction Plan (FRP) was announced in November, I looked to it as my escape. I did not want to end my military career, but I was in a bad spot. So I made my application for the FRP. It required my CO's signature and although he hesitated for weeks, he eventually signed it. The next day, he called me into his office to tell me that he wished he could have taken it as well but as a Major he could not. He made it clear to me that he was both angry and jealous of my being able to apply for the FRP. At the NICS site coffee break the next day, the CO stood up and told everyone that I was jumping ship: that I had applied for the FRP.

I love the Christmas holidays and look forward to spending them with my children. But for me, Christmas at NICS ended up being a nightmare. In November, I submitted my Christmas leave pass for approval and it was approved. Of the three officers at the NICS site, I was the only one with children and being a single parent with a mostly absent father in my kid's lives, I simply needed to be there. New Year's leave would have been okay, but I preferred Christmas leave and I was pleased to see that my CO's hatred of me didn't extend to my children.

In early December, I received an invitation to the DCEEM Christmas party. I had some friends at my last posting and I was interested to attend. Due to the tense situation at NICS, I didn't not accept the invitation until I first asked my CO if it was okay that I attend. The party was being held during the afternoon of our last day of work before the Christmas leave period and it would be a time when most of the NICS site personnel would be absent.

I had hoped he would approve in part because I suspected that both he and Captain Thorne had also been invited. I was wrong. Neither had received an invitation even though we had all come from DCEEM. I didn't know what to say when my CO told me that he hadn't been invited. I was to later learn that I was the only one invited back for the DCEEM Christmas party. Yet, it wasn't until I asked for this permission to attend the party that I learned that they had not been invited. Even though the CO gave his permission for me to attend, it was obvious that he was not happy about doing so.

The morning of the Christmas party, I attended meetings at the Fire Department at the Uplands Base before heading to meetings downtown at NDHQ. Since the closure of CFS Carp, our fire support was done out of Base Uplands, while our administrative support was done by NDHQ and the meetings I attended were regular meetings that I attended each month as the NICS site's Chief Network Controller.

My meetings ended at noon and a girlfriend and I grabbed a quick lunch together in downtown Ottawa before I left to the Canadian Building and the DCEEM Christmas party. I was at the party for about 40 minutes when a woman I knew who was a secretary came up to me and told me I had a call from the NICS site and that I could take it at her cubicle.

I should have known, but I didn't. No worries, I thought until my CO ordered me back to the NICS site. He didn't give a reason why, he just told me to get back there and do so NOW. Unwilling to piss him off, I left right away and headed for the NICS site. During my drive there I would wonder what was up this time. I should have been scared as the CO had a special Christmas gift for me.

Have you ever heard the saying that it doesn't rain that it pours? Well, it must have been one of those days as on my way back to the NICS site, my car broke down on the Queensway. It took an hour to get a tow truck and as it was a time before cell phones, I couldn't get a hold of the site to let them know until I got to the repair shop. Yet as soon as I got there, I called the NICS site to let them know where I was and why.

I was told that the CO was on the phone so I told the clerk in the Orderly Room to inform the CO know where I was and that I would be back to the NICS site as soon as I could. In addition, I gave the OR MCpl the repair shop's telephone number so that I could be reached.

In the six months that I had been posted to the NICS site, the CO had never been to my home, yet on that day, the CO left work early and drove to my home on Base Uplands knowing that I was not there: knowing I was still at the repair shop. My home was about 25 miles from the NICS site and it was out of the CO's way. I was disconcerted when I called to my home and learned from my babysitter that my CO had visited my home when he knew I was not there. I had called to my home from the repair shop as I would be later than usual in getting home from work. When I got home, I learned that he had hand delivered my cancelled Christmas Leave pass. And to add insult to injury, he had told my children that their mother would not be with them on Christmas morning. He was cruel!

There's a lot about this visit that bothered me but what bothered me most was that he knew I wasn't there! In fact, he knew that I was at a garage dealing with my broken down car as he had telephoned me there after I'd left a message for him with the Orderly Room Clerk. I was sure of one thing: my CO's visit to my home was malicious in nature. He had gone out of his way to stop by my home and distress a nine and a seven year old child just before Christmas.

Also, he had worried my babysitter who was now concerned that she herself might have to babysit over the Christmas holiday when she had planned to be with her family on vacation. My CO told my children that their mom won't be around for Christmas because she had to work before he gave my babysitter the cancelled leave pass and told her to make sure I got it. He also gave her a revised work schedule for the NICS site which had me working even on Christmas Day.

But this wasn't his only Christmas gift to me. As if the sexually harassment at the site wasn't enough, he'd now distressed my children over the holidays and then he tops it off with his abuse of his authority with this unfounded and malicious attack on me.

When he and Captain Thorne returned from their holiday leave, my CO called me into his office and tells me that I am being counselled for absenteeism from the site. He tells me that he tried and failed to have me charged for absenteeism so he was counselling me instead but warned me that I would be charged if I did not change my behaviour.

My next big assignment came the following spring, when the CO asked to represent NICS site at SACLANT Meetings in Norfolk, Virginia. Our site had been slated for closure and there were a lot of administrative tasks to be done for that closure to take place. Before I went to Norfolk, I was first sent to our subordinate units at CFS Debert and CFS Folley Lake to oversee NATO audits at both these subunits and then I was to attend the SACLANT NATO meetings in Virginia.

After the Christmas fiasco, I'd promised my children that we'd take a vacation during their school Spring Break. The trip to SACLANT (Virginia) was horrible timing as it was during the spring break holidays. When the CO ordered me to SACLANT, I asked if I could drive there instead of flying there and I was granted permission to do so.

I did not share with the CO what I had planned and I thought it best not to tell him. Thinking outside the box, I next asked my babysitter if she'd like to take a two week working vacation to Virginia with the kids and me. I felt that this would be a wonderful opportunity to make up to her what had happened over the Christmas holidays when she had to work because I had to.

I was so pleased when she said she'd be happy to come with us. We left Friday after work and drove to my sister's home in Pennsylvania where we spent the weekend skiing at Camelback Mountain before heading south to Williamsburg where we spent the day sightseeing. Then it was onto Norfolk and SACLANT. I got a beach side hotel at Virginia Beach so that while I attended meetings, my babysitter and my children could spend their days enjoying the beach and hotel pool. On the drive home, we spent the weekend in Washington, DC and visited the museums. I was happy to share this with the kids and our babysitter. We'd made the best of a bad situation and it felt wonderful. What might have been a nightmare turned into a joyous vacation even though I was working. When you get served lemons, make lemonade!

In February, I heard that I was accepted to retire under the FRP and I saw this as my escape from the hound dog that my CO had become yet he wasn't done trying to destroy my military career. I had just returned from our subunits at Debert and Folley Lake and the trip to SACLANT when I was unexpectedly called into the CO's office and again he notified me that I was being absent from the site too much. Absenteeism from the site! For goodness sake....I'd just returned from multiply business trips which he'd sent me on.

This time he told me he had submitted the paperwork to have me charged and shares with me that this time he got it right as he'd "dotted his 'i's and crossed his 't's and I believe that is what the "counselling" was all about.

Yet, there was a problem with this disciplinary action: the six month probationary period. I was due to retire in few months and wouldn't even be in the Canadian Forces for half of the disciplinary action period. In addition, the disciplinary action's probationary period's purpose was to save an officer's career and I wouldn't have a military career in a four months. It was early June and I no longer had a military career after the 4th of July.

I shake my head now and I did then as my CO threatens me that with this on my record, I'll be dishonorably released and I will lose my FRP benefits. Then I understood what he is trying to do. Scared, I contacted the Colonel as I had been instructed to do should anything more arise. I let him know what is going on and somehow he got the charges dropped.

Yet my CO wasn't done with his maliciousness. Whenever a site closes, there is a closure parade that takes place and my CO took great joy in telling me that I was not going to be on the parade. And, then to rub salt into that wound, he sent a memo throughout the NICS site telling everyone that I will not be on the closure parade. In an abuse of his authority, he had removed me from the NICS Site Closure Parade because he was pissed off that he'd had to drop the charges against me.

I found it difficult to explain to NICS site personnel the reasons why (which I didn't fully understand myself). It was horribly embarrassing. Still, I did not let the CO's behaviour affect the execution of important tasks that I was responsible to do such as the postings for site staff. We had over thirty NCMs at the site so this was no easy task. Most of the members directly under my command were overseen by my MWO and I worked closely with him to do the best by our people as possible.

I was concerned about him and with the site closure happening, to protect him from the maliciousness of the CO, I arranged for him his first choice of postings.

A friend of mine was the CO at a unit in British Columbia and this was where he wanted to go. I contacted my friend and talked up my MWO before asking her to request him for her unit. He repaid me with a letter to the CO, dictated by the CO, which contained lies about me. Again, I had been naïve. I wouldn't learn of his for years and when I did, I felt like a total idiot but more than that, I felt ashamed of him.

You would think with my impending retirement and the site closure happening, the CO would be too busy to mess with me, but he obviously wasn't. He'd exposed his maliciousness once too often and a smart man would have known when to quit. I was reinstated in the closure parade, but he'd ensured that I was not on the closure flyer and in another foolish act, he removed my troops from my command.

After the closure parade, I was taken out of the workplace and would only return for my retirement party. I had only two weeks left

in my 18 year military career. My retirement party was held at the NICS site and had been arranged by the site personnel. Our Colonel attended and presented me with a NATO plaque, while the site personnel gave me a china set of tea cups on a beautiful tray. It was a considerate and moving gift: they really understood me as the tea drinker I was.

I smile as I remember this gift which I still keep in view in my kitchen in my home here in South Dakota. The NATO plaque is prominently on display in my home office and I was honoured to receive it from the Colonel. My

CO even gave me a gift that day although I wish he hadn't. He didn't present it to me the way the other gifts had been presented. Instead he came up to me during the party and told me that of the loss of my job with Valcom. My CO smiled as he told me, "The C&E world is a small one!" Then he wished me luck trying to find another job! At the time, I didn't believe him.

Our Colonel vouched for me and I found my final military assignment to be a very interesting one as I was asked to step in and be our C&E Branch's General's Aide at our Branch Headquarters in Tunney's Pasture. I was pleased....it was quite the consolation prize!

I no longer lived in a PMQ on the Uplands Base and I was soon no longer be in the military, but I had a job with Valcom (a military contractor) and I had bought a house in Kemptville just south of Ottawa. I thought my future was set. Yet, my CO had been correct when he told me that I no longer had a job at Valcom. I hadn't believed him because the job had been a done deal. I didn't know they could change their mind and even today I wonder how they could do this after they had guaranteed my income and job to my bank for my mortgage. It would be financially devastating for me to have lost this job and this income.

When I queried why to my friend at Valcom, I was told that my CO had badmouthed me to senior military officers at the RCAF Officer's Mess and these same senior officers had told Valcom that they didn't want me working on either of the projects (TEMS or HADCS), that they had contracted with Valcom for work. Basically, Valcom couldn't use me on their military contracts. And, although I worked hard to find another job, I had been black-balled and the very same potential employers who had previously asked me to work for them, now wouldn't touch me with a ten foot pole. With the bad-mouthing of my reputation, the only way out was for me to leave the Ottawa area. But I had a problem with that as my divorce agreement did not allow for me to move my children more than 250 km from the Ottawa area (that is, 250 km away from where their father was). When I made this agreement, I have thought it wasn't a problem as there were hundreds of potential postings in the Ottawa area for a CELE officer.

Having applied for and been accepted for a FRP (Force Reduction Plan) retirement while I was posted at NICS Carp and it was a God-send as I had this hound on my tail. I just had to get out of there and if that meant getting out of the military, that was something I was willing to do. When word got out that I was retiring, a few company representatives approached me to work for them and one of them was Valcom. As a military contractor, they wanted me to work under a contract they had gotten with DND for TEMS. I would basically be doing the same work I had done before with DCEEM but as a civie. It was a good fit and I looked forward to the work. We negotiated a start date and a starting salary of $59,000 a year, which was more than $10,000 above what I was making as a salary in the CF.

Now I had a job and because I had to move out of PMQs on Base Uplands, I went house-shopping. I ended up buying a home in a new development in Kemptville which is just south of Ottawa. At first I wasn't approved for a mortgage as I had been honest with the Mortgage Representative at my bank and told him I was retiring from the CF but he approved my mortgage after Valcom confirmed my future job and future income to him. Then, in the spring of 1995, we moved. We had a beautiful new home where the kids each had their own bedrooms. Our dog, Mimi loved it. We were in the country and she had much more space to run about. She even liked our swimming pool. We had an above ground pool and a deck between it and the sliding glass door off our kitchen. I'd gone all out with this home as I wanted it to be something very special for the kids. It would be our forever home: no more moving from PMQ to PMQ.

I took a few days of annual leave to make the move and as the kids had to change schools, I wanted to be there for them. It was a few months from the end of the school year, but I believed that it would allow them to make new friends in their new neighbourhood before the end of the school year and that would work well for them to have friends over the summer. Having heard that the Catholic school in Kemptville was an extremely good school, I tried to get the kids enrolled into it, but I was not a Catholic and so they said no. No worries, I thought.....had to give it a try. I enrolled the kids into the Kemptville area public school and arranged all the utility and services we would need for our new home over that few days.

A few months later, I would lose my job with Valcom even before I began it and I would learn about the loss of this job from my CO at NICS who, at my retirement party, shared with me that the C&E World was a small one and that I should check on my job with Valcom. I called Valcom and was told that our agreement was not solid and that, in fact, I no longer had a job with them. I was shocked. Later, I spoke directly with the fellow that had hired me and he explained that the Colonel that my CO used to work for and who was within DCEEM threatened to stop all business with Valcom if they hired me. Oh, and by the way, this Colonel just happened to be a close personal friend of my harasser at DEEM, the LCol who I had worked for. Complaining wouldn't do me any good, so I went looking for a different job but suddenly the people that had sought me out in the past (when I first got the FRP) were now not even returning my calls. I found that I was an unwanted entity.

Luckily I still had people who believed in me. One of these people was a retired LCol who now worked at DEEM as a civie. Mr. Mike Proctor had previously written me a letter of reference to help me find a job back in January and although I hadn't needed to use it then, I needed it badly now.

January 16, 1995

o whom it may concern,

I had the privilege of supervising Dawn Lavigne as an engineering officer on ly staff in a defence Space System engineering office for over a year. She is a oroughly accomplished professional well versed in space science and related gineering who eagerly accepts tasks and responsibilities related to both her positi id the engineering profession in general. She has an enthusiastic, out-going rsonality and is effortlessly at ease with senior personnel while achieving an ceptionally good first impression. She can be depended upon to perform ceptionally well those tasks involving protocol and the sensitivities between fferent levels in an organization and between agencies.

She thoroughly researched numerous space policy, scientific and planning cuments while establishing an international network of contacts in order to provi fective direct support to the definition of a major defence project involving very lvanced and challenging Space technology. Her understanding of the state-of-the a the fundamental technologies was such that her engineering guidance was accepte ith confidence by policy and requirements staffs at the Lieutenant Colonel level ring meetings where she was the sole participant cognizant in space technology.

She eagerly sought out and accepted responsibilities that complemented her basic duties and benefitted the Canadian scientific and engineering community. The benefits of her ability to work with others were evident in the contacts she establish and pursued with important foreign and Canadian individuals in both government an non-government capacities. Noteworthy, among many examples, were her significa contributions to the work of the 1994 APCEA show committee; the initiative and se starter characteristics shown by her organization of a show event which brought influential US and Canadian women together to discuss the status of women in engineering and science; and, her participation in Women in Science and Engineeri (WISE) discussion programs in high-schools. Her support of WISE was commende by the National Chapter President in a letter to the General Manager APCEA Cana

Dawn demonstrates a strong sense of integrity in dealing with individuals sh encounters in a professional and social capacity. I am confident that she will be a significant and reliable contributor to the success of any activity involving the planning for the application of advanced technology within a complex governmental or commercial organization.

Michael A. Proctor

Michael A. Proctor CD PEng

I also met with my college buddy's mom who was a prominent person in Canada. She also had a good opinion of me and had been mentoring me for years. Celine came to my aid contacting business friends of hers trying to help me get an interview. She understood my financial need to find employment as I had two children to care for.

Sadly, none of this ended up working out for me but I did end up finding a job and a very good job at that. I was going to work on the very best satellite project in the world. The only problem was that it was in the United States and I would have to move and that was a concern on multiple levels including my custody agreement of my children. At the time, I didn't know if my ex-husband would allow our children to move but I need not have worried because he didn't want the kids, he wanted his own life back and he was also motivated by money.... especially after he heard from the children about my Motorola starting bonus. We ended up making a deal and I was allowed to move our children with me to Phoenix, Arizona after I paid him off and it only cost me my starting bonus. To this day, I consider it money well-spent.

After I got settled in my new job as a spacecraft engineer on the Iridium program with Motorola and felt safe due to the distance between Phoenix and Ottawa, I used my regained strength and took action against my CO: I filed charges against him. Away from the harassment, I felt stronger and capable of dealing with the effects of it and ready to move forward with correcting the problem that he was to the Canadian Forces. Yes, I blamed him for ending my military career even though there had been other events of harassment, he had been the straw that broke this camel's back. What I accused him of in my charges was valid and I believed that he wasn't done harassing CF women and that given the chance, he would go on to hurt their military careers. I didn't want any other woman soldier to have to face what I had been a victim of because of him.

Although I was worried about doing this, and it took a lot of courage for me to move forward, I felt bringing this to the attention of the Department of National Defence was the right thing to do and that was my motivating factor. I formally filed charges of sexual harassment and abuse of authority against my last CO as I knew in my heart that he had to be stopped. And if not by me, then who?

Unhappy that he'd been caught and had charges levied against him, my last CO turned his hatred towards the Canadian Forces and DND. He tried unsuccessfully to have me charged in return. More than twenty times, DND told him that he didn't have a case. When all of his attempts failed, he retired from the Canadian Forces and tried to sue the Department of National Defence for over three million dollars. I believe he was narcissistic and could not let go of his hatred.

What a mess! He even went so far as to hold a press conference and tell the world about his lawsuit. He named me at the press conference and when the story went nationwide, I got an email from my cousin who tells me all about this. His email had the subject line, "Dede's famous!" When asked by the Canadian Forces to testify against him, I readily agreed and he ultimately lost his lawsuit.

Chapter Five: EPAR and Escaping to the USA
KINGSTON, ONTARIO (1995)

Rape spelt backwards is "EPAR" and that is a word my husband and I use to discuss events that are triggered by flashbacks to this horrible event that would shape the rest of my life.

It happened in 1995. I still ask, why then? I was already retired from the Canadian Forces and out of uniform and I had accepted a job in the USA. I would be moving out of country within the month. I don't have all the answers and I expect I never will. Sometimes I wonder if this is why it happened then. Maybe this guy (my rapist) thought he could get away with it. Sometimes you have to stop and look at things differently....and sometimes you end up feeling the same way as you did decades ago.

I know I have to write about this but my heart is racing and there are tears in my eyes. Tears of fear. God, I'm so afraid! Twice each day, I flashback to this memory. Every time I get dressed and when I undress I remember how my bra was torn off me and I remember how scared I was to be seen. I remember how I pulled my torn clothes about me to cross Princess Street and I feel the fear of being seen all over again. I remember how desperately I wanted to get to the safe haven of my car and how getting there became an exercise in escape and evasion for me as I hid in an alleyway waiting for the traffic to clear and then how I hugged the sides of buildings and looked away from the few people I passed.

As hard as it is for me to admit to having been afraid then, it is even more disconcerting now....after all, I was a soldier! The first couple of time I felt this fear, I chastised myself and figured it was because it was a fresh memory but even today, I feel the same level of fear. It has not gone away. I don't know why but I have come to accept that the feelings are there. It is what it is!

Okay, so I just took three deep breaths and restarted to write. I wrestle with my memories wanting to forget them and knowing they simply are not going to ever go away. Writing about what happened to me is the most difficult thing I have ever done.

In early September of 1995, I drove to Kingston to get my hair done one last time by my favorite hairdresser, Tim. I had taken a job working for Motorola in Phoenix, Arizona but before leaving Canada to move to the USA, I was going to treat myself to a beautiful haircut with highlights and the whole works! Tim had been my hairdresser for years and I was heading to Kingston with an appointment to spend the morning letting him do his magic. I would never return.

I was being practical, I told myself. It would take me time to find a hairdresser I liked in Phoenix and getting my hair done now gave me a few months to look. It was supposed to have been a fun day but that's not how it turned out. My hair appointment was in the morning but I was going to stay in Kingston for lunch and then I had time to take a leisurely drive home to Ottawa.

Having arranged to have lunch at a pub near my hairdresser and with a military buddy of mine was just what I needed. He joined me at the pub and we had a great lunch. I had a beer and some wings but I don't remember what he ate. We talked and talked for the next few hours…catching up and he mostly talked about his last posting having just returned to Kingston from a posting where all of his living expenses had been paid.

After we ate, he asked me to walk back to his apartment with him as he'd forgot to take something in that morning and we walked and continued talking just like friends do. I thought nothing of it. He'd said it would only take a few minutes for him to pick up something before he headed back to the Base.

I had at least an extra hour and had planned a leisurely drive back to Ottawa anyhow and considering that my buddy had not only gotten off work early to join me for lunch, I owed him that much. Besides, with my moving to the USA, I may never see him again. I remember feeling sad knowing that I would probably not see him again.

My move to Phoenix ultimately meant that I would probably lose touch with most of my friends but I knew I would develop new friendships in Arizona and I planned to stay in touch with my friends in Canada. This buddy and I had worked together for years at NDHQ in Ottawa for years and we'd been on two Adventure Trainings together. We'd developed a close friendship and deep respect for one another. Or so, I thought. I trusted this guy fully, yet it was a trust he didn't deserve.

I would later regret having not paid attention to where we were walking but at the time, I was letting him lead the way and I was simply following him. When we got to his apartment, I sat on the couch and looked over his apartment while he looked for some papers he said he'd brought home the night before and had forgotten to take back to work that morning.

It was a nice apartment and I could see that he'd adopted a modernistic theme to his decorating of it. Nice! Before searching out his papers, he'd gone to the bathroom and I laughed thinking it was probably to get rid of some of the beer he'd drank at lunch! From the bathroom, he went over to his desk and I figured that was where the papers were that he needed as I continued to look around his apartment from my seat on the couch.

He surprised me by sitting down beside me on the couch and I felt the hair on my neck stand up. Although we'd not stopped talking during a short walk to his place nor after we'd arrived, it was now very, very quiet. When he didn't say anything, I noticed how very quiet he'd become as if he was mentally weighing something. It was like he was thinking deeply and I wondered what was up.

When he'd sat down on the couch, he'd sat awful close to me and it invaded my personal space but when I went to move further from him, he put his arm up and behind me on the couch. This was so strange. Then with the arm that was behind me, he pushed me towards him and when I resisted, he grabbed my hair at the back of my head and pulled it backwards so that I was looking at the ceiling.

Caught off guard, I didn't respond. He was so strong and he was using that strength on me. I was disconcerted. We didn't say a word to each other but my wide eyes spoke volumes. The element of surprise is known as a powerful took and here it was being used on me. I didn't know what was up and unable to back away from him, I went numb.

My friend wasn't the best looking guy but now with this awful look on his face….a look of pure anger….he looked ugly….very, very ugly! He didn't yell at me or call me names or anything. Neither of us said a word….. I was stunned into silence.

When I did not try to pull away, he yanked me forward and turned me around before lifting my skirt. I don't know how he did it, but somehow, I now had my knees on the carpet and I was facing the couch. He briefly let go of my hair to push my back down to the seat of the couch while he pulled my undies to my knees with his other hand.

Once he'd pushed me as far as he could into the couch, he again grabbed a fist full of my hair and I stayed put. I'd like to say what I was thinking but I wasn't thinking. Nor was I fighting back. I wasn't doing anything. I was numb and it was surreal. I've never been raped before and I didn't know what was happening. He'd had the element of surprise and I believe I was in shock.

I felt his penis near my privates and that's when it all became real for me. He must have undone his pants after pushing my undies down. What surprised me was his inability to penetrate because his penis wasn't hard. Time and time again he tried to enter me but I was closed for business and with his being soft, he could not get the dirty deed done.

He got more and more aggressive as he got angrier. He pushed me down again into the couch….more aggressively this time and when he again grabbed my hair, he yanked my neck to and fro in his futile attempts to guide his penis into me with his other hand.

At some point in time, I must have zoned out because I remember seeing the kitchen behind his couch and that is what I focused on. I don't know how much time passed: a minute or an hour. I didn't know and I didn't care. I just wanted it to be over.

Eventually, he got so frustrated with his inability to get hard and finish the job that he shoved me away from him and I went hard face first into the back of the couch. I stayed put until I was sure he had moved away from me and then I slowly backed up and stood up.

I did not turn around and look at him. I couldn't. I pulled my undies and skirt back up and tucking my blouse into my skirt's waist and then

I turned to leave and that's when he moved. He got to the door before I could and blocked my exit.

He continued to not say anything but when I looked at his face, I saw only anger. Then he grabbed the front of my blouse and pulled it towards him so hard that buttons flew in all directions and my bra clasp gave way and scrapped its freed claws across my back.

When he had pulled open my blouse and my breast were exposed, he looked at me with disgust before moving to the side and shoving me towards the door. I didn't need to be told twice and I quickly opened the door and ran.

My legs felt like rubber but I ran anyhow. Confused, heart-broken and scared out of my wits, I stopped in the alley next to Princess Street and looked down at myself. I was still exposed. I didn't want anyone to see me so I pulled my blouse around me as best I could and when the traffic had slowed, I raced across the street. I hid in the exit ramp of the S&R Store while I caught my breath. My heart was racing out of control. Then again I pulled my ripped blouse together and with rubbery legs I hugging the walls of the building as I struggled to get back to my car.

I did not even consider going to the police station just a few block away. What for?! I had little faith that they would do anything..... after all, they had turned a blind eye so many times before. So, I found my car, got in and headed out of town. As I drove home, I made the decision to not tell anyone. I hoped to get home before my kids got home from school so I could clean myself up.

I didn't tell anyone. I don't know why and even today when I think about it (twice a day as I put on and take off my brassiere), I feel shame. My move to Phoenix a few days later was a God-send and I vowed never to return. I had served my country and felt as if this was the icing on the cake.....I'd been served up! I was so angry so I got the heck out of Dodge (spelt C A N A D A).

I'd been a soldier and I would have died for my country and this..... THIS.....was how I was repaid. My anger knew no bounds as I blamed the whole country and everyone in it. I recognize that my anger was displaced but I was running on raw emotion at the time. I know now how I came to blame Canada, but back then, I never ever wanted to go home again.

So ashamed for having been so stupid to trust someone who didn't deserve it, I didn't want anyone to know although I did consider telling my sister and once, I even tried to. We had been so close and with her being a nurse, I hoped she could help me to understand why I felt so much anger and so very lost. I had hoped that she might help me to understand why I felt so ashamed.

So with the plan in mind to tell her, I had to figure out a way to do that without going back to Canada. I needed her to come to me. I had to do this in person. When next we talked on the phone, I invited her to Phoenix for Christmas and when she said they would love to but they couldn't afford it, I offered to pay for the plane tickets. I bought plane tickets for her and her family to come and see me at Christmas and then I spent days planning what I would say.

But that was a waste of my time. My selfish sister decided to change her mind. I call her selfish because when she rebooked the Christmas plane tickets and booked the trip for a few months later, she pocketed the difference in the plane fare and used it to do her Christmas shopping. When she did come to see me in in February, she told me off. She made it clear to me that she was unhappy with my having moved to the USA and she didn't want to hear about my military woes. I never told her and we remain distant to this day.

This memory haunts me. As recent as last Sunday, after I went to confession, my husband touched my back and I flashed back to the rape. Although I didn't say it out loud, I thought "Fucking Asshole!" and that was why I didn't go up for Communion. It was a good thing I didn't say it out loud or my husband may have thought I was saying it to him!

The Priest's sermon had to do with forgiveness and yet I have not found it in my heart to forgive this guy and I don't know if I ever will. I guess I'm just not that good of a Christian. Unable to handle the flood of emotions, I left church and as I walked back to my car, I let the tears flow. Ahhhh.....my car.....my sanctuary again!

PART TWO: In the Ranks

Chapter Six: A Call to Adventure
TORONTO, ONTARIO & VANCOUVER, BC (1978)

Living in Toronto was exciting and there was so many people. It was not long before I found a boyfriend, a 'looker' by the name of Richard Bennett* and not long after that we got engaged. Richard was from a well-to-do family and he was a silver-spooned, annuity child on many counts – not needing to work nor worry about the hardships of poverty as had been my experience.

Although many a woman would see Richard as a solution to their toils, I simply saw him as the attractive man who could fit the bill of my storybook fancies; those Harlequin romance novels. Even though I didn't have to, I continued to work and endeavour to make changes to my world through my own efforts.

Yet he was not the man I thought he was and this was first brought to my attention when we visited our apartment's pool and stumbled upon a group of drug-intoxicated men who were holding children under water for ill sport. I charged forth and stole their attention – giving the kids a chance to escape. The men immediately chased after me and they caught up and began to smash my head into the coarse concrete of the pool deck.

They were strong and the drugs they had taken enhanced that. I was at their mercy as they threw me into the water half-conscious and ignored my struggles as I attempted to stay afloat in the deepest depths of the pool. I held onto a fraction of a breath and tried to manoeuvre limbs that were unresponsive at best. Somehow, I managed to flutter kick my way to a pool ladder where I desperately tried to catch my breath. My vision was blurry and I tried to climb out of the pool, but the heavy sole of a work boot met my jaw with a staggering force. I heard a sickening pop and was propelled back into the water.

When I surfaced, I could only focus on trying to recover my breath. Relying on my body's natural buoyancy, I was able to regulate my breathing and my vision straightened. I saw they were distracted and not looking at me and I swam for the shallow end. Cautiously I climbed out of the pool praying that the men wouldn't turn around and see me.

That's when I looked around the pool for Richard. He was nowhere to be seen and I realized he was not there. I would later find him hiding in the alcove of the apartment's tenant-storage room where he was cowered in the fetal position without a scratch on him. I was pissed that he had run away and left me to take a beating. Little did I know, he was capable of being dangerously rough.

I forgave him and then two months later, I found out he was having an affair after finding a name and phone number in his wallet. I verified my suspicions with mutual friends and there was no doubting that he was two-timing me. I decided to confront him. "So, tell me about Susy*," I said to him as he sat down to a meal I had cooked for him.

His face told me everything – yet, he insisted that he did not know whom I was talking about. He ignored my second prod and left the table to take a smoke on our balcony. I insisted on pushing the matter as most scorned people would, and so the argument traveled onto our little balcony eight stories up the apartment complex.

My persistence made him angrier and I saw a glint in his eye that I had never seen before as he grabbed me forcefully. Richard was a tall man and he was stronger than I had anticipated for he was able to lift me above the wall of our balcony. Furious, Richard looked me in the eye and – without words – threatened for me to say one more thing on the matter. His snarl and my dangling legs let me know what the end result would be.

My anger knew no bounds and without hesitation, I glared back at him and coldly said, "Go ahead…be a hero." I had lived a life of fear and I refused to give Richard the satisfaction of seeing me afraid. He twisted his torso and threw me onto the balcony's floor where I sat catching my breath and thanking my lucky stars. Richard left our apartment but he returned later that night and acted as if he had not come close to committing homicide.

In fact, he seemed confused when I slept on the couch. I continued to sleep on the couch for the next few days but I was not without a plan. I posted advertisements for my furniture in the Toronto Star newspaper and put the apartment up for sublet in a separate ad. Sure that one day soon Richard would return to a mostly empty apartment and a notice of eviction while I would use the proceeds to leave Toronto. My plan went off without a hitch, and by the end of the week, I was on a train to Vancouver.

It was August, 1978.

Leaving my hometown was difficult, but it was a mixed act of adventure and a yearning for a better life. At the age of twenty, I wanted to make my life mean something after it had been reduced to nothing, and the city across the country represented a new beginning for me. My mother – who had moved to Vancouver the previous year – met my train, and we lived together for a time.

Still, I wanted more and soon rediscovered an interest that I had encountered when I was seventeen: I wanted to join the military. Originally, I was unable to since only men were able to join the military while under the age of eighteen; women had to be older. Now the proper age, I was able to follow my dreams and entered a Vancouver recruiting office to start the next chapter of my life.

I was highly patriotic and the notion of serving my country while experiencing a life apart from the norm was exhilarating. I loved my mother, and I loved my friends, but I loved my country and what it represented most of all. Canada was always out for the underdog – the 'little guy' – and I'm kind of like that. My country provided hope within a world that desperately needed it and I envisioned myself as a soldier that held this responsibility on her shoulders. So, with a romantic chip on my shoulder, I was entered the recruiting centre.

The Sergeant in the recruiting office was quick to inform me that there was no global position dubbed 'soldier' in the Canadian Forces and that I would need to select a specific occupation. This was genuinely news to me; I had been ignorant of this basic fact. He led me through a list of potential occupations as I dreamed of how I could benefit others within each position. I settled on the job of 'Cook' as the description for the job was enticing. Next, Sergeant Dylan* gave me a standardized aptitude test to complete and when it was done, he said to me, "You don't want to be a cook, you won't last six months!"

I was shocked and disillusioned and as a high school dropout, I wasn't confident in my academic abilities and wondered if I would even pass the test. Still, how much schooling did I need to be a cook? I had entered that office with determination – knowing that I was tough – and had prepared myself to make any sacrifice necessary to be a member of the Canadian Forces.

Seeing my horrified face, Sergeant Dylan clarified, "No, no! You did great on the test. Really great, actually. I said that because you'd be bored because being a cook is one of the most gruelling, unsatisfying jobs available in the military. They need to play it in the pamphlets to get recruits into the field."

I felt cared for. In having processed the results of my test, the Sgt didn't want me signing up for the wrong trade and told me that I would be better suited as an electronics technician based on my test results. He told me that I would be taught everything I needed to know and that no existing knowledge was needed. The only requirement was a good head on my shoulders.

I signed a contract too cumbersome to read and was slotted to depart for Basic Training in Cornwallis, Nova Scotia in a few months. After that, time seemed to bend in on itself. In Vancouver, it was the rainy season and it rained most days and the hallways of the apartment building we lived in continually smelled of wet wood. I didn't like the damp atmosphere but I ignored it as best I could. At the time, all I was concerned about was the future that now lay before me.

Daily, I headed to the running track at the school across the street from my mother's apartment to get some physical exercise in preparation for the physical demands of Basic Training. I was concerned that I was not in good enough physical shape and wondered if I would meet those demands. I had my doubts but I was going to give it my best.

I had to tell my boss that I would be quitting and I wasn't looking forward to it. I had a job with a small accounting firm walking distance from my mother's apartment. I'd only arrived in Vancouver a few months earlier and my boss had taken a risk in hiring a high school dropout like me. He was a nice man and I was worried that he would be disappointed. I liked him very much as he was easy to work for and a kind man. I knew that the best thing to do was to be upfront with him.

He was seriously pissed with me.....that is, until he found out why I was quitting. At first, he asked me to leave his office and didn't allow me the opportunity to explain. He told me to pack up my stuff and leave right away. As I was packing up my stuff, he came into my office and asked me why I was leaving. When I told him I had joined the military and wouldn't be leaving right away, his attitude totally changed.

A few weeks after I had joined, we received a surprising telephone call. It was Sgt Dylan from the recruiting office and he wanted to know if I could leave for Basic Training right away. He told me that a girl had backed out and there was a slot for me if I wanted to go earlier. I accepted and Mom and I headed downtown for me to be sworn in and to do some shopping for some of the basic necessities that Sgt Dylan had said I would need.

I let my boss know right away and instead of the required two-week's notice, he allowed me to give him two days. I'd only been with them for a few months, still the people at my office arranged a small going away party for me. A few days later, my mother helped me pack my bags with the required kit and saw me to the airport. I was excited to leave but it saddened me to leave my mother. I was embarking on my first ever airplane ride and truly the beginning of my new life.

When I had moved to Vancouver from Toronto, I'd taken the VIA train and it had taken five days to cross the country. With flying, I'd arrive in Halifax the same day as I left. I found this amazing.

It was late November of 1978.

Chapter Seven: Basic Training
CFB CORNWALLIS, NOVA SCOTIA (1978-1979)

I loved Basic Training. It was everything I'd hoped it would be and more. When I arrived in Halifax, I was directed to a large tour bus waiting outside of the airport. The bus was half-filled with women between the ages of eighteen and twenty-five, and more joined the roster as flights from around the country arrived. When the bus was mostly full, its door were closed after a final roll call was made.

Many of us were nervous and kept to ourselves while others chatted boisterously with new friends. I was one of the ones keeping quiet – staring out the window at the darkening landscape and envisioning what lay in store for me when I arrived in Cornwallis. I was outside of my comfort zone and had little idea how drastically my life was about to change.

The drive was slow-going, but we eventually arrived at the gates of CFB Cornwallis. We had been able to see some of Halifax when we boarded the bus, but twilight had quickly overtaken the landscape, and most of our trip was through darkness. The street light at the entrance of the Base caught our attention. It illuminated the perfect grass at the front gate and warded off the dark abyss our bus had been travelling through. Caught in the light were five imposing shadows that led to uniformed women who were watching the bus roll to a stop.

I was drowsy after the long trip but that didn't seem to matter as one of the uniformed women entered and ordered us off the bus. In a demanding tone, we were instructed to line ourselves into three ranks as our luggage was removed from the bus by the driver. We then grabbed our respective bags and followed the uniformed women onto the Base. We arrived at a two-story building with an H-shape. This and the other identical buildings we had passed were called 'H-huts' and they were the barracks that would be our home for the next three months.

We were Platoon 13 and we would be housed in half of one of these buildings with Platoon 14 using the other half. There were three all women platoons on base and 12 male platoons yet each of the male platoons had twice our numbers and used a full H-hut. In our platoon, there were two troop known as Troop A and Troop B.

One-by-one, our names were called out, and we were told which barrack bed space we were assigned to. We were told to listen attentively to the location of our bed spaces as this would define which troop within our platoon that we would be assigned to. My bed space was on the main floor and I was a member of Troop A. Troop B occupied the second floor. As the list of names continued, I  could smell the salty fresh ocean scent on the wind and although it was much colder than Vancouver, I felt a sense of home. I forced myself to ignore it as the stern look on the face of these uniformed women reminded me that I would not be visiting a beach any time soon.

When the last name was called out, we were informed that we had five minutes to place our suitcases in our designated lockers, tie our hair into buns, and form ranks outside. When we returned, our instructors introduced themselves and informed us that we would have to earn their respect over the next eleven weeks. We were told to retire for the evening and reform outside at 5am.....That time was 2am Vancouver time!

Before the sun broke the horizon, we were marched to a warehouse and assigned military uniforms, footwear, and weapons. The uniforms were essential for the cold of winter we would face and we now looked the same regardless of where we had come from. We were dubbed the 'Valentine's Day Platoon' as we were slotted to graduate on the 13th of February (the day before Valentine's Day) and ironically, our actual platoon name was '13 Platoon.'

We were one of three female platoons on the Base and we learned we were considered the 'fresh meat' upon our first trip to the mess hall. Each morning we were marched up to the mess hall where we quickly scoffed down a breakfast before reforming up outside to march

107

either back to our platoon or to where training for that day was being conducted. We had classes that taught us about the military, weapons handling, physical fitness, first aid, drill and combat and they worked us hard to see if we would collapse under the pressure that the daily training schedule involved.

A few of the women in my platoon were not comfortable with the difficult training routine. One girl in my platoon had been sent to Basic Training due to disobedience in her household. She was a rich kid and had never used an iron in her life, nor had she ever cleaned anything: she had staff to do that, she told us. I wondered how lost she must have felt as I felt out of my element here at Basic. She didn't last 2 weeks.

And, we lost other girls as well....mostly due to injuries. I was surprised to learn that some of the girls had joined to earn a steady paycheque, but most of us held onto the ideals that had brought us from our corners of Canada to be this Valentine's Day Platoon. I admit that the difficult training environment shocked me in many ways too, but I found solace in the group of girls I was with and we bonded quickly.

As an idealist, I became known as "goody-two-shoes" because I refused to cuss. The girls in my platoon were amused by this and began to make bets on who would be the first to get me to swear. The bet lasted for three weeks and although that may not seem like a long period of time, in Basic Training, it was a lifetime.

In our H-hut, the instructors had offices at one end of the barracks and we had a meeting room directly above them. This same room would often also be used for training. It was across the barracks from civie lockup: when we first were given our uniforms, our civilian clothing

was packed away in our suitcases and they were put in a special room known as "civie lockup." The door to the room was kept locked at all times and only our instructors had the key to it.

As recruits, our only sanctuary was in the middle of the H-hut where we had a large bathroom. Each troop had its own bathroom which had four distinct sections: the toilets, the sinks, the showers, and the laundry room. We would congregate in the laundry area to wash and iron our uniforms or to sit and shine our boots. Mostly we would gather here to talk, laugh, and joke while we worked on our kit. We called it a shoe-shine party.

Our days were stressful as planned by our instructors who intentionally made it so we would have little time to eat as they worked us from sun-up to sun-down weeding out those not suited to this life. After a few weeks, we were to march ourselves individually to breakfast, but that's not exactly what happened.

With the brutal schedule assigned to us, we were up most nights until the wee hours of the morning getting our kit ready for inspection and we didn't want to wrinkle our new pressed uniforms or scuff our newly shined boots by dressing up and heading to breakfast at the mess hall. I'm not sure who came up with the idea, but it was adopted immediately and truly saved us a lot of time. We teamed up and sent a "runner" to the mess hall to get food for all of us.

We simply had to fuel our bodies as the physical demands that would be placed on us that day demanded that we eat something. Our runner would return with a whole loaf of bread that was a bag of peanut butter and jelly sandwiches. It was never the same girl as we switched up daily, but it was sure a life-saver for us. We would eat the sandwich while continuing to work on our kit or bed space or whatever we needed to do to get ready for inspection. I ate PB&J sandwiches for breakfast for over two months.

One girl decided to profit from our hunger. This girl knew "the system" and had stocked up on boxes of chocolate bars. We often didn't take the time to go to the Mess Hall for any meal and that included supper because we only had so much time and not enough time to do everything we had to do. So, we went hungry.

Not surprisingly, we paid her whatever she asked for those chocolate bars and she made good money. She was making money on our misery and we all took exception to it. There had been some talk about giving her a "blanket party" but many of us thought that was too severe. A blanket party is when you throw a blanket on top of someone and then beat the piss out of them. With the blanket on top of them, they can't see who was throwing the punches and it was thought necessary so that no-one could get in trouble for the assault. We never found out if that was true because not a single blanket party was thrown in Platoon 13 although this girl came close. Instead, someone poured coke into her iron and unknowingly, she ruined a blouse and she had to buy a new iron. No, it wasn't a nice thing to do but neither was selling desperately hungry girls chocolate bars at twice the price. We were not concerned about her having to buy a new iron.....she had the money!

The more major tasks assigned to our troop, required our full attention and we quickly learned to delegate these tasks between one another in order to get all the work done. For example, the toilets, sinks, and showers of the bathroom had to be cleaned until the porcelain shined. And, each night, we had to strip and re-wax the floors of our barracks. It was on one of these nights, where I was assigned to wax the floor that the girls got me to swear.

The wax could only be applied after another girl had stripped off the previous coating of wax and then another had washed the floors. Once dry, I could apply the wax. When I had finished waxing the floors and while we were waiting for them to dry, the girls and I were polishing our boots and ironing our uniforms while the floor dried.

"Where's Skater?" one of the girls asked shortly after I got into the bathroom. The instructors called us by our last names and we'd started to do the same.

On the verge of turning twenty-six, Kerrie Skater* was the oldest in our platoon, and we colloquially called her 'Mom'; she was friendly and reliable so it was odd that she was missing. I left the bathroom door to the bed space area and saw a figure tip-toeing toward me from the direction of her bed space. I called out into the darkness and the figure jumped; unquestionably it was the figure of Kerrie.

We were all concerned about our floors because if they were anything but pristine, it would spell punishment for us and here were tip-toe marks left in the wet wax. I ended up having to redo the floors and I was furious with her for causing me the extra work but she apologized and I found it easy to forgive her. C'est la vie! After I had rewaxed the floors, I returned to the bathroom where everyone else in the troop were working on their kit. I was calmed down by then and fixated on the circular motion of polishing my boots.

A short time later I heard, "Oh no, has anyone seen Skater?" She had disappeared again from the group. My heart sank as I guessed where she had gone and this time I ran to the bathroom door and when I looked outside into the bed space, I found a series of toe prints stamped into my glistening floor and the trail led directly to Kerrie's bed space. "Fuck you, Skater!" I shouted, startling her. The other girls in the bathroom ran toward me and began to laugh. They were enjoying the fact that Kerrie had been the first person to get me to cuss. Skater and I still laugh about it.....35 years later!

Releasing that outburst of emotion truly helped me to release some stress. Kerrie and the other girls helped me reapply the wax and collectively, we returned to shining our boots in the bathroom. This time we all waited until the floor was completely dry before we ventured out of the bathroom. It felt as if a small wall had been lifted

as we laughed and joked with one another and somehow, I felt more in-tune with them than I had before. We had a lot of comradery and when the first snow fell, we were out playing in it.

My life in the military had truly begun as I threw caution to the wind and embraced this feeling of comradery with those who would be my sisters-in-arms. We had each other's backs and I felt immensely welcome within the group. And even though our 13 Platoon's instructors were strict and prepared to give us punishments for the slightest infraction, we knew they were on our side. Still, their punishment of choice – the one that they would hand out like candy – was a 'fire picket' duty and I got lots of those: I was practically the Fire-Picket Queen! At those times, I felt the instructors truly had it out for me.....but somehow, I wasn't alone!

A fire picket duty involved waking up at a predesignated hour during the night to patrol one of the other girl's barrack buildings to ensure it was free of fires and the duty lasted two hours. Toward the end of my shift, I was required to wake up the next punished person and once they were on duty, I was allowed to return to bed. Some shifts would leave me with as little as one hour of sleep a night because I still had to get my other duties done and my kit prepared for the next morning's inspection.

We had an instructor who I admired greatly. She was called "Mitch, the Bitch" by most of the girls in the platoon but she was God-send to me. Early in my training, she'd caught me crying and wisely, she had advised me that the military could not use my tears. She told me that the next time I feel like crying, I needed to get angry instead because the military can and will use my anger. I never cried again.....in uniform.

Ahhhh, but then there were Sundays! Sundays were always fun for me because as a platoon, we were marched to Church each Sunday morning to attend the service there. We could choose either Catholic or Protestant but we had to go. The only other choice given was to not attend the religious service upstairs in a church but proceed downstairs and wait for the others to join you for the social hour. The service was fine although many of us had a difficult time keeping our eyes open through them, but what made it so special for me was the sing-song that went on in the basement after the service. About 50 of us would gather around the piano where all sorts of tunes were being played. Music sheets were handed out and we'd simply sing and smile....a lot! I loved it.

Drill class was always a challenge for me and it didn't help that due to my height, I was designated as the 'left marker' which meant that whenever we marched, I was responsible for controlling the speed and accuracy of our steps. I was so bad at drill. During a parade practice, our instructor ordered us to wheel left, and we obeyed, I changing my pacing to guide the recruits beside me in a counter-clockwise fashion. However, our new direction led us straight toward a wall and without a further command I didn't know what to do. So I began to march on the spot and everyone followed suit. Our instructor became infuriated and ordered us to "Halt." She believed that I was being coy with my actions to make a fool of her and we did look rather stupid. "Smart asses don't belong in the military!" she shouted at me before informing me that I was supposed to guide the troop into a second left wheel to avoid the wall.

This ended up being when I was issued my first fire picket duty as a punishment and it set a prevailing theme for the rest of my basic training. Over the course of the next few weeks, many of us were made targets and we receiving a copious amount of these punishments - sometimes uncalled-for. I believe it was meant to teach us to accept life as being unfair. A few of the girls had difficulty handling the pressure that this produced, but most of us took the attention in stride and used it to excel.

We dubbed one such girl 'Push-up Girl', and her claim to fame occurred any time we had physical training (PT) classes. Carol Allen* was a short woman, but little of her frame was due to fat; she was built like a body builder and had the stamina to outdo one. The first time we had PT, she was put in the punishment spotlight because she was not doing push-ups which involved using our knees for added support but instead were doing push-ups from her toes and she was counting them off as if they were easy.

One PT instructor noticed this and moved over to where she was. He told her, "If you want to do push-ups like a man, then you need to prove that you're as strong as one," and then with a smug grin on his face, he ordered her to carry out a hundred consecutive male push-ups. We were all done our mere 25 push-ups and stood to watch as she pumped them off.

When she had surpassed eighty, the other PT instructors came over to watch. They were incredulous when she made it to a hundred with ease before standing up. Determined to break her, they began to heckle her and then they ordered her to do an additional hundred male push-ups and this time they told her to make it one-handed ones. Carol dropped her body to the floor and easily, with one hand behind her back, pumped off those 100 push-ups. Blown away, the staff then ordered her to do another hundred and this time, they wanted her to clap her hands between each of the push-ups. Carol did not disappoint as she launched herself to and from the gym floor clapped her hands together each time before returning to the ground in time to repeatedly launch herself up once again. This time when she got to 100, she did not stop but continued until she was ordered to stop by the instructors. After that they stopped giving her a hard time although there were the times when they showed her off as an example to us during subsequent PT classes.

In PT, we got to swim as well although the experience wasn't always fun. During one memorable pool PT class, we were ordered to jump off a ten meter diving board to simulate jumping off a ship. We were instructed to keep our legs straight, but that meant hitting the water like a bullet and going deep and I didn't want to go too deep into the pool so I bent my knees a bit and paid dearly for it. The water hit my butt like a knife. I wasn't the only one foolish enough to not do as I was told and this small group was visible as we were the ones walking, marching, and running awkwardly for the next few days.

Yes, we all have weaknesses and Carol had them too. She shocked all of us one day when she collapsed and was raced away from the barracks by ambulance. Earlier that day, she had returned from the MIR (Medical Infirmary...the base's medical facility) with some cough medicine after experiencing the signs of a common cold. Fearing that she might fall behind the group, she continued training instead of taking the prescribed bedrest with her medicine. We knew she was weak from the effects of the cold, but we learned an even more valuable lesson that day. She quickly taught us that even the most commendable soldier could be brought down by the slightest weakness; Push-up Girl was allergic to alcohol and one of the ingredients in the cough medicine she'd been given was alcohol. Rushed to a nearby hospital and then was there for a few days, we became concerned that she wouldn't rejoin us. Medical absence during basic training was almost always cause for either a release from the CF or being placed back at the beginning with a different squadron. We feared that we might have seen the last of Carol. However, after a meeting between the Platoon WO and the Capt in charge of Basic Training, it was decided that Carol had every merit that a soldier in the Canadian Forces ought to possess and she was allowed to resume training with us. This was under the provision she did not consume anymore cough syrup.

Such an idea is comical in reflection, but it was a serious issue at the time; a few of the girls in our platoon wished to get out of the training and would feign illness – sometimes outright causing it – in order to be medically released. One girl ate tobacco to look unwell but they found out what she had done and she got a couple of fire picket duties for that stunt. The training was genuinely tough, and it proved to be too much for some of the girls.

Almost all the girls that truly didn't want to be there were let go but it wasn't an easy process. One girl decided to leave on her own terms and simply walked off base. We had been training for two weeks, when one dark night one of the girls broke into civie lockup and after changing out of her uniform, she walked out the door and off base. We later learned that she had simply followed the railway tracks off base and then hitch-hiked to Digby. During role call the next morning, she wasn't there.

A hush went over the troop and the whole base began to stir with commotion when the word got out. We checked her bed space before discovering the door to civie lockup had been jimmied opened. She was then declared as AWOL, absent without leave and we wouldn't learn what had happened until the Military Police picked her up in the nearby town of Digby where she'd been waiting for a bus to Halifax.

She was taken into custody and returned to Cornwallis where she was placed in a jail cell. It was brave to venture through unknown terrain in the dark of night, but it was stupid to take off the way she had. She would be dishonourably released and returned home. It could have been much worse for her as she could have faced charges to imprisonment for her actions. We were then schooled by the military police on base about the repercussions of being AWOL and they made sure to reinforce the fact that this was a grave offense. We never did hear what happened to this friend of our after she was returned home..... and we were too afraid to ask.

We continued this game of trying to stay out of trouble, trying to avoid injury, and trying to maintain the motivation that had led us from our safe and comfy homes to this inhospitable environment. Collectively, we were able to handle the worst they threw our way, but I still found difficulties in unexpected areas: who would have thought that ironing a blouse was so hard? For weeks, I was picked up on inspection for having not used enough starch when ironing my blouses and each time I got a fire picket duty. By the 4th week I was tired of it so after I ironed my blouses, I had two of the girls hold the arms of the blouse outward while I sprayed starch on them! I laughed at how they sat stiffly on the hangers in my locker. And, again, I got picked up on inspection....this time it was for "too much starch" and this time, I was given two fire picket duties which I deserved. These missteps were my greatest chance at downfall.

I had been on Basic Training for about five weeks when I got a telephone call from my Mom. It was great to talk with her. She wanted to know everything that I was doing and as I told her, she was eating it up. That week, we had been at the firing range and had learned how to fire the SMG. I didn't initially tell my mother I had learned how to fire a sub-machine gun until she asked.

First off, when I told Mom we'd been at the range shooting, she shared with me how she used to ride shotgun on the corral fence, as they were slaughtering the pigs back home on the farm where she grew up. Then she asked me what gun I was using and I said an SMG. "Hmm" she said, "I don't know that one. What's a SMG?" I guess I shouldn't have said anything (hindsight being 20-20 and all) but at the time, I was pleased with myself and proudly told her, "A submachine gun, Mom" and that's when she started to cry! Although she knew I was joining the military, she didn't have a clue what that meant and she just could not imagine her little girl firing a sub-machine gun. Literally, it blew her mind.

Although I had begun to cuss and continued to adopt much of the bravado that was encouraged in recruits, there was still a deep level of naivety that remained part of my person. This was exemplified two-thirds through our training when we were ordered to the meeting room unexpected. It was just before the 7th weekend. This is very important as the 7th weekend was going to be the first weekend when we'd be allowed to have a real weekend and could travel off base to wherever we wanted to go as long as we were back by Sunday night. All the girls in the platoon were making travel plans and myself and a few of my friends made plans to take the ferry from nearby Digby to Saint John (New Brunswick) and see the sights that weekend.

But, I didn't get to go. Why? During the week just before our 7th weekend, the whole platoon was unexpectedly ordered to the meeting room where we were told that nurses would be coming to inspect our private parts. A military nurse explained the awkward situation to us, stating: "We have been informed that a girl on base – most likely in this platoon – has crabs. Every precaution must be taken to ensure this does not spread. This is why we have brought you all here today." "What are crabs?" I asked. I genuinely did not know. "Well..." the nurse began – visibly uncomfortable with the situation, "Crabs are little red spiders that can reside in a woman's private parts and they spread easily via toilet seats. To make sure they haven't spread, we'll be checking each of you."

"Gross!" I interjected without thinking. My words left a silent echo throughout the room that was quickly replaced by laughter. I was immediately pulled away from the group by one of our instructors and taken downstairs to the offices where the instructor informed me that my comment was unforgivably rude – especially since the girl who had the crabs was in the room with us at the time.

I was caught between being grossed out and feeling ashamed and while I struggled with my conscience, my MCpl whispered with another instructor about what to do. I had never meant to offend anyone with my outburst; I was disturbed that I was being forced to put my privates up for inspection. I was given a full weekend of fire picket duty and schooled about my less than kind behaviour. This really hurt as we were now at the point in our training where we were allowed to leave the base on weekends – a luxury that felt eons away with yet another series of boring fire picket watches ahead of me.

I was assigned to patrol the barrack of the new 15 Platoon. The old 15 Platoon had graduated a few weeks earlier and the newest batch of female recruits was now on base. We were no longer the "new meat!" They were still 'green' and had not learned the ropes yet. I decided to make the most of my situation and help this group of girls and I shared with them what we had done to survive their first few weeks of hell (aka, Basic Training).

I warned them that Basic Training was a difficult combination of exerting oneself and then pretending that nothing had happened during inspections. They would be expected to clean off sweat and mud-stained clothing in a matter of minutes. That not being possible, I showed them the rope of how to make it appear as if they had done the impossible. I told them how they needed to have two sets of their kit: a model set that would permanently be left in our lockers – pressed and folded to perfection – and a set that we would wear daily and hide in pull-out frames of the ceiling whenever inspections were called for. I even told them about our bras which were subjected to these demanding standards. We had compensated for this by buying any size bra we could from the CanEx (the store on Base), even though their stock of such items was lousy. Many of us had uncharacteristic triple-D cups set out for inspections. The girls of 15 Platoon appreciated the help to no end, and I eventually became a mother figure to them and I began to look forward to fire-picket duties.

Still that weekend, every time I returned to my own barracks, they were empty. Everyone was gone....everyone except me! When Saturday afternoon rolled around, I was given a bit of break as my instructors let me go to Digby for a few hours. I walked to the front gate and called a taxi which drove me to Digby. Once there I had lunch at a Chinese food place and then walked around town for an hour or so before taking a cab back to Base. It was brutal for me that Sunday night when my friends returned and I heard all about the great time they all had in Saint John.

By the 10th week of Basic Training, it was early February in Nova Scotia and it was bloody cold. My platoon and I reached our penultimate week of training, but a terrifying obstacle loomed before us: Field training at Granville. Our regular activities had been difficult enough in the snow, but roughing it and sleeping outdoors in sleeping bags in the woods without any basic amenities was something we were not looking forward to. Yet, whether or not we were prepared, we were put onto a deuce-and-a-half and trucked off to Granville; an isolated area to the east of the base that would be our home for that week.

We slept in 'hootchies' which were simple rectangular shaped tarps that when strung between two trees or poles made a tent-like shelter without walls. We slept on the cold ground with only our sleeping bags to keep us warn. My assigned 'hootchie mate' had been kind enough to erect our shelter while I heated water for the IMPs. IMPs, or Individual Meal Packs and that is all we would be eating this week. They were meals sealed in a silver foil pouch  and were heated up by placing the whole pouch in boiling water. They were mostly awful to eat but we had to eat so we ate them.

My hootchie mate, with absolutely not a clue about camping, had placed our hootchie over a sunken part of the ground between two trees – making it so that any melted snow or rain would pool beneath us. Great! While I opted to sleep under the stars, she slept under the hootchie only to wake up in a puddle during the night. Two girls in a nearby hootchie pulled her in and had her sleep between them. Everyone was in their sleeping bags, although my hootchie mates was wet. It was a beautiful night as I pulled the sleeping bag over my head and zipped it closed. My boots were off but inside my sleeping bag to stay warm and dry and I wore my coat and combat clothes to bed. During the night, we had freezing rain come in and when I woke, I discovered that I could not move; my sleeping bag had been frozen shut and I could not get out of it. I punched upwards to break the ice and eventually it gave way and I was able to escape from the cozy cocoon. I was warm and dry and I grateful.

Almost everyone encountered difficulties with the harsh cold that week. Being in the field was rather unhygienic since we were unable to shower, wash, or even brush our teeth for the whole week. Unable to stand this, one girl found an outdoor sink and decided to wash herself in it. Her hair began to form ice crystals within a few minutes and she got an awful cold. We concluded that being smelly was better than being frozen. Frost bite and hypothermia were serious concerns that we fought off each day and none of us felt we could jeopardize our training: we were so close to the end of it. A few of the girls were returned to the Base due to cold-related injuries and watching them being driven off was a grim reminder of what was at stake.

Our days revolved around firing rifles at the Granville Firing Range  and undergoing various field exercises that replicated actual combat situations. Between these events, we would carry out our tri-daily ritual of eating our ration packs, the IMPs. This always felt like gambling with our lives as most of the meals seemed virtually inedible. Some days, we would receive half-decent IMP's such as Salisbury steak, but more often than not, we received dubious meals such as the omelette – which we dubbed 'Lung in a Bag' due to its unsavoury smell and texture.

When the final day of our field training arrived, we were informed that we would not be driven back to the base and instead, we would march there. The journey would be over fifteen kilometers in length, and we would have to carry our packs and rifles the entire way; beyond any doubt, the trip would be gruelling, but victory was in our sights. We packed up our sleeping bags and hootchies into our backpack and tightened our boots for the trek. We were prepared for the long march ahead of us. As we got formed up to leave, our instructor to us, "Alright, ladies. You've made it this far, but your greatest challenge is up ahead," she told us. We had heart of this march and knew it to be our last major test. Fully geared up, we headed out on our three hour march.

I was highly aware of our surroundings when we initially began the march taking in the sights as we passed by but I lost interest after the first hour. I had realized that the ground ahead of us suddenly elevated before veering into a steep decline. "Welcome to Heartbreak Hill," our instructor said, "This is where most medically-released recruits fail their Basic Training." She told us. And, then to motivate us, she said, "Your warm bunks and a graduation parade lie just beyond the hill, but one wrong step and you won't make it there." In order to climb the ridge, we broke ranks and once we hit the top, we peered over the edge where we saw that the ground seemed to drop sharply vertically – the tips of some trees ending where another's trunk began. We still had our backpacks and our rifles to carry through this difficult forested area. The implication of this final stretch worried all of us.

With the number of punishments I had received and with a paper-trail performance that was anything but exemplary, I would never receive the pardon that Push-up Girl had received. One wrong move here could end my military career before it had begun. We worked together helping one another as side-by-side, we tackled Heartbreak Hill. Our movements were slow and deliberate at first, but we eventually gained confidence and sped. At times, I felt like an orangutan since I had to use branches for support as I moved down from one level to the next.

Some of the girls simply tried to walk down the hill without support, but the loose gravel underfoot often gave way and they would find themselves sliding precariously for several meters until they grabbed onto one of the small trees. If it was not for that foliage, we would have needed climbing gear to make it down the hill safely. When we were able to see flat ground through the declining canopy, we knew we were close.....but we were not quite there yet. Two girls took a tumble during that final stretch – losing control and some of their kit. Luckily, they were not seriously injured and were able to join us when we gratefully reformed our ranks at the bottom of the hill. Having caught our breath, there was a buzz of excitement; we had completed the final obstacle and were on a direct route to victory.

There was no fanfare when we returned to CFB Cornwallis except what we felt in our hearts: we each felt as though we had won a marathon. Our instructors told us to wash up and prepare for an inspection and just that quickly, we returned to our game of hiding unkempt attire and pretending that we cleaned our equipment to perfection in record time. However, the general feeling in the air was no longer one of fear and worry; we were happy and smiling and so very full of hope.

Throughout the final week, we practiced drill manoeuvres on the parade square multiple times a day until we arrived at the moment we had been working toward for over seventy-five days; it was finally Valentine's Day. Our parade was held at the indoor drill hall because of

inclement weather – so any parent that travelled to see their daughter graduate into a soldier did not experience the frigid cold we had known for so long. Neither my mother nor sister were able to attend, but it did not bother me as I was surrounded by my new family. We were proud of one another and we reminisced about each and every hardship, every cold day, and every fear. In the Drill Hall, we stood to attention, pivoted, marched, saluted, and stayed neatly in unison for over an hour. I wore my position of left marker proudly as we marched past the families of my new sisters. The instructors who had treated us like weathered dirt now stood proudly before us – knowing that they had trained us well. The cadence of our steps, the music from the band, and the eruptive applause formed a fanfare symphony that made it hard not to smile.

Chapter Eight: POET and Radio Tech Training
CFB KINGSTON, ONTARIO (1979)

Sorrow pierced our pride as the girls of Thirteen Platoon realized they would be saying goodbye to one another. As we said farewell to one another, foremost in my thoughts were the way we had become sisters during the hardships of Basic Training. We'd developed bonds that could surpass any distance, and we had come to think of the Canadian Forces as a family – one we hoped would have many opportunities for reunion. Friends like Kerrie Skater – whom I had become inseparable with – were destined for a variety of training bases across Canada.

And so we went our separate ways; Kerrie flew to Montreal to begin training as a Weapon's Technician, and I got on a plane headed for Toronto with a majority of the newly-validated soldiers: we were no longer recruits, but we weren't fully trained yet either. When we arrived in Toronto, most of the girls got onto buses destined for Base Borden where most of the trades-training was done and where I would have gone if I had decided to become a cook.

However, I was on a different route and I didn't get a bus. Instead, a passenger van met a handful of us and we were driven to Base Kingston  where we would become students at CFSCE (the Canadian Forces School of Communication and Electronics). The driver dropped us off at the administrative building and we were assigned barracks and told where to go to start our training. I was destined for Delta Squadron where I would begin POET (Performance Oriented Electronics Training). POET was a six month long electronics training course and although I knew I would receive training intended to benefit the military so that

I could be a resource they could call upon, I felt more valuable than I had any other time in my life.

After arriving on Base we were assigned our barracks and I was overjoyed. I actually had a room instead of a bed space. I shared my room with Barbie Fowler* for the next few months. It was a blessing to have only one roommate instead of 50. Before we started POET, we were given a two-week math course to get our mathematics skills up to speed and ready to handle the demanding academics we would encounter on our electronics training courses.

I found the math course easy and ended up having a lot of free time; which was a pleasant contrast to my time in Basic Training. I had always loved math in school and had done well; there even being placed in a scholastic class where we were did three years of math in two years……that was until I dropped out of high school. It was a good refresher for me to do the math skills review course and I ate it up. I loved it.

We were brought up-to-speed on math equations, especially the ones we would need throughout the six months of POET and I was excited to begin and made the most of each class. Once POET began, I became a very serious student. My fellow students learned to accept my eccentric study habits as I would often skip breakfast so I could study ahead before each day's class. My purpose for joining the military was to serve my country, and I had discovered a niche that allowed me to grow and challenge myself.

I was not all work and no play. The trainee's mess, the Lamplighter Lounge, held barbeque nights every Thursday to bring us together before many left the base for the weekend. They had several barbeques – enough to feed an army, we joked – which were built into a circular brick wall that encompassed a picnic area and the patio portion of the BBQ area even had a cement dance floor.

All trainees from the four CFSCE NCM squadrons who were attending the school were invited to congregate at the Lamplighter Lounge. The music of the outdoor dance could be heard half-way across the base. It was so much fun and I loved attending these parties in part because I loved to dance. There were 16 of us in my class and we

such, when I saw John in the Lamplighter Lounge one day, I called out to him, "Hey, Clit!" I shouted as I approached him.

He was standing by the bar as I got there yet he ignored me and focussed his gaze on the world outside a window. I walked up beside him and tapped his mug to get his attention. His eyes traveled from the glass of the window to the cold beer mug he was holding. "You know what, Dawn?" he said quietly – looking into his drink, "You can be a real bitch sometimes."

He let go of his mug and walked out of the mess. I was bewildered and felt as if the floor had been removed from under me. I looked around the room to see if anyone else had witnessed the exchange. My friend, Anne had been sitting at a table not far away. She waved me over to her and said, "How could you be so mean to Cedric after everything he's done for you?" she asked – disapproval coating her expression.

"What do you mean? I don't get what happened," I replied. "'Clit'! You keep on calling him Clit!" "Well, yeah," I said, "That's his nickname."

She stared at me incredulously for a few seconds, then told me, "His actual name is John, Dawn. Do you even know what a clit is?" she asked me. When I shook my head no, she explained, "Clit is the short form of 'clitoris'."

The blood fled from my face as the gravity of my mistake became clear. Ann told me how John Cedric had been given that nickname during his Basic Training, and he loathed it to no end. My mind could not fully come to terms with the realization; for over three months, I had called out to him in the halls, lazed about and chatted with him in the mess, and went on trips to Ottawa with him and the gang – all the while calling him 'Clit'. That entire time, he did not say a word to me about his unsavoury nickname. I wanted to blame someone else for having been led astray, but I was only outraged at myself for how clueless I was.

Regret from this misdeed still haunts me today. Here was someone I admire and think so highly of and my stupid, unknowing nature had torn a chasm in that friendship that could never be healed. I wanted to do everything in my power to make amends. Unfortunately, I never had an opportunity to fix what I had broken as I was called away to Toronto the next day.

That Friday morning, a senior staff member excused me from class and brought me to the CFB Kingston's Admin Officer's office. My mother had contacted Base Kingston and informed whoever she spoke to that my sister had been admitted to the hospital because she needed an urgent lung operation; a cyst on one of her lungs had imploded. My mother was unable to be with her and asked if I could be let go to go and be with my sister.

I was asked if I wanted to go and I answered positively with little thought. I was told to go to my barracks and pack and return as quickly as I could. When I got back, an Admin Clerk gave me a $500 pay advance in cash and a train ticket. I was told that a taxi was waiting outside to take me to the train station. "Go be with your sister," the Admin Officer said, "Return when you are able to."

So many things had gone wrong in a single month, and now my younger sister's life was in danger. Under normal circumstances, anyone might have cracked under the pressure, but I was able to remain strong with the help of that clerk's kind, understanding demeanour and the assistance that the CF had provided. I was not expected to return within a fixed number of days as they trusted me to do the right thing and return when I could. I have always appreciated the opportunities the military provided, but on that day, I was eternally thankful.

I travelled to Toronto and was there by the time my sister came out of surgery. I spent a week and a half with my sister. Her operation went smoothly, and I did everything in my power to help her recover once she was discharged from the hospital. It was strange being in my home town once again. I was surprised that I did not receive any pleasant feelings of nostalgia nor was I stricken with a desire to stay. My thoughts remained in Kingston and on the future that was ahead of me as a Radar Technician.

I said farewell to my sister and returned to Kingston via train. That day, the weather was bothersome; heavy winds buffeted the train cars, and a strange chill loomed in the air, but my heart was lifted as I returned to the one place in the world that I now called home. I would apologize to Cedric, finish POET, and impress Sergeant Dylan in Vancouver and all the others who had helped me embark on this journey.

Unfortunately, my heart's ascent was halted and yanked to a low level. Upon returning to CFSCE, I was informed that I could not be allowed to rejoin my POET course due to my absence and would be placed on the next available course. Ultimate ly, I did not become a Radar Technician like my friends had, instead I was slotted to become a Radio Technician. For the first time since joining the Canadian Forces, I felt alone.

I completed my training to become a Radio Technician in August but I felt displaced. For me, the sanctity of my CF family had become disjointed and I wondered if I would ever see Cedric or Ann again. Gone was the daily comradery we had and I grieved the loss of those special friendships.

I began my Radio Tech TQ3 training at Charlie Squadron in the summer of 1979. While at CFSCE, I'd lived in Beamont Hall and ate my meals at the Vimy Mess Hall and when at Delta Squadron, I'd had to commute from the Vimy side to the McNaughton side of Base Kingston to attend classes for those first six months at CFSCE. Each morning, we'd caught that bus and we would talk and laugh: it had been a special time for us girls and I missed it immensely. Charlie Squadron was right across the parade square from my barracks so after breakfast, I would walk to class. To every cloud there is a silver lining. In addition, it was summer and it was Kingston and I loved it in Kingston. It is an historic and fun town.....especially in the summer!

Chapter Nine: Working in Newfoundland; 226 Radar Squadron
GANDER, NEWFOUNDLAND (1979-1981)

My first posting as a Radio Technician was to CFS Gander in Newfoundland. The year was 1979. CFS stands for Canadian Forces "Station" as the military installation was small. So small, in fact, that it could not be designated a "Base" as in CFB (Canadian Forces Base). At CFS Gander, there were three main operating squadrons: 103 Search & Rescue Squadron, 770 Communications Research Squadron, and 226 AC&W Squadron.

I was posted to 226 Squadron. Commonly known as a radar squadron, this NORAD Air Control & Warning Squadron controlled the military skies over a large portion of Canada's Atlantic coast. We had two large radar antennas that found any aircraft's distance and height from Gander. In order to communicate with these military aircraft, we used radios and I was one of the crew that maintained and serviced the radios.

As part of my responsibilities, I was a member of the Base Defence Force (BDF) and attended meetings and participated in exercises. The purpose of the BDF was to defend the Station in the case of an attack. On the BDF, I enjoyed this opportunity to truly be "military" as I spent most of my days checking on and repairing radios. We practiced basic military protocols such as establishing a line of soldiers to ward off any invasion, we checked on the fence around the station and ensured it was in good repair, we tested radio communications between our Operations Center and those deployed to sentry positions, we conducted searches of buildings, and we captured bad guys (fake ones of course). I remember one misbehaved "bad guy" who just wouldn't do as he was told. In the end, he was lying face down in muck.

226 Radar Squadron was part of NORAD and was officially called 226 AC&W Squadron where AC&W stood for Air Control and Warning. In the Rad Tech Shop, we had rows of old radio equipment (most of it from the WWII era) and I got to work on radios of all different frequencies including HF, VHF, and UHF. My work was not boring especially when fighter aircraft were scrambled from Moncton, New Brunswick to intercept a Russian MIG that "accidentally" flew into our air space. We knew they were simply testing our defences, but it really pissed us off when each Christmas morning, we'd be scrambled to attend to the uninvited MIG.

One day, while I was working behind one of the rows of equipment, I overheard a conversation between a Cpl and a MCpl in my shop that had to do with me. There was a Rad Tech Shop Christmas Party being held at the Cpl's home. I had been posted into the shop in October and yet, this was the first I had heard of it. The MCpl was asking the Cpl why he hadn't invited me and the Cpl responded that his wife didn't want me there. She had said it was bad enough that her husband had to work with a woman, she wasn't going to have her in her home. This saddened me but it would not be the only incident like this as the "wives" excluded me a great deal. At an isolated posting, I found myself even more alone. It was especially hard for me, as these get-togethers were my rare opportunity to be with other women.

Still, I enjoyed the comradery shared during meals at the Mess Hall. Often we'd listen to the stories told by the SAR folks from 103 Search & Rescue. My adventurous spirit couldn't help but dream of doing that sort of work. And during my two years in Gander, a few times I got to ride along with the SAR folks on training missions and even once on a rescue. It wasn't supposed to be a rescue, but they were called to assist while on a training mission and I just happened to be aboard. It was very, very exciting and as we had perfect weather, it was not scary at all. Still, the adrenaline pumped hard in my veins.

Once invited to visit 103 SAR, I would visit there a lot. And, eventually, they got used to seeing me. I was as pleased as punch when I was invited to be a spectator on my first of many SAR training missions. During training missions, they would take the Chinook helicopter up and execute a fake rescue. The purpose was for the SAR Techs to get exposure to multiple potential rescues that were native to Newfoundland and the pilots would get their flight hours in (needed to maintain their pilot's licenses).

One story a MCpl SAR Tech told us about over a meal at the Mess Hall was how they were called to rescue one of the seal hunters off an ice flow that was flowing out to sea. I listened closely as the story unfolded about how a large chunk of ice that the hunter was on had broken off the main sheet of ice that was connected to the shore and how he would perish if not rescued as the ice flow. They got the call at 103 SAR and were able to find him. That's when one of the SAR Techs, using the guide wire, was descended to him and the hunter was then lifted off the ice flow and into the Chinook (a two propeller helicopter painted mostly yellow).

I flew with the SAR Techs on a training exercises to the deep woods at the center of the Province of Newfoundland where the flies were as thick as thieves. And, even though we were suspended a hundred feet (or more) above the tops of the trees, and even though we had two huge blades whop-whopping above us, the flies still found their way into the helicopter and bit us mercilessly. The rainbow to this cloud was the fantastic photos of the CFS Gander and 226 Radar Squadron that I took as we flew over them and our unexpected coffee break. Nowhere in the military, do we miss coffee break! I was amazed that it happened on a SAR Chinook. During the flight, the load master broke open small cans of apple juice and small packages of cookies and handed them out so we wouldn't miss coffee break!

The most memorable trip on a 103 SAR's Chinooks, happened one day in winter when we flew to the city of St. Johns. As we flew south, we hugged the coastline and the scenery was outstandingly beautiful. But,

more beautiful than that was the iceberg we came across. Just off the coast, an iceberg jetted up so we flew over to it to get a closer look.

The iceberg had two humps and between them, light blue waves rushed over an ice bridge connecting the two parts. I was amazed and stood up and headed towards where the Load Master was hanging out a half open side door.

For safety, he connected me up to the SAR Tech equipment and then I was allowed to lean out of the helicopter and look. I took this opportunity to get pictures….I'm always taking pictures!

Next we landed near the "Hole" along the coastal edge and again I took lots of pictures. The "hole" was a 20 meter hole in the ground that went all the way to the sea. After my amazement at the iceberg, I believe they stopped here just to show it to me and I

felt honoured that they would make the effort. A few pictures later we were on our way to St. Johns.

Our final stop surprised me as much as it did the people in the restaurant. We put down in the parking lot of a McDonald's! The Load Master got off and headed indoors where he ordered a few hundred burgers. I helped load them up and we took off. I'd long known that I could buy a McDonald's burger out of the big freezer at the SAR hanger, but I'd never thought about where they came from. Now, I knew!

No other trip with the SAR group was as good as that trip had been. Yet we had a few exciting things happen on the station....including a visit from a royal. Prince Phillip is a pilot and in order to maintain his pilot's license, he had to get flying hours in. So, he would fly across the pond (Atlantic Ocean). As a Private, I didn't even get to see him but I knew he was there and even just knowing that was thrilling for me.

After two years at my posting at 226 Radar Squadron in Gander, Newfoundland, I was approached by my MCpl and asked what posting I would like next. Being remote, my posting was only two years long but I loved it in Gander. I was told to make three choices but having made them, did not guarantee that I would get any of them. That's the way it is in the military.

I so loved being posted in Gander that I wanted to stay yet the only posting option open to a Private Radio Technician was the Tech Shop at 770 Communication Research Squadron. So, that was my 1st choice. I figured it was a shoe-in as 770 Sqn found it hard to get technicians willing to be posted to Gander and they were scrambling for them. Not a lot of people (and even fewer Radio Technicians) wanted to move to an isolated area such as Gander, and the Station at Gander had little to recommend it for a young person not interested in hunting or fishing.

In general, it was expected that I would get my 1st choice simply because no-one else wanted it! Administratively and financially, it made sense: the Canadian Forces wouldn't have to move anyone as I was already there. My hopes were raised even more as my posting message came in. I'd got my first choice.....I was posted to 770. But it was not to be.....It was explained to me that there were no women allowed at 770 Squadron and so my gender got in the way of this posting.

I didn't see the problem but, obviously, there was one. So, in 1981, after spending two wonderful years in Gander, I got a revised posting message and instead I was posted to 764 Communications Squadron in Ottawa.

Chapter Ten: Ottawa and 764 Communications Squadron
OTTAWA AREA, ONTARIO (1981-1985)

When I first arrived at my new posting, I found myself on a large base in a large city. Besides the downtown Headquarters of the Department of National Defence in Ottawa there were a number of Bases and Stations in and around the city. One of these bases is Canadian Forces Base Uplands and it is located adjacent to the Ottawa International Airport.

CFB Uplands is an air base and our air squadrons shared the same runways as the airport. My job was to work at the 764 Comm Sqn Tech Shop on the Uplands Base. I was responsible for fixing and installing radios for the military police and the fire department on Base, set up public address equipment, and technically supporting air shows....

.....and entertainment tours in wonderful places like CFS Alert on Baffin Island in the Northwest Territories. It was a tough job, but someone had to do it! Like any job, there was good and bad but it didn't matter, I loved my job.

Unlike 226 Radar Squadron in Gander, I was working on state of the art radio equipment and I loved the challenges that presented me. I got along with everyone and enjoyed the comradery. Coffee breaks were always fun.

To fix the handheld radios used by both the military police and firefighters, I worked in a cage that shielded radio signals. A RF (Radio Frequency) cage is the size of a closet but was built exclusively to stop any radio frequencies from penetrating into or out of the wire cage. While learning specific equipment repair skill, I often worked with

Guy* (another Private, like me, but one who'd worked at the squadron for years). Guy was French and had a thick accent but we worked well together and I knew he was my source of information as I developed my skills as a Radio Technician in this work environment.

So, it was not surprising to me when Guy leaned over me while I was tuning a PRC512 police hand held radio and staring at my chest asked me if I wanted to fuck. I was a Private too, but junior to him. At the time, we were in a RF cage and he was showing me how to tune the radio. Anyways, Guy was leaning over me watching me tune the radio and advising me when out of the blue he says to me, "Wanna Fuck?" Later I thought of all the things I should have done or said, but at the time I was caught off guard and simply replied, "No thanks."

Guy had gone too far with his overt passes and so I told our boss, a MCpl. That was a total waste of time as the MCpl simply told me that's just how Guy is and that I should ignore it. So, I did just that. I went about my work and ignored Guy's advances as best I could. I still felt like a piece of meat and was wary not to be caught in the storeroom with him. I didn't make a big deal of it as there was simply nothing I could do about it.

I got on with the job and soon I was on my way to being a really good Radio Technician. Like I said, I loved my work and any time I fixed anything, I got this surge of pride in myself. It was amazing. One day a lady military police officer who I was friends with, came into the shop with a busted PRC512. The thing was in a box and was in a hundred pieces. Jayne explained that she's accidentally ran over the radio and asked me if I could fix it for her so she wouldn't get into trouble. She didn't want to tell her boss what had happened. Hey, I was good.....BUT not that good! So, I apologized to her and told her it was BER (Beyond Economical Repair) and she left with her head hung low.

While I was at the Base Uplands 764 Comm Sqn Tech Shop, we got a new CO. This Commanding Officer was an amazing fellow: a true blue soldier. When he'd first arrived at 764 Comm Sqn, he was determined to make some changes and "the memo" came out. This memo caused an uproar at the Tech Shop as the new CO had spoken of his disappointment regarding the lack of physical fitness within the squadron and I was impressed: it was great to see an officer as gung-ho as he was. For good reason, I referred to the new CO as "G.I. Joe" but I doubt he knew that. His memo was the topic of conversation at our coffee breaks for the next few weeks and I could hardly believe my ears when I heard a Sgt exclaim, "Who does he think he is?" I wanted to say back to him, "Duh, he's the CO!"

We often had dignitaries arrive on base via plane and when they did, 764 was responsible for setting up the needed PA equipment so they could hold a press conference in Hanger 11 (where the reception area was for military aircraft). As a newbie, I got to do a lot of PA system work and although it was not a favorite job, I didn't mind.

The following summer, I was asked to help out with the local Air Show when a senior technician assigned to help with the setup for the

Ottawa Air Show, took ill. I was overjoyed at being asked and gave every single chore my fullest attention. For instance, while up in the control tower of the Ottawa International Airport, I lent a hand at repairing an Air Traffic Control radio that had gone kaput during the show. Our military Air Traffic Controllers shared a control room with the civilian ATCs and this radio was needed as it was used to communicate with our military aircraft and on this day it was the aircraft flying during the Air Show.

The next work day, I was permanently assigned to work at the airport. Now that may sound exciting and at first I was excited about it. That was until I learned that the job was a lot of sitting around waiting for a radio to fail (which didn't happen very often). I guess I shouldn't have spoken up about Guy and I wondered if this was my punishment for doing so. I was kept at the airport for over a year and to keep myself from screaming with boredom, I brought knitting with me. I was learning to knit and I needed something to do. I also read a lot of books while there. I was bored out of my mind each and every day and to add insult to injury, I was on call 24/7 so I had to carry a pager with me and was unable to take leave. I wanted to scream!

I was only called out to do a repair a few times but the call out that makes me smile is the one I got in the middle of the night when the ATC told me that the equipment was not working. I raced to the airport at 2am for the stupidest thing that ever happened to me. If it wasn't so serious, it would be laughable. As Air Traffic Control is critical to safe flight, we have to react as if it is a national emergency. On this particular night the Air Traffic Controller claimed that the radio wasn't working yet when I got there, I checked on it and it was working just fine. It wasn't until I went to the ATC's console that I noticed that his "On/Off" switch was in the "Off" position!

Soon after getting the Airport assignment, I received a message telling me that I was soon to be promoted to Corporal. When I graduated my initial trade's training, I was a no rank Private then while in Gander, I completed my TQ4 certification and got my first echelon (a single "V" on the arm of my uniform). A corporal has two echelons yet in the Radio Technician trade, we are not considered a real Corporal until we complete our TQ5 training. Still, we got to wear the rank and we got a pay raise.

Within a few days later, I received a message saying I would be heading back to C Squadron to do my TQ5 training. I was so grateful to be leaving the airport job. The year was 1983 and Training Qualification Level 5 (TQ5) is a course in advanced electronics for technicians that was six months long. Taught at the Canadian Forces School of Communications & Electronics (CFSCE), I would be on TD (Temporary Duty) for six months.

As I was on TD, I would once again live in the same female training barracks; Beaumont Hall on Base Kingston. Soon after I started my TQ5 training, I met and became friends with Cpl Alice Gillis who was a Teletype Technician. She was on also on her TQ5 training and that training was in my squadron. Alice, being posted to CFSCE in Kingston was on temporary duty from Kingston and in Kingston. It just works like that. Where she worked was the Teletype Tech Shop in C Squadron, so she didn't even have to change buildings.

Being posted to Base Kingston, she had a PMQ (Personal Married Quarters....a house) on the base with her husband, MWO Al Gillis and their daughter, Laura. Although I don't remember exactly how we met, I do remember how easily we became close friends. We really hit it off and before long she was inviting me to barbeques at her home. Alice lived on the south side of the Base between the Vimy and McNaughton sides of Base Kingston, while my barracks were located on the Vimy side of the Base and therefore, a short walk to her home.

Alice's husband's name was Al and at my first meeting with Al, I found him imposing. Maybe it was because of his rank or maybe it was that he was so much older than Alice and I, but Al was a good guy who was young at heart. He epitomized a true soldier in my eyes having served with the Army and then with the Airborne and during that time having risen to the rank of MWO (Master Warrant Officer), but he never "wore" his rank when he was off duty. He had an easy going way about him and I was soon feeling at ease in his presence.

I had many fun times in Kingston that summer when I was doing my TQ5 training. I was away from Ottawa and serious about doing well on my course so I rarely returned to Ottawa. My Military Policewoman friend, Jayne came to Kingston one weekend to visit me and stayed for a weekend of fun and partying.

It was summer and Kingston is at its finest in the summer. That Friday night we caught up on all the happenings in Ottawa and Kingston and on Saturday, we drove to the beach and spent the day there before returning to Base and dressing up and heading out to eat and dance.

After supper, we ended up at a pub and that's when Jayne tells me that I have to try this new drink. "It's called a Bang-Bang," she says. I'm a bit of a lightweight when it comes to alcohol and Jayne is a Brit with the drinking constitution of one. So, she has the bartender give her a tumbler with a shot of tequila in it and then she pours a bit of ginger-ale in the glass. She puts the palm of her hand over the glass and then bangs the bottom of the glass on the table twice…hence, Bang, Bang! The ginger-ale fizzes up and she downs the shot before the fizz dissipates.

So, I try one……then I try another one. I'm sure I wasn't feeling the effects of the alcohol yet as I ordered a third and then a fourth. I couldn't have as they went down easily. Soon, the reckoning happens as I start to feel the effects of the first one starts kicking in and in no time, I am drunk like never before.

About that time, Jayne sees an outstandingly cute guy at a nearby table and asks me what to do. ME! "Go say Hello, "I tell her. So she does and then turns around and heads back to me when a beautiful blonde woman joins him at the table before Jayne reaches it. Frustrated she just looks at me, orders another Bang-Bang and then decides in typical British fashion to saunter over there and say hello anyway. I hide behind a pillar and watch as she gets to the table, stands there for a moment and then heads back towards me. She joins me behind the pillar and explains to me what happened.

Wanting to talk to the hunk, she tells him that he has a phone call in the lobby hoping he'll leave the table and she will follow him out and talk with him. Unfortunately for Jayne, the pub wasn't part of a hotel and didn't have a lobby! The blonde with the hunk explains this to Jayne who turns tail and heads back towards me. I still laugh about this.

A half hour later, Jayne bumped into a cousin of hers who is with a group of friends and we join them for some friendly banter. The hunk and his blonde have long ago left the pub (thank goodness) but the experience is fresh in Jayne's mind as she tells her cousin about it. We all had a hearty laugh at her expense but the evening is about to get even more interesting.

I could say the evening got better and better, but by better, I mean worse! As a lightweight when it comes to alcohol, I'd overdone it and I wasn't feeling so good. So I excused myself and headed outside for some fresh air. Yet, once I'm outside, I feel stupid standing alone on the sidewalk, so I cross the street to where my car is parked and get in.

My stomach is rolling so I put the seat back and open the window and promptly "fall asleep" and that how I was when the cop found me.

I opened my eyes when he tapped me on the shoulder. He was leaning over me and gosh, was he cute. I smiled widely at him and said something intelligent like "Hi." All business, he asked where my car keys are and I thought for a minute and then told him that they were in my purse and my purse was in the pub. Then, I asked him if he would get it for me!

It was obvious to me (even in my drunken state) that he wasn't keen about getting me my purse, so I told him that it was okay as my girlfriend in the pub was a cop too! He just smiled. Then he asked me to get out of the car but as I sat up my stomach came up and I quickly turned sideways and threw up out the open car door......and all over the cop's shoes and even his slacks. Not my proudest moment!

Preoccupied with cleaning off his pants and shoes, the cop moved away from the door of my car and I lied back down and low and behold, I fell back to sleep! He should have woke me up and arrested me and put me in a detox cell overnight but he didn't. Instead I woke up as the sun shone into the window of my car. When I woke up, I didn't know where I was but a quick look around reassured me that I was in parking lot behind the Kingston City Hall. The parking lot was deserted except for my car. So, I raised my seat up and that's when I felt my purse behind me. Honestly, I didn't know it was there before that moment.

On my mind is my concern for Jayne.....where was my friend? I pulled the car keys out of my purse, turned over the car and drove back to Beamont Hall on base. Once parked outside the barracks, I made my way up the stairs to the first level where my room was hoping to find my friend there. But, the room was empty. The girl next door, my barrack neighbour has her door open and comes out of her room when she sees me. Then she points back into her room and asked me if "that" was what I was looking for.

Jayne was safe and sound in a deep sleep on the second bed in her room. Her roommate had been away for the weekend and she'd been able to accommodate my friend. I shook Jayne awake and was she ever pissed at me. She told me that after I disappeared, her cousin invited her to a party and she went with them until one of them lit up a joint.

Being a cop, Jayne was in a car where marijuana was being smoked. "Perfect," she'd thought before making up some lame excuse about having to go back to the pub. They dropped her off and she didn't know where she was. She described how she sat down on the curb and waited for a car to come by. Yet, it was the early hours of the morning and there wasn't a car in sight. She sat there for about an hour. She said she would have walked back to Base if necessary, but she didn't know which direction to head in. I felt so bad.

Eventually someone did drive by and Jayne showed her ID and asked for a ride from this stranger and they drove her back to the Base and dropped her off at the Military Police Shack just down the street from Beamont Hall. She walked to the barracks and told me how when she got there, I wasn't there and that's when she lost it. She banged on my neighbour's door and asked if she could crash on the empty bed in her room.

Jayne was still mad at me an hour later when we headed to the mess hall for breakfast. With some food in her, her sense of humour returned and then she was laughing at the events of the night before. I shared with her what had "happened to me" and she laughed so hard that she had to grab her aching stomach.

After that, I didn't go downtown to party. In part because I was afraid of being recognized by that cop and I was sure I would never live that down. My secret was safe with Jayne, but I wouldn't tell anyone about that night for decades. And, instead of partying, I worked hard to achieve top marks and when all was said and done, I'd done well. The CFSCE TQ5 school was impressed with how well I'd done on the course that I was asked to stay on to be an instructor but my CO at 764 Comm Sqn said no, not at this time.

A few years later, I would get posted to C Squadron to teach the TQ5 course but for now so I returned to Ottawa and 764 Comm Sqn and then was assigned to work in the Tech Shop at the 101 Colonel By building which was part of NDHQ. This is where 764 Comm Sqn had its head offices and the work for a technician there was diverse and exciting. There were a lot of people working for 764 Comm Sqn and I got to know many of them. What a great group of people they were. I was grateful for the extensive gym at the main NDHQ building which

I took full advantage of and it paid off because while there I had the resources to truly get into great physical shape. I worked out so much that I even won a few physical fitness awards.

My work at NDHQ included providing tech support to anyone who needed it including the Operations and Intelligence Centers for our Department of National Defence. The work was wonderful. I even got a written commendation from the Minister of National Defence when I was called to his Conference Room because a VCR wasn't working and there was only a half hour left before he was to hold a Press Conference in that room. I quickly assessed the problem, fixed it and his Press Conference went off without a hitch. My CO was very happy about the commendation from the MND. When the MND Commendation arrived at our squadron, the CO came looking for me himself and thanked me personally for doing such a good job. I didn't know him very well and I was in awe of him. He was a striking figure of military might and I was proud that he was our Commanding Officer.

When the opportunity came to go an Adventure Training, I signed up and it was great. We spent a hard and fun week in Quebec learning how to cross-country ski. It was the first winter after I had returned from my TQ5 training and every one of the 25 people that were a part of the

training were from 764 Comm Sqn. I'm still not sure where we went but it was someplace remote in the hills of Quebec and I was grateful that many of the other participants also didn't know what to expect. This was my first Adventure Training and all I knew is that they promised to teach me how to cross-country ski and that was enough for me. I'd be in the fresh outdoors and I looked forward to the training. It would be a week of hard physical work but it would also be a lot of fun. I wasn't a natural at cross-country skiing...not even close! But with the help of my new friends, I soon got the hang of it. With a common goal, we linked arms and soldiered on. The best part was that suddenly I felt like I was back in the military again.

A year after the Adventure Training, GI Joe visited our NDHQ Tech Shop to speak with me personally. He'd learned that I was doing night school and correspondence courses and asked me why. When I told him that I hoped to one day go to university, he told me about the UTPM (military university training program for members) and suggested that I should consider doing this. He said he believed I would make a good officer. I never forgot that and years later, when I felt ready, I did apply for UTPM.

Although the CO had denied my staying at CFSCE as an instructor, when it came time for me to be posted, I was again asked to consider CFSCE and so when asked by my MCpl if I wanted to go to CFSCE to teach, I said yes. I loved the idea and it wasn't long after that when I received my posting message.

Chapter Eleven: Life as an Instructor at C Squadron, CFSCE
KINGSTON, ONTARIO (1985-1987)

I was posted to the electronics school, CFSCE and assigned to teach TQ5 training in C Sqn in 1985. I was overjoyed at this posting: pleased to have been considered smart enough to be an instructor at this level of training. Still, as I reported to Charlie Squadron, I wondered if I was worthy.

Within my first few weeks, I was first sent off to Base Borden to do Instructor Training and when I returned I was given a desk in an open office format and asked to work on the Master Lesson Plans. I had figured this was my learning curve and got right to work. It wasn't until months later that I learned the task they had given me was the lowest task they could have assigned me and the Master Lesson Plans had not been updated for 10 years. Still, I was determined to do the best job I could.

I was a Corporal and I would be teaching Corporals but I wasn't the only one. One of my fellow instructors was also a Cpl yet the difference in our teaching style was staggering. He was a short fellow with bit of a Hitler complex and in his classroom he strongly asserted his authority and he was at times was known to be mean.

A few months later I was finally assigned my first class to teach. I would be teaching Advanced Electronics Theory which consisted of the last few weeks of this six month long TQ5 training. By then, I'd been in the CF for long enough to realize that in the military, women in uniform were either a whore or a bitch. There was no grey in this black and white scenario. So, while I was an instructor at Charlie Squadron, I let my internal bitch came out to play. I was very strict with my students and much like my fellow Cpl instructor.

I felt I needed to be strict as early in my teaching career at C Sqn, I had been shown multiple displays of disrespect as my students pulled various stunts on me that they would never have pulled on a male instructor. One day in the C Squadron cafeteria, I heard one of the students refer to me as the "Dragon Lady" and I smiled. Hey, I didn't have a problem with that one little bit! It became my nickname and I embraced it. Known as the "Dragon Lady" who made students do stand by your desk inspections on a daily basis, I epitomized the bitch I had become.

Many of the students thought they should be given some slack as they had done their time (four years in the military) and they weren't just cooks, they were technicians! They thought they were somehow privileged. I didn't care if they were now Cpls and they grew to understand that as far as I was concerned, they were military first and technicians second. I became a hard-ass believing that since I had to wear the same uniform as they wore, they had better look sharp in it.

And, when they didn't, I took serious action much like I did whenever one of my students showed me disrespect. I wore the same rank as my students, but I was their instructor and therefore they were to show me respect. One day, a student spoke back to me in a disrespectful tone: he'd told me to go to hell and then laughed at me in front of the class. I ordered him to stand to attention in the doorway facing the hallway and with the door open, he could listen to the lesson as the class continued. He didn't want to follow my orders so I asked him if he would prefer that I call the Military Police. If that happened, he would be charged with failing to obey a direct order. Only then did he get up from his desk and stand in the doorway and, just as I had planned, when Sgt-Major walked by, he stopped and asked him what he was doing there and he was forced to explain himself. The Sgt-Major smiled at me and moved on down the hallway.

It was no surprise to me that after that, the students in house were more respectful towards me. Well, most of them were. A few courses later, I had just put on an instructional video for the students to watch when one of my students took out his Walkman and put the earphones on his ears. Seriously, I thought! Momentarily dumbfounded at this, I walked over to his desk and asked him what he was doing. That's when he explained to me that it was only background music!

I don't know who was more surprised when I left the room without saying a word, him or the class. They did not know what I had planned:

I went downstairs to the Tech Shop and borrowed a pair of wire cutters. When I re-entered my classroom and he saw me coming towards him with the wire cutters in hand, the earphones quickly came off and the Walkman was put away. I hadn't said a word....I didn't need to as he got the message loud and clear.

There were some awkward moments in my class and one of these happened when one of my students ended up being a fellow I had dated years early. We hadn't dated a lot.....actually, he'd only asked me out that once as it had been a horrible date. That evening, I hadn't wanted to go out as I was exhausted after a day on parade. It was the only time, I'd ever fallen asleep at a restaurant. I'd closed my eyes for a brief second between the salad and entrée courses and woke up when he was finishing his desert. Like I said, it wasn't a good date and now here he was in my classroom. Can you say awkward!

I was shocked at the level of sexual misconduct at the CFSCE School as my Troop Warrant Officer made multiple unwelcome advances toward me. I rejected his advances because I wasn't interested and because I was in a relationship and he was supposed to have been  married. It got difficult for me, but it was manageable until one day when he went too far. The Squadron had just come off of parade and we were all in our dress uniforms when he called me to his office. Once there I was asked to sit down because he said he wanted to talk to me. I didn't know what was up and I wasn't worried. He starts to talk but I can't remember what he was talking about because he also started to undress right there in front of me. I asked to be excused but was ordered to sit back down. First he took off his formal dress uniform and once down to his underwear, he walked directly in front of me. I averted my eyes and got up to leave again but he then firmly orders me to sit back down. I stood still for a second and seriously thought about leaving anyhow but my military training was strong and it took over and I complied and sat back down. Shocked by this behaviour, I continued to try to not look straight ahead as he stood in front of me without saying a word. It was hard to miss the imprint of his penis against his underwear as he was aroused. Did he expect me to jump his bones unable to control my reaction to his hardness? Honestly.....I just about puked and wondered if this man was crazy. I stayed put and did my best to ignore him. When my WO had completed his prancing about, he returning to his desk and took a position behind it while he finished getting dressed in his work uniform and only when he was finished dressing, did he tell me I could leave.

I headed back to my office and just sat there at my desk staring into space. I didn't know what to do. I wondered that if he would go this far, how far would he go next time? And that's when I got up and headed out of the building. When I arrived at the Military Police Shack, I asked to speak to a police officer and a Sgt came out to the front desk and guided me into one of the back rooms where he asked me why I was there. He had opened up a notepad and had a pen in his other hand and wrote down my name and the date. I wasn't sure what I was going to say to the Military Police, but that's where I walked to. My best friend was a Military Policewoman and so I felt safe going to them.

I figured he was going to take notes but when I started to tell him what happened, he put the pen down and didn't write another word. Although he appeared to be listening to my story, he didn't take a single note and when I was done talking, he took a deep breath before cautioning me. He asked me who I thought "they" were going to believe: me or the WO? He then asked me how much time I had in the military and I told him seven years. I'm sure I looked confused because next he explained to me that my WO had 12 years in and with my only having seven years in, he repeated his question, "Who do you think they're going to believe?"

I didn't know what to think as I left the MP Shack: I was so confused. Weren't they supposed to help me? I never forgot what the police sergeant said to me that day and it played a part in why I did not come forward after future assaults.

I put that aside as there was nothing more I could do: it hadn't been the first time I had experienced sexual misconduct in the CF and I suspected it wouldn't be the last.

Chapter Twelve: UTPM Application
KINGSTON, ONTARIO (1987)

My friend, Alice and I reconnect while I was posted in Kingston and her MWO husband, Al, also friend, would become mentor and guide me as best he could. Alice and Al knew I was continuing my education and that I might one day apply for the UTPM program and we discussed it from time to time. Al shared with me that in his lengthy military career, he'd had many COs and that in general, he had a distaste for officers. Yet, he also told me that he'd seen a handful of good ones and that he believed that I would be one of the good ones. I was honoured that this long-in-the-tooth MWO believed I would make a good officer. This was the second time someone I admired had told me that they thought I would make a good officer and this type of encouragement was empowering.

In early 1987, I submitted my application for UTPM. Almost right away, I ran into road block after road block. For instance, the Base PSO (Personnel Selection Office) kept "losing" my file so that my Commanding Officer was unable to see it and without it, he couldn't make a recommendation of me as he hardly knew me. And, this was when I felt the need to make a record of all that was happening and I started to write everything down. At the time, I wasn't sure why I was doing this, but today, I'm grateful that I did although I still wonder how I ever got into the UTPM program with so many road blocks in my path.

I had settled into my teacher position within CFSCE and started doing night school classes at Queen's University: I was both a teacher and a student. At Queen's, I was completing the final courses that I needed to be eligible to begin an electrical engineering degree. This high school dropout was desperately trying to make a better life for herself and her family. It had already been a long road to finishing all my high school classes. All in all, it had taken eight long years of night school, correspondence, and university prep course work to get here. I had worked so hard for years to complete my high school in part because I didn't want my kids to say to me what I had said to my mother when I quit high school. She had not wanted me to quit and had tried to talk me into staying in school but I wanted to get out into the world and make some "real money!" The part-time jobs I'd had just weren't cutting it. When she wouldn't get off my back, I angrily said to her, "How can you tell me not to quite when you yourself are a drop out?" I sorely regretted those words and I never wanted to hear them come at me.

My hope was to successfully apply for UTPM. The acronym UTPM represents the University Training Plan Men and it is a program for serving soldiers who are aiming at becoming an officer. If my application was successful, I would be sent to a university full time for four years and at full salary. So, it was a big deal and the only way I could afford to go to university.

On the Monday morning of January 5, 1987, I requested to see the Base PSO and not for the first time. Yet this day was different as soon after I made that request, I was asked to sign my annual PER (Personnel Evaluation Report). The PER is a report on how a soldier is doing and is provided once a year unless special circumstances warrant an additional report being prepared. I had some expected to do well as I had done in the past but I received very low scores. They were not scores that someone applying to be an officer should be achieving. I was shocked and surprised as I had no idea how my scores had plummeted from the previous year.

I didn't know what was happening so later that morning, I met with my Captain in charge of our Troop, but the meeting did not go well. In fact, the meeting lasted less than 30 minutes and he broke it off with the promise to again talk to me that afternoon. Yet, in that short 30 minutes, I shared with him about some of the problems I had with two of the Warrant Officers that worked for him. Having written down and then typed up the details regarding the many challenges I had in making my application for UTPM, I was able to give him my typed sheets of paper. Then I asked the Captain why my Personal File and even application for UTPM had both been lost. At first, he blamed one of his Warrant Officers and then he blamed the changeover of the Commanding Officer of our squadron for the lost documents.

I had learned that my documents had been being "lost" since the previous year and frustrated, I directly asked how it was that these documents could have been misplaced all the way to February, 1986. The Capt said the outgoing CO of C Sqn (a Major) had been slack due to his impending retirement and then he told me that my previous request to see the Base PSO had sat on the acting CO of C Squadron's desk for a long time. Yet he then told me something totally different and said, this new acting CO (a Captain) had tried to get my PERS file but had difficulty getting it and that had added to the delay.

During the interview that reconvened after the Captain had lunch, I was told that I was being over sensitive and I disagreed. I told the Capt that someone threatening to hit me as the WO was not being overly sensitive, nor was my speaking up about it. He laughed at me and said he didn't believe it! I emphasized to him that I was telling the truth and his advice to me then was that I should take care of it myself by speaking directly with the WO about it.

I then started to tell my Capt about what his other Warrant Officer (my supervisor) had done and he interrupted me and told me that he didn't want to hear anything bad about this WO. He went on to say how this WO was a good soldier and how I should be more loyal to him. I was surprised when he said he'd already heard about the incident from the WO himself. I was absolutely sure that whatever version he'd been told wasn't close to the truth and I said to him that I thought he should hear both sides of the story.

I was shocked when my Capt told me that his WO was just doing as he had instructed him to do. It couldn't be, I thought and giving him the benefit of the doubt, I figured he'd not heard a true accounting of what had happened so I offered him my type written record but he refused to look at them. My Capt said he didn't need them. That's when I noticed that he hadn't written down any of the details of our discussion. Not surprisingly, I was very disappointed and severely disillusioned at the conclusion of this interview.

Taking the Captain's advice to speak directly to the Warrant Officer who had threatened to hit me, the following morning I met with the WO in a one-on-one. At first he denied having threatened me but I persisted and eventually he admitted he may have said that but that he had in no way intended to follow through. The meeting went well until he asked if I had mentioned this to our Troop Captain and then he explained that if I had, it would make him look really bad.

I avoided directly answering the question and instead told him I had talked to the Captain about something totally different but that I would prefer not to mention it to him just yet. The next morning, our Troop Captain called a meeting in the Squadron Theatre at 1000 hours. In this meeting, he spoke on the matter of loyalty specifically with respect to subordinates to their supervisors within the Troop and he emphasized how a problem within the troop should not be complained about outside of the Troop. He then launched into a speech about how his position was administratively mishandled before he stepped into it and how he hopes all this is now straightened out.

I was pretty sure that nothing will be done for me at the Troop level but waited to hear directly back from the Capt. Two weeks passed and I heard nothing back and decided to wait a bit longer. Two weeks stretched into four weeks and still I haven't heard anything back and I knew my suspicions had been accurate and that nothing would be done. I put this matter (although well documented) aside with the determination that if a single more incident happens, then I would follow up on this matter to the highest level. Even though the matters of being threatened and sexual misconduct were ignored, I need to move forward with my UTPM application and with my future. My first action had to be to find out where my "lost" PERS file was and why my PER scores were so low.

Not surprisingly, I felt like I was in a nightmare not of my making. Also, I wondered if the way administrative matters were handled was this questionable, then how could the handling of my PER not be? And, very importantly, what had happened to my UTPM application? Was I being recommended and had it yet been sent to Ottawa? I needed to find out the answer to these questions but none of my supervisors within my Troop would give me the time of day. As a Corporal in the squadron, how was I to have confidence in the administrative abilities of my supervisors? It was an important factor of my job, that while I tended to my instructor duties, it was only right that I have confidence that my supervisors are looking out for my best interests.

I felt ready for the next step in my academic life. I had two young children and a husband to support and my only option was the UTPM program. The only hiccup was that I couldn't move forward without my Commanding Officer's approval. In addition, I hoped he would support my application with a recommendation. Taking the bull by the horns, early one morning, I telephoned the Secretary for the Commanding Officer of C Sqn and asked for a meeting with the acting CO and when she asked me what the purpose of the meeting was, I told her that I wanted to ask the CO for his recommendation in support of my application for UTPM.

She called me back with a scheduled appointment. The CO's office was on the Main floor of a large building that was Charlie Squadron on Base Kingston and the CO had over 50 corporals working directly for him and another few hundred on course in the squadron. It was impossible for him to know us. I had never spoken to him personally and the only time I had ever seen him was when he was in front of the troops on the parade square.

I was a no body to him: just one of many faces in the C Sqn Troop on the parade square. As the classroom where I taught was on the 3rd Floor so we never ran into each other. Somehow I had to make myself into a "somebody" who was known to him. In my effort to let him know about me, I prepared a legal size folder to give to him. On the flap, I wrote "All about Dawn" and inside the folder I placed copies of my academic transcripts as well as my military technical training coursework. He might not get to see my PERS file, so this might have to do. In the folder, I included a few letters of appreciation I had received as well as two letters of recommendation I had received. I felt ready for this very important interview.

The first time I met with the C Sqn CO, I didn't share with him the challenges I had with the Base Personnel Selection Officer (who had lost my application twice over the last few months) nor the events that had happened in my Troop. Instead, I focused on why I would make a good UTPM candidate. I sat and waited for him to review the folder I had provided for him and then I answered his questions as completely as I could.

I noticed how he paid particular attention to the letter of recommendation from the Padre on Base. I was a Sunday school teacher at my church and had organized and overseen the previous year's Christmas Pageant and had received a letter of appreciation for it. This letter was also in the file. At the end of my meeting, the CO said he would consider my request and get back to me. I left feeling hopeful for the first time in a long time.

When I did not hear back from the CO for weeks, I telephoned his secretary and was told that he had not made a decision yet. I was crest-fallen as I didn't have a Plan B and knew not what my net step might be. Then I got the phone call: it had been three weeks since that all important meeting so when his secretary called me and asked me to stop by, I raced downstairs with my heart in my throat.

I knew I was holding my breath as I saluted him and took the seat he offered. His head was bent over his desk as he told me that he had decided NOT to recommend me. That's when my breath whooshed out and numb, I just sat there. I didn't ask why. I was numb and embarrassed and I couldn't wait to leave his office.

Yet, I remained put as the CO continued to talk although I was only half listening after that. With the challenges I had previously had with the PSO, I was struggling to accept his decision. The CO explained that he, being "only a Captain" didn't think his recommendation would be perceived by the UTPM Selection Board as worthwhile and that is why he went to the Commandant of CFSCE and had asked him to recommend me. I was stunned as I listened to him explain to me that the Commandant had just gotten back to him an hour ago with a "yes" and instead of a Captain's recommendation, my UTPM application would be receiving a recommendation from the Commandant himself and I almost fell off the chair. I don't remember anything that was said after that and I believe I floated out of the CO's office on a cloud.

I was notified that my application for UTPM had been successful by a fellow at church. One of my church members, who I did not know well but had often seen in church, came up to me after the service. Then, after confirming who I was, he congratulated me. When I asked what for, he told me that he had been on the UTPM Selection Board and was impressed with the completeness and organization of my application as had been the other board members. He went on to say that he didn't know I had applied and was pleased to see that I was doing so well.

I was not formally notified for another few weeks when my CO called me to his office. We left from him office and headed over to Alpha Squadron (where the C&E Branch officers trained and where the Headquarters of CFSCE was). With the CO and I were two other NCMs: a CPL and a MCPL who had also applied for UTPM and been selected. In the CFSCE Commandant's Office, the school Commandant, a Colonel and the Deputy-Commandant, a LCOL congratulated each of us and then they stood on either side of me and removed my CPL rank epaulets off my work dress uniform and replaced them with OCDT epaulets.

Next, these two powerful men walked the three of us new OCDTs to the C&E Branch Officer's Mess where we were welcomed to the Officer Corp. We had coffee with them and it was a very special day for me and one I will always remember. When I got back to the squadron, I called Alice and soon Al was calling me.

I valued Al's opinion and when I was thinking about applying for UTPM, he told me that he thought I should go for it and that he thought I'd make a good officer. At the time, I wasn't sure if he was serious or just pulling my leg, but he made sure that I knew he was sincere. I appreciated his guidance and mentorship and I would miss him a great deal. He told me how proud of me he was when I was accepted as a UTPM and even prouder when RMC accepted me as a student there.

He told me he looked forward to my graduation day and promised he'd be there. But it was not to be. Al was a paratrooper and having served with the Airborne and because CFSCE was a stagnant posting (non-operational) posting for Al, he kept himself in parachuting order by jumping with the Gananoque Sports Parachuting Club near Base Kingston. Having served out of CFB Petawawa more than once, he proudly wore a white maple leaf on his paratrooper insignia. And, to stay current, each weekend he'd head out to the club to get a few jumps in.

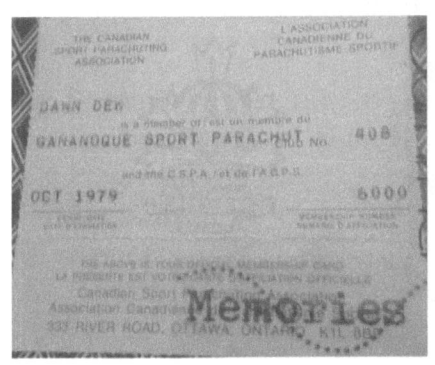

I knew the club and had even become a member back in 1979 when my friend Terrie and I had joined the club. We wanted adventure and we got it even though neither of us ever jumped more than once. My first and only jump was a bad experience for me. With one foot out the small door of the single engine Cessna, my jump instructor told me that when I jumped I should throw myself as far out the door as I could: he suggested that I reach for the end of the strut.

And that's when my first jump became my last jump. I did stretch out to reach for the end of the strut, the problem was that I caught it. We were lucky the airplane didn't crash as my weight hanging from the strut caused the small plane to tip.

My jump instructor, thinking I was good to go, had thrown my pilot chute out the door after I confidently threw myself out the door. When the pilot chute opened up, it pulling my main chute out and I was yanked hard and fast off the strut. Down I went like a rag doll until I was yanked back by the opened chute. Whew....I would live another day! But, would I ever jump again....Nope! Still, it was amazing to float to earth like a feather and I'll never forget that.

The investigation in what had happened to Al concluded that the parachute had been at fault and that it had been wrongfully packed. Ironically, Al was anal about always packing his own chute but once a year, it had to packed by a qualified parachute packer at the Gananoque Sports Parachuting Club. It would be under the "professionally packed" chute that Al would thunder in.

A friend who witnessed his jump that when his chute had opened as a streamer, he pulled out his knife and starting cutting it away but it had taken too long and without an AOD (Automatic Opening Device), he didn't have time to deploy the reserve chute. She said, he screamed all the way down and I suspect he knew it was not going to end well for him. She was also unkind enough to share with me how his body left a half inch deep hole in the ground where he impacted the ground. Yeah, I got all the unwanted details!

The ILC (Independent Learning Center) is an Ontario-based correspondence school which I took courses at and it ended up being where I achieved most of my high school credits. When I was in Gander, I dissected a frog for a Biology course and I guess I shouldn't have done so on the dining room table in the barracks. I was quite unpopular as the smell of formaldehyde lingered for weeks. As I did course after course, I found one major stumbling block: Chemistry!

First I enrolled in Grade 13 Chemistry but quickly realized that I was in over my head. I was not academically ready for this course and there was no way to learn all I needed to know so that I could pass the course. So, I stepped out of the course and signed up to take Grade 12 Chemistry. Once I had the basics down, I again signed up for Grade 13 Chemistry and was able to pull off a mark of 97% in the course. I believe it is very important to know one's limitations and stepping back allowed me to step forward strongly later on.

I took both Grade 12 & 13 Chemistry via correspondence courses from the ILC (Independent Learning Center). Not long after I started at RMC, I received a letter from the ILC notifying me that I had won an academic award for having achieved such a high mark in the Grade 13 Chemistry course. The letter said that my Grade 13 Chemistry teacher was so impressed with my work that he nominated me for the award. I wasn't aware of this until I learned that I had won.

The letter informed me that the award would be presented at the Conference Room of the Kingston Ramada Inn and I was asked to give a short speech. I'd been an instructor for a few years by then and I'd gotten used to talking publicly so I felt okay about doing so. A few months later, I won an academic prize at RMC for top student in 1st Year Chemistry bringing it home how important a solid foundation in the basics of any course of study is.

PART THREE: A Career after a Military Career

Attending an Iridium launch with my test team at Vandenberg AFB

As a National Wind Senator in the USA

CanDew
Scientific

Chapter Thirteen: Working for Motorola
PHOENIX, ARIZONA USA (1995-1999)
MANSFIELD, MASSACHUSETTS (1999-2000)

After retiring and leaving Canada, I went to work as an engineer for Motorola on a satellite project called "Iridium." In my professional life, I continued to work hard and excel.

That's when I heard about a "High Tech Career Exchange" where companies outside of Canada were looking for engineers. But, there was a problem....the High Tech Career Exchange was happening on the same days as I had full day meetings. My meetings were being held at NDHQ and the High Tech Career Exchange was taking place downtown just blocks from where my meetings were. Maybe, I could drop in during my lunch hour.

Unwilling to give up, I did just that and ran over to the High Tech Career Exchange during my lunch break. I dropped off my resume with a number of potential employers and Motorola was one of them. They there looking for engineers to work on Iridium: a satellite project consisting of a constellation of low Earth orbiting communications satellites. It was the most exciting satellite project of its time and I would have loved to get a job there. Still, I didn't have much time.

So, I raced over to where they were conducting interviews but there was a long line down a hallway. I was in uniform and was able to get to the front of the line so that I could simply drop off my resume. I'd used this tactic to drop off three other resumes. I didn't have much time and I had to be back at my meeting by 1pm.

I asked the HR guy from Motorola where I could put my resume and he pointed to a nearby box on the counter, but advised me to hang around. He said, I would do better if I stayed and spoke with one of the HR people. But there was a long line of potential candidates down the hallway and I simply didn't have the time. So I put my resume in the box and said, "No, thanks. I think my resume speaks for itself!"

Yes, it was a cocky move but I was on an adrenaline high and racing around to get my resume to as many of these companies as I could. I'd just come from a meeting where I'd been regarded as an expert and I was full of confidence about my skill set. Besides, I had to do something to stand out from the throngs of engineers lining the hallway that day. The HR guy from Motorola later told me that he went right to the box and grabbed my resume, curious as to who I was.

The following week, Motorola called me and asked me to do a telephone interview. It was my last day in uniform and I agreed to do the interview on a prescribed date unaware that I would be travelling with my children on that day. A week later, from a cattle ranch in Red Deer, Alberta, I did the telephone interview with Motorola. As I stared out the window at the Charlois cows and their calves, I answered the many questions put to me and the interview went so well that they asked me to come to Phoenix for an on-site interview. I agreed and we set a date. The kids and I completed our vacation and as soon as we got home, I flew to Phoenix.

Motorola impressed me as they flew me 1st class and put me up in a Hilton Hotel in Phoenix. They'd gone all out and even made arrangements for me to spend a day visiting the Grand Canyon. The four day trip was wonderful although the interview day was long. They'd arrange for me to be interviewed by 11 different people that day. It was a marathon of interviews and by the end of the day, I was exhausted and exhilarated.

My most memorable interview from that day was with the Manager I would work for if I got the job. Why was it so memorable? Well, because I wasn't really serious about moving to Phoenix. I'd thought about it seriously and I desperately needed a job, but I had served my country for 20 years and I'd just bought a house and was financially committed. Besides, I'd just moved my kids with the promise that this would be our last move, so no, I wasn't seriously thinking about making the move. Yet, I sure did want to learn more about Iridium and the day trip to see the Grand Canyon was a big draw for me as well. I know it was shallow of me, but it was a dream of mine and I have no excuse for my behaviour. It is what it is.

Then something happened that changed my mind. During my interview with the fellow who would be my new Manager, he claimed that the constellation would do something that I knew it couldn't do. I don't know exactly what gave me away but I suspect it was my body language.....it was obvious to him that I'd lost interest. The Manager stopped what he was doing and looked straight at me and simply asked, "What?" Not one to mince words, I replied, "You can't do that!"

"Why can't we?" He asked. And I told him, "Because the technology isn't there!" And he replied, "You're right. It's not there....BUT....it'll be there when we get there!" From that moment on, I was sold and desperately wanted to work on the Iridium satellite project but what about my kids? Could I convince them to move to Phoenix? Would their father allow it?

That week, Motorola made me an initial offer of a salary $45,000/year but I continued to look for a job in Ottawa so as to be near my new home in Kemptville. Having just bought a house... I couldn't move to Phoenix....could I? Even though I wanted to work on Iridium, moving to Phoenix was impractical. Still, I couldn't help thinking how perfect a fit the job was for this Space Scientist.

When Motorola made me their offer, I asked for a few days to think about it and this time, I got the offer in writing. I'd learned my lesson from the Valcom incident. Even with a copy of the fax they'd sent to my mortgage lender, I was unable to convince anyone of the validity of that job as Valcom came up with one excuse after the other. I was not about to let that happen to me a second time.

During that time, I had an interview at Marconi in Ottawa. The interview went well and three projects they discussed all seemed interesting to me. The HR representative and I were taking a break in the cafeteria at Marconi and discussing the options when she blurted out that I wouldn't get to work on any of those engineering projects: Marconi was interested in hiring me because they didn't have any women engineers yet. My job responsibilities would be to go out in public, like at schools, as Marconi's woman engineer. She really saved my bacon that day as I was seriously considering the job. I wanted to work as an engineer/scientist and not be some company's token woman engineer.

When Motorola didn't immediately hear back from me, they offered me a higher starting salary. Then, a few days later, they offered me a starting bonus. I was still looking for a job in the Ottawa area and had been unable to commit to them. I was pleasantly surprised when they never gave up on me and that feeling of being wanted was powerful yet even with that I continued to hold them off until the day that the fellow that would be my future boss telephoned me and asked me if I was indeed interested.

I told him that I was but that I was a single parent with two children who had to buy into us moving to Phoenix and I wasn't sure they would. What I didn't know is that he was a single parent of two disabled boys and understood my commitment to my family. He broke off our telephone conversation asking if he could call me back in an hour and an hour later when I called him, he invited us to come to Phoenix on a "House-Hunting" trip at Motorola's expense. He told me that I was to bring the kids to Phoenix and find out if liked the area and would be okay with the move. I could not believe the generosity of Motorola and their concern about not only my happiness, but also my children's. It was so different in the military where a family was considered a burden.

In August, the kids and I flew to Phoenix for a week. It was very hot but that didn't stop them from loving it. We returned home but before we left, I signed the offer and committed to Motorola that I would work for them. Early the following month, I was raped by a fellow officer and now I desperately wanted to leave Canada and we moved to Phoenix later that month.

When we arrived, we didn't have a place to live so Motorola put us up in Corporate Housing. It was a lovely house in a gated community in a suburb of Phoenix called Ahwatukee and the kids loved that it had a swimming pool. A few months later, when I was sure about the job panning out on the long-term, I bought a house in Ahwatukee so the kids wouldn't have to change schools again that year.

Motorola's corporate culture was very different from that found in the Canadian Forces. At first, I felt it couldn't be real and wondered if everyone was putting on an act but weeks, then months, and then years passed and it stayed the same. At Motorola, there was a deep respect of women engineers and I no longer felt the need to prove my competence based on being a woman. If asked to compare how women were treated at Motorola with how women in the Canadian Forces are treated, I could only say that there was no comparison!

My workplace was very welcoming of women engineers and my skill set was not constantly questioned as it had been in the CF. I felt respected and my opinion was often sought and not questioned or criticized. I not only did well at Motorola, I thrived professionally and personally. The Canadian Forces could learn a lot from Motorola, but I doubt they will ever consider this because in my opinion, they don't want to learn how to treat their women right.

I started to work for Motorola in September of 1995 and that Christmas the Secretary for our group gave us each a special Christmas gift. She'd hand painted each of us a walnut in a Christmas theme and had attached a ribbon to the top of it. With the ribbon, she hung one of each of these decorative balls outside each of our cubicle offices so that when we arrived at work that morning, we each found a beautifully decorated walnut hanging near our office doorway.

A few days later, we had a big meeting given by the Vice-President of Motorola. During that meeting, I asked him a question regarding something he had reported to us on and although my intent was clarification and I wasn't meaning to cause trouble, a hush went through the room but the VP easily reassured me with his answer. From the meeting, I'd gone directly to lunch and when I came back to my office from lunch, I found all the walnuts were hanging outside my office! When I asked, "What's this?" I was told that the guys had done this because they thought I had more balls than anyone else in the office!

Our offices were a series of cubicles and on this particular day one of our colleagues was having his 40th birthday and to celebrate, we plastic wrapped his office (including the cubicle doorway) using the big roles of pallet plastic wrap. Once the office was sealed, we poured bags and bags of Styrofoam peanuts into his office space until it topped the cubicle walls. We then smoothed out the top with a broom and that's the way he found his office when he got back from lunch that day. Lucky for us, he had a good sense of humour as when he got back from lunch, he just stood there and the look of shock on his face was comical. He didn't get any real work done that afternoon as he spent hours emptying his office cubicle of those nasty peanuts! And even though he was thorough, he missed a few and over the next few months he kept finding one here and one there! Whenever that happened, he throw them at us.

Motorola did have one bad apple. I guess you just can't weed them all our as there are bad apples everywhere. There were thousands of engineers working on the Iridium project and given that number, I expected to find more than a single bad apple but in my five years there, he was the only bad apple I encountered.

This guy thought women were simply sex objects and although his attitude was well known, he was a great engineer and tolerated. I avoided him. I don't remember what he said or did one day, but it pissed me off and I told him off and I'd thought the matter was dealt with but I was wrong. Unfortunately, he was on my Motorola baseball team and he was as good a ball player as he was an engineer, but day he went too far.

After winning the game that Saturday, a large number of us team players all headed to a restaurant pub for some snacks and beers. Many of us had our kids with us and I'd brought along mine. As a group, we sat at a big long table by the window and ate and drank. This guy had more than a few beers and became belligerent and ignoring that there were children present, he loudly asked me if it was true that Canadian like to take it in the rear. He was seated four people away from me and on the other side of the table and knew I was a Canadian. What a jerk, I thought, but answered him saying that it was true.....I said, "That way we can both watch the hockey game!"

Our boss was also on the team and his kids were also at the table. When Monday came, he was called into our boss' office and was schooled about what is appropriate and what is not. Then, for good measure, he saw the effects of his behaviour on his paycheck which was docked a few days' pay for his behaviour and told to take a few days off and think about it. Personally, I think he got off easy and I was so impressed. Motorola didn't have to do anything yet they did and in so doing made it very clear that they will not allow discriminatory behaviour. A site wide memo came out a few days later making it clear their position about the matter. And, again I was impressed. I wasn't surprised based on the corporate culture that existed there, but after 20 years of feeling under the gun, it was so very nice to feel protected.

Not long after I got to Phoenix, I had my first panic attack. Nightmares were the norm for me but I found running helped keep them at bay. It helped that I was working long days and got up at 5am each morning to go for a run. On weekend days, the kids would come with me. My son would wear his roller blades and my daughter rode her bicycle and they would share custody of the Mimi's lead as she came with us.

I was having nightmares almost every night. Luckily my work exhausted me and I threw myself into it. Still, I had nightmares so I sought professional help to deal with them. I saw a Psychiatrist and he prescribed some medication and sent me to a Therapist to do talk therapy.

I did these things to help me deal with what would later become known as PTSD which got worse after a morning news report told me about a man in a white panel van who had abducted, raped and murdered a young girl in our area of the city. That triggered me. I had been raped and knew what it was like.

I didn't know I had been "triggered" until I was driving to work that morning. It was when I had my first panic attack. I didn't know what was happening. Like a movie rolling in my head that I just couldn't stop, I saw my daughter abducted and thrown into the van. Then I saw her raped in vivid detail before her rapist killed her. It felt surreal and as if I was right there in the van watching.

It threw me off my kilter. My heart raced and my hands were shaking and I was sweating in my air conditioned car. Unable to continue driving, I pulled the car off the road as I thought I was having a heart attack and maybe this is what it felt like. I was so very frightened and so I headed for the nearest hospital. A few hours later, I was told that it was anxiety and that I'd had a panic attack. I was told that I should see a psychiatrist and already having one, I called him and he saw me the next day. That's when he prescribed me a med known as Effexor. I stayed on Effexor for years and I kept running too. In time, I would end up running three marathons and four half-marathons.

I knew that running was helping me keep sane and the gym at work was key to my sanity. I would get up on a treadmill and run and run and run. One day, a friend of mine, Chuck Parsons, would approach my treadmill and ask me when I might be freeing it up. Caught up in my thoughts, I'd not realized that I'd been on the treadmill for 50 minutes. Being fit has its advantages and needing the exercise as I did, I got into other sports sure that they would also help me. First, I joined a Motorola baseball team, then their ski club and eventually their hiking clubs. I loved to downhill ski and because of the many ski trips put on by their ski club, I got to ski every mountain that the western United States had to offer. Once, they had

a ski trip to Whistler (just north of Vancouver) and I wanted to go so badly but I was concerned what the effect on me psychologically if I ventured into Canada. My love of skiing won out and unable to resist the 5,000 feet of vertical that Blackcomb Mountain offered, I bit the bullet and signed up for the trip. I loved it. I had an unsettled stomach during the whole trip, but I loved it. The base elevation at Whistler is 2,000 feet while ski hills in Colorado have a base elevation closer to 7,000 feet: I did not get the headaches associated with altitude sickness that usually plagued me for a day on the Colorado ski hills and that made it possible for me to take in more time on the slopes. I loved it!

With Motorola's Hiking Club, I got to hike the Grand Canyon three times. They say in the Grand Canyon, you will have a moment and that moment will have you to return or will have you stay away. My moment came as we were climbing out of the Canyon. We'd backpacked down the Kaibab Trail to the Colorado River, spent a few days at the Bright Angel

Campground there and we were hiking back up to the top via the Bright Angel trail and had stopped at Indian Gardens to camp for the night. I had wandered off to be by myself as is my nature and that's when I had my moment. I saw a Mull Deer and her two fawns in the nearby forested area. I stood stock still and watched her eat looking up periodically to check on her babies. It was a special moment for me and I felt a kinship with this mother as I also had two babies to watch over. It was my special moment and I knew I would return again and again to this beautiful place.

That was during my first backpack trip into the Grand Canyon. On my second trip, I hiked down to Havasu and camped by Mooney Falls and came away from that trip with giardia. Guess I didn't boil the water for long enough! On my third backpacking trip, I lead a group of eleven on the hike. This trip was made even more special for me because my daughter came with  me. I would end up carrying most of her stuff, but I didn't mind: I was so glad that she wanted to be there. Where my son wasn't interested in hiking, my daughter loved it and would often accompany me on hikes. She'd asked to come on this trip as her birthday gift and I'd agreed and figured I'd be keeping watch over her in the Canyon, much as the deer had kept watch over her young ones.

Work was going very well for me and it wasn't long before I was watching my first launch. My mother and father came to Phoenix to watch it with me and as a group we celebrated its success at dinner that night with balloon hats and lots and lots of stress relieving laughter. Motorola is known for being a global leader in wireless technology and cell phones and had now ventured into satellite phones. I was hired as a staff engineer and been promoted to a senior systems engineer two years later after spending an extensive amount of time at Lockheed in California. For over six months, I'd fly over to Sunnyvale each Sunday night and work 12 hours days so I could fly home on Thursday and spend the weekend with my kids. The work was fabulous and all consuming.

Once after my children's father had cancelled a vacation that my son was supposed to have with him, I took him with me to California in the hope of taking the sting out of his disappointment. And although I had to work, there was a basketball court at the hotel and a swimming pool: neither of which I knew about. My son, now a teenager, spent my work days keeping occupied at the hotel on the court or in the pool although I did get off work early most days. It was the only time at Lockheed where I begged off early so that I could go for a run with him.

My son had joined the cross-country team at school and during our runs, he was kind enough to cut his pace so his mother could keep up. One day it started to rain heavily during our run and we returned to the hotel soaked like drowned rats and laughing our heads off. My trips to Lockheed were all about work and this was the only time where I would spend the weekend in California. That weekend, we headed to San Francisco and took the boat across to Alcatraz. I had a rental car and we used it to drive all around the city and even down the winding road of Lombard Street....it was amazing!

A few months into the job, I was assigned as a team member of the 1st launch test team and I was thrilled. Motorola had a test team that performed testing at the Closed Loop Test Facility (CLTF) in Phoenix and it was an amazing privilege to be part of this team. When I had started at Motorola as a staff engineer, I'd managed the development of procedures for network operations at the Iridium gateway and later at Lockheed I performed systems integration and test of the qualification model and so when I was I asked to be on the test team for the 1st launch, I jumped at the opportunity. I was then trained to become an expert in the Attitude and Orbit Control Subsystem 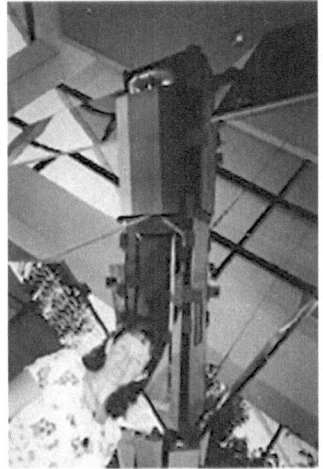 (the AOCS) and the Electrical Power Subsystem (the EPS), although I did some of my training on battery technology at George Washington University in DC.

After a year on the team, the head of satellite engineering approached me and asked me to be a test team lead. The test team was running two shifts in preparation for future launches and they needed to run a third shift and if I agreed, I would become this team's leader. Of course, I agreed. The leader of the other two test teams had nick-names: one was called "Captain Kirk" and the other was called "Captain Picard," so it wasn't surprising that I got a nick-name as well: I became known as "Captain Jainway!"

Asked to develop the architecture for a new test facility which would handle overflow CLTF testing, I felt challenged. I was scared that they had picked the wrong person: I knew a lot about my area of specialty (the EPS) but I was no way near the depth of understanding that the members of my team had on each of their areas where they were experts. I soldiered on and daily, I picked their brains. They already had a job to do and wanted to go home to their lives and here I was asking them a whole lot of questions and taking their time away from them. So, they weren't that thrilled when I asked them to come back in and rerun a test one fate filled day. In the analysis of the data from that day's testing, I'd seen a problem in the test results but had to confirm it and that meant rerunning the test. Running the routine again would take six hours.

In my analysis, the deployment sequence had not executed properly: the onboard software executed an autonomous deployment of the satellite subsystems immediately after launch. My team members, like me, couldn't just stay at work and one test team had been disbanded as we wound down from the peak of the project. I needed my team to rerun the test before the launch the next morning. Yet, they had other responsibilities, had just worked a full day, and needed to recharge. And, I had children to care for.

So, at 4pm we all headed home to take care of whatever we had to take care of and then returned to work at 6pm to rerun the test. I headed home to feed my kids and get a babysitter for them before returning to work. My whole team headed out yet at 6pm, they were all back ready to work. By midnight, we knew there was a serious problem with the LBCS (Lockheed Bus Control Software) and that the solar panels would not deploy properly.

Lockheed (who was responsible for the spacecraft bus), had modified the software at the last minute and the LBCS change had screwed up the timings on the solar panel deployments. They would deploy, but their extended arms would lock before fully deployed and in this configuration, they would not be unable to capture enough solar energy to recharge the onboard battery. If we launched these satellites with this software onboard, we'd be launching five 25 million dollar rocks into space. Yet, the launch was scheduled for 8am the next morning.

Having confirmed the earlier test results, I called a colleague of mine to look at the results and confirm them. After he'd done this, he called our boss. It was now 2am. Our boss came in right away and reviewed the data and when he had also confirmed the result, he called the vice-president of the Motorola with his recommendation. And, even though it cost Motorola five million dollars, the VP called Vandenberg and scrubbed the launch.

Motorola was hesitant to scrub the launch as doing so cost them so much money, but if they hadn't it would have cost them a lot more. My team's test results were confirmed over the next few days and my boss and Motorola were very happy with us. Everyone received big bonuses and a few months later, we were on a plane to Vandenberg AFB to watch a launch. This would be a special launch as on one of the satellites (SV75) was attached a plaque with the space systems engineering test team members names on it. Years earlier I had applied to become an astronaut and that didn't pan out but here was my name on this plaque being launched into space and I was thrilled. SV75 is still my baby and I continue to watch over her. With the naked eye, you can see the Iridium satellites. They are steady dots of light flying that pass over us in the night sky and whenever I see one, I imagine it is SV75.

A few years later, when the Iridium satellite constellation was filled and launching had slowed down to a trickle, Motorola started to plan for their next satellite project which was known then as "Iridium Next." Honoured to be asked to attend the Iridium Next meeting as an EPS expert, this French speaking Canadian would become invaluable. Potential contractors of the future spacecraft were vying for the opportunity to build the bus for this satellite at these meetings and at this particular meeting, engineers from a Europe-based company were pitching their design. There was concern on Motorola's part regarding one of the design elements of the EPS and our selection committee was seriously questioning this technology even though the potential contractor company gave heartfelt reassurances that the technology was ready.

During a break, I went over to the refreshment table to get some Pepsi and overheard their engineers talking. They were speaking in French but I understood every word and grateful to be able to practice my comprehension skills, I listened to them talk. Yet, what they said concerned me so I headed over to my boss and blew the whistle on them, telling my boss that the technology wasn't as ready as they had told us it was. They had lied to us.

The next generation of Iridium was put on hold when it was discovered that the constellation would last much longer than originally predicted. Jobs and people started disappearing as the project continued to wind down and that's when I decided I had to make a job move. Wanting to stay with Motorola, I looked for job opportunities on their internal job posting site and I found one in Massachusetts that looked interesting and I applied for it. The Cable Data Systems office in Mansfield needed a senior software integration and test engineer to work on a new technology they'd been developing known as VoIP (Voice over Internet Protocol). I went to the Cable Data Products group in Mansfield for an interview, got the job and moved to the nearby town of Hopkinton in Massachusetts.

The year was 1999.

I continued to work for Motorola but only for a year and the only reason why I lasted that long was because they had moved me and if I had stayed a shorter period of time, I'd have had to pay Motorola back for my move across the country. I liked my new job well enough, but I did not like the work atmosphere. Again, I was into an unwelcoming work environment for women. My new boss was "doing" his secretary and they were not shy about it. When she'd go into his office, he'd draw the blinds and when she came out, her clothes were wrinkly and her hair disheveled. Once, they were caught fooling around in the conference room. It was not a good work atmosphere for me and to make matters worse, the head of the software engineering team was overtly flirting with me. A married man and horribly unattractive, he was always trying to get me to go on a business trip with him because he said he wanted a pretty woman along. I never did go on any business trips!

I felt like I was in the Canadian Forces again and I was surprised that Motorola condoned this until I learned that Motorola had only recently purchased a cable data products company and had placed them under their umbrella and this is where I now worked. It wasn't long before I sought the help of a psychiatrist and I ended up on medication again. For those of you who don't know much about PTSD, it is cyclic. That is, it cycles back around on you and in this work environment, I was being triggered daily. I started to go out for walks every lunch hour just to clear my head. It was on these walks where I made new friends. Two fellows, one that oversaw the maintenance of the lab I worked in and one of the guys that worked with him also went out for a walk at lunch hour and we were soon walking together. These two guys are still dear friends today.

When we heard there would be a layoff at our facility, the women hid in the bathroom. Why? There were no women managers and so they could not be laid off that Friday. It was a well-planned and well executed maneuver. The clerks and secretaries had drafted the memos and knew the details so they arranged a bathroom potluck. Unaware of what was going on, I was surprised when I walked into the bathroom and saw couches, tables and chairs, and the sink counter lined with crock pots and serving dishes. You got to give it to these women, they were well organized.

When I could not take the sexual harassment by the head of software engineering, I went to HR for help but nothing happened and that's when I started to look for another job elsewhere. I was determined to reduce my commute. Mansfield was a 40 minute drive from my home in Hopkinton along Interstate 495 and although I didn't initially think that would be a problem, anyone who has driven in the Boston area can attest to how horrible it is to drive there during rush-hour. I found a job right in Hopkinton and the commute would great....all 2.4 miles of it.

Chapter Fourteen: Disabling Accident

HOPKINTON, MASSACHUSETTS (2003)

EMC Corporation is a world leader for information storage and management products. And, I'd been hired to work on the testing of new PCBs (Printed Circuit Boards). The PCBs were large and slotted into large test chambers to execute testing. An engineer would have to sit for hours and watch the output on a computer screen and although they used to computers to control the chamber's conditions, it was a very manual process.

At first I liked my job at EMC as I was developing test software for their HALT (Highly Accelerated Life Testing) and HASS testing (Highly Accelerated Stress Screening), which were executed in test chambers. I was using LabView and TestStand and I was able to create routines that saved the company hundreds of hours weekly. Personally, I loved the challenge my job had of automating a test. My office was on the main floor but the test chambers (and my lab) was in the basement of the building.

What I didn't know when I was hired, or I didn't realize, was that I was eliminating engineering jobs, thereby saving the company money, but this made me very unpopular with my fellow engineers: a relationship that was already strained by my gender. Being a Senior Engineer, I assigned tasks to my fellow engineers and they just didn't like being told what or how to do anything by a woman. Still, I was hired to do a job and I did it. My fellow engineers did not want to work with me; they certainly did not want to test a software designed to get them laid off.

Not long after I started the job, I overheard a disparaging remark about my wearing skirts to work, so I stopped wearing skirts and dresses but then I heard that I was wearing too feminine attire and determined to fit in, I started to dress more like a boy. One day, when I was getting dressed for work and looking for something that would be

174

found appropriate by my colleagues, I got pissed. Really pissed! That day I showed up to work wearing pink....bright fuchsia pink!

I loved many aspects of my job at EMC, after all it was a core-engineering company and I was in my element working on automation test software, yet I found the work environment difficult and socially isolating for women. Within my group, the fellows I worked with headed out to play basketball in the back parking lot after lunch most days when the weather permitted and I tried to join them. As soon as I would arrive, half of the guys would walk away and sometimes all of them would. I gave it up after finding myself alone with a basketball and a hoop too many times. I started to get lunch over at the main EMC building which was larger and had a cafeteria instead of eating lunch with my colleagues: that was so uncomfortable and my efforts to make friends was going nowhere.

The upside of working at EMC was that no-one hit on me and so I no longer had to deal with that. Still, I found the work atmosphere was not good for women engineers. I was socially outcast and I wondered if dealing with the sexual advances wouldn't have been easier because at least I'd have friends to enjoy my lunch hour with. And, even when I lunched over at the other building, I'd most often eat alone. There were very few women in this large engineering company and even fewer women engineers. I wondered if I was the token woman engineer hired so that the company could declare that they hire women engineers.

The toxicity of the work environment got worse as time moved on. Each day, I swallowed down my fear of men knowing that it had its roots in the PTSD I suffered with, yet I was careful to never be alone with any of them. In the cafeteria, I sat with my back against the wall and which gave me a view of the whole room. Although irrational, my fear had me always watching my back: knowing a fear is irrational didn't stop me from feeling it. It was very real for me. Being afraid of men and now being surrounded by only them daily un-nerved me and when my efforts to integrate within the group had failed, I socially isolated myself.

I'm mistakenly made friends with the only other woman in the building; the group secretary and that would end up being a really bad judgement call on my part. She was so jealous of my success, but I didn't know this at first and when I found out, it hurt me badly. Where most women promote other women in their efforts, this bitch would show her claws more than once and I would become even more isolated as a result. I was good at my job and earned bonuses for finishing deadlines ahead of schedule. Every time, I got a bonus, she would get pissed at me and I didn't put two and two together until my boss told me that he knew I was thinking about leaving the company. I thought about moving jobs but realized it was too soon to make a move. When my boss got wind of this (from his secretary who I had confided in), instead of getting fired, I got promoted to Principal Engineer. This made her even more vicious and I didn't help matters by asking her how her boss knew I was thinking of leaving. I thought about thanking her for the promotion, but I didn't want to make matters worse. When my salary increased, she stopped talking to me altogether. With the bonuses I'd received that year, I was finally making six figures. I took the promotion and stayed put: it was hard to turn down as it was expensive to live in New England and my teenage kids were already looking at colleges. I needed the money.

Not long after that I joined SWE, the Society of Women Engineers as I found this organization an avenue where I could comfortably mix with other women engineers. We held monthly meetings and it was good for me to commiserate with these other women. I wouldn't complain about my work environment, but I would listen to others complain and that helped me a lot as I no longer felt alone. At a locally held events, I got to meet an impressive lady by the name of Oprah Winfrey. She was the guest speaker at a SWE event held at the Simmons College. Simmons College is a private women's college that has a strong tradition of empowering women and within its rich history of inclusion, they graduated their first African-American woman way back in 1914. I suspect that Oprah knew this and it must have been near and dear to her heart and that's why she graced us with her presence. My take away from this event was a saying which even today crosses my mind a lot: she told us what Michelangelo once said. He said, "The greater danger for most of us lie not in setting our aim too high and falling short; but in setting our aim too low, and achieving our mark." It hit the nail on the head for me being profound and the way I've always felt.

When the stress at work re-activated my PTSD, I sought professional help. A psychiatrist diagnosed me with depression and told me I needed to get away from the stress that was activating me. I took short term leave from work and looked and looked for a therapist. I tried a number of them, but they were all men and I was unable to even tell them why that didn't work for me. I was still very protective of Canada and the Canadian Forces and even though I blamed both for my PTSD and even the rape, I could not go so far as to badmouth either. It's not like I was in Canada and talking to a military psychologist who had the security clearances that allowed me to speak freely, I was out of country and speaking to civies and somehow, it just didn't feel right so I kept quiet. On the advice of my psychiatrist, I contacted a rape crises center. I must have somehow let the cat out of the bag and he was concerned about me.

My first phone call with them went very well as did the subsequent calls. When I was confident that they would keep my secrets, I went to them and visited with one of their therapists. She talked me into attending a group therapy session and this ended up being fantastic for me. Who would have thought that a group therapy session at a rape-crises center would be described as a "fantastic" experience! Certainly, not me! I was quiet for the first few weeks of the 16 week session, but as the other women spoke up and shared with the group, I felt as if they were talking about my life.....about me! Gaining strength and feeling less alone and like mine was an isolated incident, I also spoke up. This was one of the best things I ever did for my mental health. I still had a long way to go, but for the first time, I felt hope. I'd accepted my PTSD and depression as being something I'd have to deal with the rest of my life and being paid a military pension, was in some weird thought pattern of mine, a monthly reminder that I was being paid for having been screwed up.

In the year 2003, I would often think of Michelangelo's saying when another life challenge came my way. I had an accident in March where I sustained brain damage. Now, my family has always suspected I had brain damaged and now they had medical proof. I was bed rested for four months and those months in bed were made even more difficult for me as I was no longer able to keep my military memories at bay. It wasn't like I could get up and go for a run to clear my head: where I used to run marathons, now it took me 45 minutes to walk a quarter mile in my walker.

On March 20th of that year, I was working for EMC and with my office upstairs and my test chamber downstairs running a test of the latest version of my software, when I was called to a 7pm meeting at the Headquarters building where they did the R&D. I had been babysitting my automation test software even though the software captured the test results. To prepare for the meeting, I headed upstairs to my office and when I was on my way back downstairs to check on the test, I fell down the stairs.

The cement stairs to the basement had a doorway to the left and right at the bottom and I landed somewhere outside the doorway to the left and against a wall. I had blacked out and when I came to, I saw two pairs of shoes in front of me: one pair was light brown and the other were running shoes. I figured they belonged to the two other engineers still working that night. I went to raise my head from the floor but pain made me pass out again and I fell back to the floor. When next I opened my eyes, there was a pretty light blue blanket perfectly folded on the floor in front of me and beside it were a different pair of shoes. These ones were patent leather and shiny black. I figured they belonged to the security guard for the building and I was right.

He helped me get up and then picked up my organizer when I pointed at it. It had somehow gotten away from me and was on the floor about 10 feet away. When he picked it up, he turned it to an angle and let the water drain off it. Looking up the stairs, he commented that they were wet and had probably just been washed. He offered to call me an ambulance, but I declined the offer and he helped me to my car parked outside the back of the basement door. I drove my 2.4 miles home in a daze and I was glad that the roads were empty as I swerved badly.

Once home, my daughter helped me to bed and gave me some over the counter pain medication. Yet, the pain was intense and wouldn't allow me to sleep. At just before midnight, with her hovering over me, I gave in to her demands to take me to the hospital. I was diagnosed with a closed head injury and told that I would have some pretty big bruises. Over the next few days, I mostly slept. My daughter, Tracy called into work for me as I was unable to. Two weeks later, I tried to return to work but I was so dizzy that I couldn't walk properly and hugged the walls. I left after only an hour at work and my daughter was called at school to come and get me. I couldn't drive due to the dizziness.

A hump had grown on my right side and stretched from the back of my head to my shoulder blade. I looked like the hunchback of Notre Dame. I couldn't wear a bra as they didn't fit and it hurt to have one on. I'd taken to wearing sports bras as they rarely caused flashbacks to my rape and although I sometimes wore a bra that clasped in the back (just like I had on that awful day back in 1995), I avoided them. I often did not wear bras on the weekends and so it suited me just fine not to have to put one on. I still get flashbacks to the rape whenever I put on one of these bras.

The bruising was extensive and the doctor figured I must have tumbled when I fell down the stairs. On my right hip, I had a big ugly black and blue patch that was at least six inches in diameter and on my left thigh, I had a slightly smaller, but still ugly bruise that was about four inches big. I felt dizzy all the time and it didn't matter if I was standing, sitting, or lying down. It reminded me of those times when I'd been really drunk and had lied down on my bed and looked up only to find the ceiling going in circles above me. I was nauseous from the dizziness and the pain medication the doctors had prescribed at the hospital wasn't doing the trick. It decreased but did not relieve my pain.

The day when I went back to work, I was called into my boss' office and present was an HR lady and my boss' boss. Something was up! I was let go. I was told the test team was downsizing and I would no longer be needed. Of course, no one else was laid off. The timing was spot on! We all knew what was really going on, but we all played our parts and I packed up my office and the fellows happily helped load my stuff into my car when my daughter showed up. I later heard how EMC hired three engineers to take over my work but at that point in time, I didn't care, although I found it to be a great compliment. My world as I knew it was an existence between pain meds and sleep and would never be the same.

I went home and went to bed. I was given a walker so that I could navigate my way in my home between my bedroom and the bathroom. Once let go by EMC, I was on a new medical coverage known as COBRA coverage. I don't remember a lot about the paying of bills and such as my 16 year old daughter took over this function. At first, she took me to doctor and bi-weekly physical therapy appointments but she would have to take time off school to help me: to be with me on the bad days and to get me to and fro from these appointments. I mostly slept (day and night) and she had no company except when I woke up in pain and then I was bitchy. I was miserable to live with but she put up with me. I still don't know how she managed it. My son, off at university, didn't bother to come home to see me. He was living it up at university and discounted my accident and my illness. I am still ashamed of the way he behaved. When it came time for him to begin his second year of university, he did contact me. He wanted me to pay for courses he'd failed or done badly at. Before going to university, he'd been an honour student but the partying had taken its toll and his academics were weak. He'd not be allowed to continue in his academic program at Queen's University with redoing almost every single one of his 1st year courses. With my pain making me very irritable and my PTSD rearing its ugly head, and with his rare phone call and limited contact, I wasn't tolerant of his bullshit. He wanted me to pay for another year at Queens and I said no. We were almost broke. I'd used up my emergency savings, taken a loan on my 401K before having to cash it out, and eventually we got behind on our mortgage.

When he got mad at me for not paying for his university studies, which he considered a financial obligation of mine, he told me off. He was selfish and disrespectful and so I sent him an email......this is one email I remember sending! I told him that he'd have to take a college loan and that I wasn't paying for his tuition. In addition, I suggested that he may not make a good doctor as the years of study needed to become a doctor would require him to dig deep and that he would find that difficult since he was so shallow. I was really hurt and somedays I regret what I said in that email and others days I applaud myself for taking a stand. Still, he broke off all contact with me and made up all kinds of lies about me further isolating me from my family in Ontario.

Later that summer, in August of that year, the neurologist at Lahey Clinic advised me that I may never be rid of the severe head pain nor vertigo associated with my brain injury. He told me that I may never ever again walk without the assistance of a walker. I became distraught and over the next few days, I was even more difficult than usual with my daughter. I'm not proud of the bitch I had become between dosages of my pain meds and now I was angry because I was in pain and I now knew that this pain might never go away. I found a lot to be angry about in those days: I was angry at being house-bound and I was angry at life in general.

My daughter she didn't deserve this and as it was, she had no life outside our home. She was responsible for everything from cooking and cleaning to caring for me and taking care of our pets. She paid the bills and worried about money and took me to doctor's appointments and physical therapy appointments. The poor kid needed a break from me and she took it. She left and I was alone. When she left, she told me she'd be back in a few days but it was during those few days that I tried to kill myself.

The straw that broke the camel's back happened as I was leaving the pharmacy, having just refilled my prescriptions for pain and vertigo medication. That's when I saw my son. I had not seen him since before my accident when I'd flown him home in October of 2002 for his birthday. He was parked in the car I had bought him (so that he could come home from university....ironic, eh!). He was sitting in the car at the corner across from the doors to the pharmacy and after I'd negotiated my way out of the door, I looked up and that's when I saw him. We looked each other in the eye, both surprised to see one another, and that's when he turned away from me. It was obvious that he didn't expect to see me. I lowered my head and turned my walker for home and let the tears fall. Had he seen me struggling with the walker and been embarrassed? He was all about show and the way I figure it, he didn't want a disabled mom.

I don't think my heart could hurt more than it did that day. When I got home, I collected various family pictures of him and of my daughter and put them around the bed. Then, I got a glass of water and the medications I'd just bought. I opened each of them and took a handful of pills from each bottle and swallowed them down with water before laying down to go to sleep one last time but the Lord didn't take me. I didn't wake up for three days and when I did, I'm sure it was the smell that woke me: the body continues to function even when you are in a dead sleep. I never tried that again mostly because I figure the good Lord will take me when he's ready. In 2012, I wrote a poem about this event in my life. I called it "Look Away" and it goes like this:

"Look Away"
© 2012 Dawn (Lavigne) Ottman

At college, he'd heard how his Mom had fallen down the stairs
And he'd even heard how messed up she was
When he first saw her that following summer's day
.......He looked away

He thought she couldn't see him
But she's caught a glimpse of him
And with her head hung down her tears flowed freely
.... as she looked away

Sitting in his car he lost himself in himself
As he watched her struggle with her walker
Her movements were pathetic and embarrassing
.......So he looked away

She wasn't the perfect Mom he wanted in his life
And now she was disgustingly disabled
It was just too embarrassing for him
.....So he turned away

It was bad enough that he didn't give
A single word of support or love
But he soon criticized her to justify
..... his turning away

And he conceived lie after lie to avoid her
He wove a tangled web of deceit
And lost the love of a son for his mother
......As he turned away

She heard how he said she had done him wrong
The ex-husband quickly joined the evil plan

And even seemed to enjoy watching
......as her son turned further away

Yet, in the decade that has passed
Could he have ever told himself the truth
For her, time passed ever so slowly
.....Since he had turned away

Alone, this Mom spent a decade
crawling out of the hole of disability
she had loved him too much and taught him greed
.....no wonder he'd turned away

She could not financially supported him
When his college tuition came due
As she had no income but lots of bills
....and he turned even further away

Her pain of separation was greater
Than the physically pain she endured
He'd broke his mother's heart when, from her
.......he'd looked away

She was so torn up inside
She didn't know how to go on
The bottle of pills was right there beside her
...... and she didn't look away

It was a time when the pain was too much
And her heart couldn't break anymore
He would have been so ashamed when she tried to take her life
...........good thing he'd looked away

It took three days to wake up
And the pain was still there
Grateful that her son wasn't there
......she looked away

Wondering what to do, she got up
Cleaning up was difficult but she got it done
As no one was there to help her
............having looked away

Now she is better
Not great, but better
And still her love is strong and she misses the son
.... Who'd looked away

Will he know how to make his way back home?
If he ever wants to.
Will he know how simple it is to say he's sorry?
.....Instead of looking away

I spent the next year and a half relearning to walk. I am not the type of person who believes in limits so I relearned to walk and within a few years, I had progressed to a four-prong cane and then a single-prong cane before I was able to walk without the assistance of a walker. By then I had moved to South Dakota. When I was still in the walker but migrating to a four-prong cane, I signed up to walk a half-marathon and although it took me over four hours to walk that 13.1 miles it remains my most rewarding event. Before my accident I could complete a full marathon in that much time, but it didn't matter. This is now and that was then.

Chapter Fifteen: CanDew Scientific
LEMMON, SOUTH DAKOTA (2004)

Unable to keep up with the medical bills, I sold my home in New England in 2004, when I was five months behind on the mortgage. Then I moved to rural South Dakota where I could afford to live on my military pension. It was in Lemmon, South Dakota where I met this guy at church and even though I was in a walker, he asked me out. We dated for three years and when he asked me to marry him, I thought he must be nuts but I still said yes and we have found great happiness with each other.

I was into writing then, and in 2006, I wrote a poem about this major change in my life. I called it "Possibilities" and it goes like this:

"Possibilities"
© 2006 Dawn Lavigne

When Life isn't fair
And we loose our direction
It's time for people to care
And....make a decision.

Allowed to go back to work...FINALLY.
Then WOW....EMC Corporation says, "Not here!"
My future is now (surprisingly)
Being planned over a beer.

There's more to this stew
For Dawn Dew
December, my mortgage is due
To be renewed.

I asked the mortgage company
To allow me to renew, But they say,
"Approval?? With no income....NO WAY!!"
I now have to sell without delay.

— Captain Dawn Ottman —

So, Farmer Bill I need you to command
If you will sell me a few acres of your land?

This answer I need so I can decide
To Lemmon South Dakota do I reside?
I want to build a home with a view that is wide
As seen by my kin years ago.
No worries if you should say "No"
Because then, to Arizona I'll go.

The Lord knows better what the future will hold
And, I feel as if he's telling me to be bold.
With no job...and losing my home
I'm wondering if he's telling me to roam?

I can be happy in either place:
Phoenix or Lemmon.
.... They draw me both in time and space.

As my head pain subsided, I was able to spend more time on the computer and I enjoyed this immensely. Having chosen South Dakota as my new home and my new home being near where my great-grandparents had homesteaded in the early 1900s, I got caught up in the history of the place. My first accomplishment was to write a book about the life of my hero: my great-grandmother, Rebecca Howe. Born in Nebraska, she loved the prairie but her family had returned to Illinois after her younger brother had succumb to diphtheria. Unable to save the young boy, he died and was buried in Illinois. And, it was in Illinois, where she 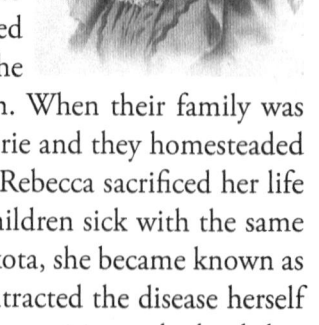 met my great-grandfather, Frank Buffington. When their family was young, Rebecca returned to her beloved prairie and they homesteaded just south of Lemmon on the Grand River. Rebecca sacrificed her life for the greater good as she helped Lakota children sick with the same disease as her brother had had and to the Lakota, she became known as the White Medicine Woman. Sadly, she contracted the disease herself and died at a young age. She is buried on the prairie on the land that her and Frank homesteaded.

I believe that certain characteristics are carried in our genes. My great-grandparents had nothing to do with the raising of my mother, who was raised by the Children's Aid Society in Canada and I certainly did not know them. Yet, our core values are the same (that is, our willingness to sacrifice for the greater good). To begin my book about Rebecca, I wrote a special poem for her. I called it "White Medicine Woman" and it goes like this:

White Medicine Woman
2007, Dawn Ottman

On the prairie
Rebecca is still
She'd helped others
And became deathly ill

You see the heart catches things
That the mind cannot see
So it was with life
On the prairie

This is the story of a hero
She was my great grandmother
And, she made us all proud
In the way she cared for another

Living in a small town is difficult for me as I socially isolate myself and am not comfortable with small town gossip. Basically, I am an outsider and I feel like one. Still, when I first arrived in Lemmon, I immediately got involved at the local nursing home as I had volunteered at one in Massachusetts. At Draper Place nursing home, I'd helped during activity sessions and I loved it. So when I arrived in Lemmon, I volunteered at the local nursing home. Although I found it rewarding, I soon discovered that I would forget important stuff and the staff there weren't tolerant of my limitations. No worries.....it happens. It didn't help that I am prideful and would not bother to explain why I had forgot this or forgot that. I was embarrassed to have forgotten and finding I was so undependable, I stopped going.

A better understanding may be gained if you know that each time I helped my husband at the farm; each time I drove a tractor, he had to reteach me how to do that. I have forgotten. My neurologist advised me to explain to folks that my memory problems stem from my brain injury and much like the woman in the movie, "Fifty First Dates," I simply have limited (or no) short term memory. So, each morning during harvest season, Bill would spend 45 minutes teaching me how to drive the combine. Then I would drive it for a few hours and he would get some work out of me. Still, the next morning, he would again have to teach me how to drive the combine. The man is a saint!

We have a cattle farm and we are a calving operation. I love calving season and seeing all those big eyed calves running about and playing. Bill jokes that when he goes and checks on the calves it takes him 20 minutes, but when I ride along, it takes an hour. I think it is the camera's fault! During the six years when we lived at the farm, I helped out a lot more (for a bit). I enjoyed giving the bucket calves (calves that had lost their mamas) their morning and night bottles. One day, when returning to the farmhouse for lunch after doing chores, Bill couldn't find me. Noticing the pickup by the west barn, he headed down to the barn and that where he found me. Not only does my memory make it challenging for me to help out at the farm, but so does my vertigo. A hungry calf had bowled me over and I couldn't get up. I wasn't hurt but I was too dizzy to get on my feet and had laid there for hours.

When I first moved to Lemmon, I bought a garage (that came with a house) and about a year after I arrived in South Dakota, I created my own company. Feeling the need to feel useful, I contacted the state's vocational rehabilitation office to see if they could find me work that allowed for accommodation for my disabilities. First, I was asked to teach at a science camp for girls held at the Computer Labs of the School of Mines and Technology but when preparing the lesson plans to teach the girls about a 4-bit Adder, I got bad headaches and a few days later in the strongly lit environment of the lab, my head pain got out of control and my vertigo reared its ugly head. I staggered and held my head only a few times during the class, but a few times were a few times too many. So, that didn't work out.

Next, the lady at vocation rehabilitation office arranged for me to do a trial work period in Pierre at state government engineering offices but that was cancelled when they found out they do not have the needed insurance for the site that would allow them to have me there. Yet, I love to feel useful and work when I felt well enough to do so.

And, although my short-term memory is not good, I still had my long-term memory and my engineering skills. When the lady at vocational rehabilitation suggested I start my own company so that I could work when I felt well, I created CanDew Scientific. When you are down to nothing, God is up to something! Having my own company allowed me to put my engineering skills to work and I became an inventor. With the diversity of writing coupled with an engineering background, I moved into the world of patenting.

Over the years previous to my accident, I had some ideas and now I could test them out. Lucky for me, I have a background in test engineering! When I'd proved them out, I submitted a utility patent application to the United States Patent and Trade Office (USPTO) and a few years later, my first patent was issued and so I went to work on my 2nd patent idea. That one was also issued and now my 3rd patent application is pending. Today, I hold two issued utility patents in green technology and one more recent patent submission that is patent pending. I do not know how to move these from being on paper to being on store shelves but figure that in time, the way will be shown to me. It's not like they are going anywhere, so I wait.

Chapter Sixteen: Becoming a WindSenator with KidWind
LEMMON, SOUTH DAKOTA (2009)

A few years ago, at Calgary's World of Science, I got the opportunity to be a keynote speaker at the Beauty & Brains Conference. After presenting to a few hundred students, I was praised for the interest I generated in a room full of middle and high school kids. After my speech, I taught lessons in solar and wind energy workshops. Not having a model to follow, I had designed the workshops myself. Where being Canada's 1st Woman Space Scientist may have given me a foot in the door, it was my ability to engage audiences and hold their attention by making the presentation/workshop theme clear and memorable that made each it worthwhile and deserving of note.

I have a strong belief in renewable energy and when combined with my desire to teach, it was suggested to me that I look into the opportunity to become a wind energy instructor: a National Wind Senator with KidWind. This looked very interesting to me and right up my alley. So, I applied and was accepted into this program. I was sent off to Albany, New York for my training and then given a five state region to handle.

I taught wind energy lessons to children at schools and science fairs and adults at community events and for good measure, I often included a solar energy lesson. I attribute my confidence to speak in front of others to be a result of my military and professional life and my ability to capture and hold an audience's attention is a skill I developed while an instructor and a public speaker when on the Debating Team at RMC.

Initially I was assigned a five state area: Montana, Wyoming, North Dakota, South Dakota, and Nebraska but when it became evident that I could not keep up with the demands of the job, I had to tell the folks at KidWind that I could no longer do the job. Ironically, this happened immediately after an event held at one of the local universities where young women were invited onto the campus to entice them into considering doing an engineering degree at that university. Statistically, young women would leave the state to do their science/engineering degrees out of state and this university was making an effort to curve that trend. Yet, all of their presenters were males. There were not a single female role models for the young women to look to and I mistakenly believed that this was, in part, I was asked to teach them about wind energy. At least they would have one role model (me) to give these young women the understanding that nursing was not the only university degree program they would be welcomed into.

I was shocked to learn, when I got to the classroom, that I would be an assistant only and that my task was to ensure that the young women got the supplies they needed to execute the workshop. In effect, I was a water-boy! To add insult to injury, I had brought the supplies: they were part of the KidWind training package. Instead of me, a male assistant from the university taught the class and screwed it up royally. Although they were using our supplies from KidWind they did not use our teaching presentation or methods. And, the superiority attitude didn't win this guy any interested young women. I was angry as he ruined a wonderful opportunity. If the purpose of the event was to disinterest young women in an engineering education/career, then a fine job was done! Being the reserved person I am, (Not!) I gave him heck and told him what I thought of the whole deal. He reported back to my boss at KidWind and shit hit the fan. My boss was more concerned with appeasing a representative at the university than sticking up for one of his people: it was time for me to call it quits.

When you are served lemons, make lemonade! During this event, one of the young women approached me and asked me if I knew of SWE (the Society of Women Engineers) and being a member, I said yes. She was one of the few female engineering students at this university and like me, she was a water-boy at this event. Sadly, we had a lot in common that way. I was pleased when she asked me if I would return to the university and give the budding new university SWE group a boost. And, of course, I agreed. She set up the venue and I returned and spoke to a small group of very nice young women scientists and engineers. One of these young women had brought her grandfather. He was a nice gentle man and we spoke for a few minutes afterwards.

He invited me to a personal tour of his business: it seems he was of the founders of Daktronics. The man had so much clout but you couldn't tell the way he sat in the back and listened. Ironically, he was the only man in the room. Usually, for us women engineers and scientists, it is the other way around. Even though I was on my own nickel (that is, I was paying for this trip myself), I stayed an extra day so that I could take him up on his kind offer of a tour of his company. I'm glad I did, as the test engineering that goes into their product is top notch: I was impressed.

PART FOUR: Advice

Chapter Seventeen: Epilogue

I didn't ask to be in a male-dominated trade in the Canadian Forces. I wasn't planning on blazing a trail for women; nor did I ask or borrow trouble, but when it came my way, I dealt with it the best I could. I was raised as a fighter; a kid from one of the poorest toughest neighbourhoods in Toronto, and then I was a soldier trained to fight. Ironic that I was trained to fight by the same organization that made me feel so very unwelcome….by the same organization that caused the events that forced me to fight for my mental well-being and my very career in that organization.

Today, I am still affected by those events and have been diagnosed with Post Traumatic Stress Disorder (PTSD). One of the blessings in my life is my service dog. He is a PTSD dog who gives me peace and erases my fear even before it takes root. At night, he nuzzles me awake as I move into my nightmares effectively stopping them before they start. For years, I was afraid to fall asleep knowing that I would inevitable wake up screaming or crying or fighting. Now, when I am awakened, I see this big strong dog that cares so deeply for me and I feel safe again. When I've had a bad night I know because I awake with my husband talking gently to me from the edge of the bed or I awake to find my dog on the bed with me in the morning. Normally, he sleeps on the floor but on those nights when he spends a lot of time working, he climbs up on the bed and lies beside me.

My PTSD dog also works during the day as he also nuzzles me when I move into a panic attack. It is as if he senses my agitation as it begins and he quietly moves up behind me and nuzzles me and I come out of the beginnings of the panic attack. It is amazing. He is amazing! By reducing the number of times these nightmares and panic attacks occur, I am able to feel less anxious on a day-to-day basis and I'm also get a fuller night's sleep………..finally!

Twice each day, I get flashbacks: when I put my bra on as I get dressed and when I take it off at night. These flashback are triggered by something as simple and elementary as wearing a bra. The flashbacks happen without control and there are days that I do not put a bra on in order to avoid them. I flash to when my rapist ripped my bra right off my chest….blouse and all. The buttons of my blouse went flying in all directions and my bra clasps gave way, they scraped along my back pulling up skin and causing the staining of my blouse with my blood. Tattered and torn, I threw the blouse out. I just wish I could also throw the memories in the garbage as well. Even to this day, I still flinch as uncontrollable fear grips me whenever anyone touches my back. I am grateful that I no longer live in a big city as I remember the crowding of the subway and the wall-to-wall people. That situation would now be intolerable for me.

Initially my sister is the one I wanted to confide in about the rape, but I was wrong to have considered that as even today my sister tells me that I need to just "get over it!" I wish I could. If I could, you know that I would. I don't know why the memories are so vivid, but they are. Even with all her nursing training, she doesn't understand why I am unable to simply let it go since it happened so long ago.

In 2003, I fell down about 20 stairs and the 18 months I spent relearning to walk was also a time when I fought off difficult memories. I was being assaulted by the mental pain from my memories or the physical pain from my injuries. Sometimes, the physical pain was more acceptable for me than the pain of my memories. At least then I could take pain medication and ease that pain. I still have not seen my son and it has been over a dozen years but I have heard the things he says to assuage his guilt for having abandoned me. I've heard through the family grapevine that he is upset that I was spending my money on me (that is, my medical needs) instead of on his educational costs. He told stories about me that are untrue in order to explain away why he did behaved the way he has. I have forgiven him and after a 21 years separation, we are now reconciled.

Marrying Bill and moving to the farm allowed me to embrace my need for isolation, but it was too isolated. In addition, my father-in-law was born and raised on the farm and considers it his home and took exception to my calling it my home and made it clear to me that it was not my home and never would be. After that, I never called it "home" again. A few years later, unable to quell the sense of feeling like I was trespassing, we moved off the farm and bought a house in town. I believe that Bill still considers the farm his home and now like 99% of the rest of the world, he drives to work each day.

Moving back into town helped me a lot. The isolation and unfriendliness at the farm was stressing me out; and with PTSD that was not a good mix. I don't always isolate myself, but when I need time to myself, I take it. Being in town allows me the opportunity to seek out company when I need it: sometimes it's a bible study group at church but it can be something as simple as visiting the local gas station and saying hi to the people there who are always friendly to me. I enjoy these few minutes so much and somedays that is all that is needed to make my day.

When I need to run, I run away: that is, I take a "vacation." Sometimes, stress causes me to flee, and other times it is a triggering event. At these times, I feel strong fear and I know I go into fight or flight response: I absolutely need to get away to feel safe. I don't understand the psych behind it, I just know it is there and I do what I need to do to relieve the fear. I am very grateful that my husband can help me at these times as he fully supports me even though he doesn't always understand me. For instance, a few years ago, I took off and then purchased a rail pass on Amtrak and took the train around the country.

At home, Bill booked me hotels for the times when I got off the train to spend a night or two at a location. I spent a few days in Portland (a city I hadn't ever visited before), an overnight in San Luis Obispo (where I wanted to see the Mission), an overnight in New Orleans (where Bill not only booked me a hotel, but also booked me one right in the middle of the French Quarter and within walking distance to "Emeril's" restaurant where he had booked me a dinner reservation), and an overnight in Philadelphia (where I got to see the Liberty Bell, the Maritime Museum and the steps that Rocky ran up in the movie by the same name). With his help, I was able to turn a running away from pain….from fear…..into a fun vacation. I don't mind travelling alone as for some reason beyond my understanding, I feel safer when I do so.

At our new home in town, we have installed a solar energy system. When we were living on the farm, a bad winter's storm wiped out our electricity and I got very cold and stayed cold for about a week. My mother called and I complained to her about the cold and as soon as the storm had passed we got a phone call from a local supply store telling us that our 10KW generator was in. Mom had bought it for us and I will never forget her telling Bill, "Never....NEVER....let my daughter get that cold again!" We'd had a generator at the farm but it was smaller and as fate would have it, it broke down during that storm. Mom was making sure that never happened again.

A few years later, it did happen again. This time we lost power at the farm for 14 days and in town for 3 days. As we had the house in town and the weather forecast was predicting the storm, Bill headed to the farm to make sure things were taken care of there while I held down the fort at our home. The blizzard blew in and with it, we lost power in town and all the roads were closed. No help was coming.

Bill was nice and cozy warm at the farm as the new 10KW generator pumped out the needed electricity. Meanwhile, I was heading out to my car and running it to get warm before coming back into the cold house. In the house, we (the pets and I) wrapped up in blankets to keep warm. Even the phones were dead as the landlines were down. We felt blessed as the cell service was still running. The problem with that was that I couldn't get a hold of Bill. The location of the farm is so isolated that there is no cell service there.

With the farm phone dead, Bill took his cell phone and drove one of the tractors through the snow and up the hill where he could get cell service and called me. We kept in touch that way. A few days later, the highway had been cleared and Bill was able to get to town. He brought in the generator having loaded it up in the bed of his pickup and was able to finally warm up the house in town. As we didn't have power in town for the next day and a half and the farm still needed to be helped, Bill travelled to and from the farm with the generator a few times each day. Not surprisingly, he was supportive of us putting up a solar system at the house in town.

For those with PTSD, know that I feel your pain and I understand the feeling of abandonment you feel when your anger and trust issues cause family to turn away from you. This is a common theme with us that suffer with mental illness. My sister was always there for the picture opportunity with her soldier sister, but when it came time to deal with her PTSD, she turned her back on me and walked away. She doesn't get it and so this is the easier path for her even if it does isolate me even more. I try not to blame her, but I do feel abandoned and misunderstood. In general, family and friends say they want to help, but helping someone with PTSD means forgiving them their outbursts and forgiving is something my family does not do. I blame PTSD for me no longer have a relationship with any of my siblings. I can't simply get over it and they won't accept me as I am. Periodically, I hear from my uncles and a few of my cousins. For those with PTSD, know that it is a lonely thing and you will have to get used to it but there are those "out there" like me who open our doors and welcome you in as family.

When I became disabled in 2003, it was very difficult as the painful memories flooded back. I was constantly being triggered by my dreams and PTSD reared its ugly head again. Unable to block painful memories, I almost became a statistic in August when I attempted suicide. I was going crazy with the assault of memories.

Over time, I have partially recovered: mentally and physically. I moved from using the walker to using a 4-prong cane and then a single prong cane and I "ambulated freely" for 15 years according to my doctors. I can no longer run due to the brain damage and vertigo problems, but I can walk and I walked a half-marathon a few years ago. I used two telescopic hiking sticks to keep my balance and although it took me longer to walk than it used to take me to run a full marathon, it is my greatest achievement! I'm now permanently back to using a walker.

In Massachusetts, there are lots and lots of people whereas here in small town, South Dakota there are few and everyone knows everyone else. As a person who kept secrets for a very long time and someone who insulates herself from others, I find that uncomfortable and I absolutely hate it when I overhear bad things said about people which just doesn't seem to fit the truth. For me, it feels very much like the military did.

Privacy is something we all deserve and with my PTSD issues, I need it more than most people. I know that. Yet, here everyone wants/ needs to know everything about you. In an attempt to protect myself, I have socially isolated myself but I've found that that doesn't seem to stop the rumour mill. When facts are not present, stories are made up and I've had to get used to this environment. Often I listen and find myself amused about the stories that are spread about me; some of which have an element of the truth in them but mostly they are amplified versions obviously made that way for dramatic effect. And, as amusing as they are sometimes, I still find this disconcerting and it does not mesh well with PTSD.

There are times when I get angry not only for myself but for others. At lunch one day, I was told how a close friend of mine here in town, had just been diagnosed with cancer. Immediately after lunch, I headed over to her place to see her and let her know that I am here whenever she needs me. The thing is, she had not yet been told this bad news by her doctor and some at the local hospital had spoken out of turn. From there the gossip mill took over and the story had spread like wildfire. Welcome to a small town!

My friend moved out of town and rarely returns to visit. She does not talk to me at all and I feel it a case of blaming the messenger. I have anger issues so this is not good for me and sometimes, I get so angry at the injustice of gossip that I cuss out the person who started the falsehood but that simply adds fuel to the fire. Now, everyone hears how I cussed out someone and I'm sure they don't hear the reason why. C'est la vie! Those that know me well have told me that I don't have a fuse never mind a short one! And, I agree.....it's hard to argue with the truth! Much of the gossip around here has little to do with truth and is horribly sensationalized. Most people here have learned that I am intolerant of it and don't share the local gossip with me, which is just fine with me: I don't want to hear it. I just want to live in peace and the few close friendships I've developed are precious to me and in general, I have gained an acceptance of the gossip that circulates in a small town.

I often look back on my days of skiing with envy. I used to love to ski and I have tried to ski but it is not enjoyable at all. Each time I tried, I hired a ski instructor to come with me and explained to the instructor the challenges I face, yet, today, for me, skiing is work, work, work and I don't enjoy it. The last time I tried to ski, I skied with a group of disabled folks who were mostly amputees and I'm embarrassed to report that they all skied much better than I could and complained a whole lot less. It's as if the whole time, I'm mentally hearing my physical therapist yelling at me, "Use your ankles.....use your hips.... slow down....take it easy." I've come to realize that skiing and vertigo just don't mix and I've stopped skiing.

My head pain is mostly gone. I have a continuous minor headache and there is those times when I feel like a knitting needle is being driven through my head. Unable to work a normal 9-5 job due to the unpredictable nature of the pain and vertigo, I started my own business so that I could do something useful and that would give me a sense of reward. To my credit, I have eight "Issued" Patents in Renewable Energy.

Unable to keep up with the medical bills, I sold my home in New England when I was five months behind on the mortgage and moved to rural South Dakota where my great-grandparents had homesteaded and where I could afford to live on my military pension. It was in Lemmon, South Dakota where I met this guy at church and even though I was in a walker, he asked me out. We dated for three years and when he asked me to marry him, I thought he must be nuts but I still said yes. That was eight years ago and we have found great happiness with each other.

These days, I have good days and bad days health-wise. I am light sensitive and grateful that I no longer live in Phoenix as too much light brings on my head pain. Stress also brings on my head pain so I try to avoid that as much as possible which at times is very hard to do for this retired soldier. I am grateful for the life I have and the ability to sleep through the night. The latter being something that evaded me for decades.

Now I am making it my mission to help other military women who have experienced sexual misconduct because I don't want them struggling for twenty years to find some peace in their lives. If there is a way to help them, then I will find it. In addition, I'm making it my mission to help effect change in the way women soldiers are treated in the Canadian Forces. We are there to serve and we are NOT there to be served up. Enough is enough!

These days, I've gone back to school and I'm working on a master's degree.....in Theological Studies and I find these studies rewarding. I don't have to remember facts for a test but I do get to ready very interesting books and write essays where I am free to express my opinion.

Chapter Eighteen: Advice to Military Women

When asked if I believe that change is possible, my answer is yes, I believe it is. The quickest and most effective way to get this done is by having the help and cooperation of the Canadian Forces. I am well aware that the Department of National Defence is a big and powerful organization who I'm about to make an enemy out of. I would prefer to effect this change with DND involvement but how do I get this done when my efforts to date to be involved in the Task Force on Sexual Misconduct in the Canadian Forces have been completely ignored.

Unwilling to give up, I contacted Madame Deschamps who recently released a report on Sexual Misconduct in the Canadian Forces. Commissioned to study and report on the problem of sexual misconduct in the Canadian Forces, she was able to collect data that dispels the reports to Parliament made by the Canadian Forces brass that there is not a problem. I applaud her courage and I am impressed that she has so accurately captured the true nature of the problem. It brought me to tears to read her report. I felt like yelling, "FINALLY!" Madame Deschamps is a hero. And, when this hero replied to me and expressed support of my efforts, I knew I was on the right track.

Yet, even with her endorsement, I have continued to be ignored by the Task Force on Sexual Misconduct which confirms to me that they are ineffective and simply a CF smoke screen effort. Timing is everything and within a few months of finding my voice and applying for veteran's benefits,

Veterans Affairs   Anciens Combattants
Canada   Canada

Decision Number: 100002184189

VETERANS AFFAIRS CANADA
OFFICIAL DECISION

Name: Dawn Emily Marilyn Ottman | Date of Decision: August 25, 2015

Condition: Post Traumatic Stress Disorder
Decision: Granted

Your Claim

You relate your psychological condition to numerous experiences of sexual harassment and assaults during your military service.

Our Decision

- You have been granted a disability award for **Post Traumatic Stress Disorder**, under Section 45 of the *Canadian Forces Members and Veterans Re-establishment and Compensation Act*, Regular Force service.

Key Evidence
We have considered all of the evidence provided, including:
- Your service records.
- Medical Questionnaire: Psychiatric Conditions, dated 26 February 2015.
- Your detailed statement.

Relationship to your military service
- You served in the Regular Force as a Radio Technician and CELE Officer between 1978 and 1995.
- Your service record show some early symptoms of post traumatic stress disorder before your release.
- The submitted medical report confirms a diagnosis of post traumatic stress disorder and relates your condition to sexual abuse, assaults and harassment during your service.

Our Conclusion
- Based on the available evidence including your detailed statement, we resolve any doubt in your favor and conclude that your post traumatic stress disorder arose out of your Regular Force service.

the Veteran's Affairs Canada (VAC) notified me that I have been granted benefits based on PTSD induced by sexual misconduct during my military career.

One of the first things I did was notified the Task Force. Yet again, I was ignored. They're reaction (or lack thereof) was opposite to the reaction of the Canadian Legion who contacted me right away asking for permission to use the decision in my case for pending cases they were helping other military women with. I was told by them that the VAC had never in its history granted benefits based on PTSD induced sexual misconduct resulting from a woman soldier's military service and how that made the VAC decision in my case precedent setting.

They wanted to use the decision in my case to move forward with other cases and they were asking for my permission because they were concerned that the details of my case (if used as a reference for other VAC benefits applications) may become public knowledge. They warned me that this would be embarrassing for me and they shared with me that they didn't want to cause me additional grief. I felt warm and fuzzy. FINALLY SOMEONE FROM CANADA CARED. Of course, I said yes and my reason is that if my case helps even only one woman soldier, then it will be worth any embarrassment that it may cause me.

I refuse to feel helpless and my passion is what empowers me enough to effect change. My experience, although not unique (sadly), gives me the passion to effect change and is invaluable in its insight into what is wrong within the Canadian Forces. My perspective is broad. Having served in the Ranks and the Officer Corp, I understand the system from a NCM's perspective as well as from an officer's perspective. I love the Canadian Forces and that is why I feel the need to step out of my comfort zone and do my utmost to effect change. It has been my experience that change can occur and I have effected change in the past: I got a Base Commander to stop drinking, I changed the attitude of an abusive LCol who became a supporter of women in the military, and I also moved a General (who hated women in uniform) to approach me when he needed help.

I have asked myself, who am I to make change happen? I have been told (by the CDS himself) that I may be too close to the problem: my "been there, done that" mentality and its associated prejudices might, just might, make me prejudge and that he says, might not be a good thing. His concerns are unfounded and I wonder if his true concern is that I might make the Task Force effective! I know I can step back as that is exactly what I've been doing these past twenty years. Yes, I am passionate about this cause and the truth needs to be exposed before change can be effected, yet Madame Deschamps has already made that happen. All that is needed now, is for the Canadian Forces to step up to the plate and admit it. Otherwise, things will continue as they have and the environment for women soldiers will continue to be hostile and dangerous from "friendly fire!"

The military brass talks about the pool of resources it will cost to address this problem yet it appears to me that they have zero insight into how sexual misconduct presently affects that very same pool of resources. My experience tells its own tale.

When I was working at Motorola, I was able to devote 100% of my energy to the job because there was no sexual misconduct to deal with…none! I became a more effective employee and as proof I was promoted multiple times, received bonuses for a job well done and paid raises as well. When women workers/soldiers are dealing with sexual misconduct, it is impossible to deliver 100% of their energy to military goals/demands and that is why I am confident that we will have a more effective armed forces once we change our attitudes and rid the Canadian Forces of this cancer.

Personally, I continue to struggle with memories from my 20 year military career in the Canadian Forces. I have PTSD (Post Traumatic Stress Disorder), diagnosed while I was in uniform and I was pretty messed up then but I am doing better now. Back then, I didn't know that PTSD is cyclic and that it would return time and again. Sometimes, it is triggered and sometimes I have no idea why it returned. I applaud the Legion for supporting the Veteran's Transition Program (VTP). The VTP helps veteran's struggling with PTSD. Most Canadian Legions have information about VTN (Veteran's Transition Network) programs as they are offered nationwide. Your legion does not need to approve you attending. So contact the VTN (www.vtncanada.org) and trust that they will help you.

I was invited back to Canada to attend a Veteran's Transition Program (VTP) after posting on a blog that a planned 6 year study of PTSD and the associated suicide rate of soldiers and ex-soldiers kept climbing. I said that the study was for academic's ears and politician's agendas and would most likely never help a single soldier. I said that in my career, there had been studies on sexual harassment that were ineffective and I didn't have any faith that this study will be any different but I felt certain that within the six years to complete the study, many more soldiers would take their lives. I was angry and I blasted off my opinion in the blog.

I was surprised to hear from the Director of the VAC who read my blog and blogged back and that's how I heard of the VTN. He suggested that I may have anger issues and the VTN might be able to help me. Always looking for something that might help me sleep better at night, I checked into it and then signed on to attend a VTP. I am so grateful to him for seeing through the fog of my anger to the underlying PTSD. Over the last few years, I've become less angry. I'm not allowed to tell you much about what happened at my VTP as I respect the confidence of the people involved but know that I have made new friends and even gained a hero in the process.

I'm also grateful for EMDR which is a treatment I started a few years ago. Understand that I didn't get mentally unwell from a single incident of sexual misconduct but the cumulative effect messed me up badly. Therefore, not a single method of treatment can, or has, fixed me. EMDR helped me to sort out my felling. When it was first proposed to me as a treatment option, I misunderstood its effect: I though it deleted the whole memory of an event but EMDR treatments don't delete the memory of an event.....instead, they delete the emotional response to a memory.

Think of it like this: your Aunt Bertha* comes to the family picnic and get so drunk that she gets her ugly fat butt up on a picnic table and does a strip tease in front of everyone in your family and a few people in the park....including the children. Now you are so angry with her you won't even talk to her. Without EMDR, you remain angry with her but with EMDR, you remember what she did but you are no longer angry.....still, Aunt Bertha doesn't get an invitation to next year's family picnic!

I attended a VTP after I'd started EMDR treatments. Still, I couldn't attend a cooed one as even seeing a cop in uniform gave me a fear response. I already have trust issues and I just don't trust anyone in uniform and military uniforms are horrible triggers for me. I knew I would be unable to attend a VTP where military men were present. There would be too many triggers for me and I would clam up. I felt sure the VTP would be ineffective as I would simply be too activated. A woman's only VTP was established the following years (2014) and I able to attend and I am very grateful for it. Where the EMDR treatments gave me the ability to speak up at the VTP, I sometimes felt I was over the top with displaced anger.

For the VTP, I travelled from my South Dakota home to British Columbia for four days three different times. The VTP has helped me deal with some of my military sexual misconduct memories and combined with my ongoing EMDR treatments, I am now capable of writing about these memories and that's exactly what I am doing. The program was perfect for me!

The VTP helped me a great deal. So, here is a lesson for those dealing with PTSD: sometimes the solution lies in multiple treatment methods. You didn't get easily screwed up and therefore the solution for you will probably also be multifaceted. Sometimes, I have to shake myself to realize that this is real. It is not perfect, but then neither am I. I used to keep a diary but stopped doing that when things got tough (some 20+ years ago). I am writing my story because I feel a strong sense of duty to do so. Yet it is not easy and sometimes I need to stop, step back, and take care of me. Still, I know that I will return to my writing once I get back from my sabbatical of healing.

Recently, I checked with some friends about how the Task Force on Sexual Misconduct was doing and the feedback I got was that it is useless. In one case, the word used to describe it was "pathetic." That broke my heart and I had hoped it would be real. The definition of insanity is when someone keeps doing the same thing expecting a different outcome. I must be insane! Again, I have let myself fall into the hope that something is being done. Told that not a single woman soldier has been helped, by this supposed task force, and that their efforts are badly organized, I am heartbroken once again. I want them to succeed but I wonder if military women are not coming forward much as I did not back in 1994 when the CF developed a Sexual Harassment Coordinator. Back then, I hoped this was going to work, but it didn't. In fact, I was told to avoid going to this coordinator unless I wanted my CO to hear about it.

The trust issue is paramount with military women. We have learned how to distrust the system which has discounted our experiences and blamed us. I have prayed that this Task Force on Sexual Misconduct in the CF would help women soldiers deal with sexual harassment and rape in the military, but from what I hear, it is not doing that. So, I've written this book and I do have some nuggets of advice. I do not know everything.....I am sharing my story to let other service women know that they are not alone as I once felt. I've been there, done that and I didn't know who to turn to so I ran. I ran for years that turned into decades and although this has been tough to write about, I can deal with it now and I feel a sense of duty to help other service women.

The Canadian Forces' past methods of dealing with sexual misconduct and especially rape within their organization is not acceptable. Why is rape illegal on Civie Street but acceptable in the military? The military brass says it is not, but evidence has shown that they don't walk the talk and I've had enough. I now feel strong enough to do something about this issue and I will no longer keep quiet to protect the reputation of the Canadian Forces. Keeping quiet has not helped and sadly, mine was not an isolated incident.

Last year I learned of a Canadian Forces woman soldier returned from Afghanistan because she had the courage to report being raped by one of her fellow soldiers. She reported this incident to her Commanding Officer. The outcome for her was bad: she was declared a "problem" and returned to Canada. Her rapist was left to continue serving in Afghanistan. I'm not sure if my story will help her, but it is time for the Canadian Forces and the Department of National Defence to act differently.

Our very own head of the Canadian Forces, the Chief of Defence Staff was reported as having said in Parliament, something to the effect of our CF military men are biologically predisposed to rape and our military women are handy! Is it no wonder that we military women are offended? Every Canadian should be offended! These women are every Canadian's sister, mother, wife, daughter, aunt, or cousin!

While this was happening in Canada, across the world, in another commonwealth country (Australia) the General in charge of the Army there, General Morrison, spoke out against the mistreatment of his military women. He publicly went on record as an advocate of women in uniform, telling the whole world that the Australian Army has a strong code of conduct and he declared that if a soldier in his army felt unable to accept that set of morals and could not adhere to the standards of ethical behaviour of their Army, then he should, "GET OUT!"

I am so impressed by General Morrison. I wanted to hug him. I find myself cheering and wishing that we had a hero like that in the Canadian Forces. Yet we do not. In the Canadian Forces, even after Madame Deschamps' report as evidence in front of them, our military brass publicly show themselves as unwilling to make this much needed change. They are reviewing what other militaries have done and looking for their easiest way out of this mess. I find them unwilling to admit that there is a problem and I absolutely hate it when they downplay any report that declares that there is a serious problem (such as Madame Deschamps Report on Sexual Misconduct in the Canadian Forces). Ironically, their behaviour is the opposite of what we were taught about military ethics: where we, as soldiers, are required to step up to the plate and admit fault where fault exists and in this way correct a problem. At Royal Military College, in our Military Leadership & Management courses (which each Cadet has to do four years of study in), we were marinated in the college logo of Truth, Duty, Valour (TDV) and what that is supposed to mean. I would like to see the Canadian Forces brass walk the talk and I am tired of lip service. What is needed is a complete change in attitude across the whole of the Canadian Forces.

To date, nothing has changed. Just a few weeks ago, I checked the feedback on the RMC Ex-Cadet website regarding an unfortunate event that took place at RMC. A civilian counsellor was brought in to teach the Cadets about sexual harassment then claimed to have been sexually harassed herself while she was at the college. Now, I don't claim to know the details of the case or even if her claim was valid (although I have a strong suspicion that it was), but what I didn't find surprising and even expected were the responses. On RMC's website for ex-cadets, there were many negative comments about her and it was business as usual and she was seen to be the problem....TYPICAL!

Given that, here's some advice from me based on my experience and present understanding of our situation. As you read these little nuggets of advice, please understand that I get it; dealing with sexual misconduct is tough. What I want you to keep in mind is that you are tough as well. You may not like the truth of my nuggets below, but they are here for you my sister soldiers:

Advice Nugget 1: Tell Someone You Trust
You can't handle it by yourself. Getting another's perspective is important. Are you being sexually harassed or is it something more serious such as sexual assault.

Advice Nugget 2: Get Professional Help
I have found getting the help of those trained to provide psychological help gives me a sense of peace. You will find them to be unbiased and like it did me, it may help you to discover what all those mixed up feelings are about. It is confusing to be treated like less of a person than you truly are.

Advice Nugget 3: Adopt Yourself
I've found it helpful to imagine whatever is happening is happening to someone else instead of me. And, then I decide what to advise that imaginary person to do or what I would do to "fix" the situation for that person. That person is you! You are valuable and as important as the imaginary friend you want so desperately to help.

Advice Nugget 4: Don't go to your boss or your Commanding Officer.
I've told you how I did not come forward and how this has harmed me psychologically but I've also told you why and the same situation still exists today....so be wary. Keep in mind that although this little nugget of advice may go against what you wish were the circumstances today, I advise it because I believe that at this point in time, the Canadian Forces is not ready for you to come forward.

As recently as September, 2015, I've learned that the efforts of the Task Force on Sexual Misconduct are uncoordinated and pitiful and they have not helped even one victim. Given this, I believe you will not be helped and that's why I feel confident in telling you this, as sad as I am at the truth of it. With my whole heart, I wish this was not the case but I would be remiss to advise you otherwise. There is a very good chance that you will be perceived as "the problem" and coming forward to your boss or Commanding Officer could very well destroy your military career.

Instead, go outside the Canadian Forces. Go to a private psychologist. Yes, it will cost you, but it will be worth it....this is your health that is at risk. If you have a hard time with this decision, know that I did too and only when I started to think of it as a cancer and that the Canadian Forces won't pay for it, was I able to get help. If you have been a victim of rape, please go to the nearest rape/crises center. There's none in the military yet although I will work towards changing that. For now, head to a civilian center. Do not be afraid. It has been my experience that they can be trusted and they will keep your confidence. It took me a long time to get this help and when I did, I'd wished I had years earlier. Know that they can and will help you.

Advice Nugget 5: Don't shut down on people.
This one is easier said than done. It is hard to trust and fear causes anger. Controlling both of these may seem impossible when you get activated. But, once you are feeling safe, reach out. Although it is true that some people will disappoint you, others will step forward and hug you and do their best to keep you safe. It is a difficult conversation to have with someone but I've mostly found love and understanding. Some have even told me of their experience with rape when they had never spoken of it before. You will find that you are not alone so please give it a try and my prayers are with you in the hope that you find comfort and help.

Chapter Nineteen: A Non-Profit to Help Canadian Military Women (CanMW)

I needed to do something so I decided to do something big. So, I've started a non-Profit in Canada that will help Canadian Military Women. It has been registered in British Columbia and is call the **CanMW Support Association** and its purpose is as follows:

a. To help and support Canadian Forces women in crises as a result of sexual misconduct including sexual discrimination, sexual harassment, sexual assault, and rape.

b. To address the following TWO main areas of deficiency in the Canadian Forces with respect to sexual misconduct:

i) VICTIM ADVOCACY - This will be healing centered and could include face-to-face therapy, group therapy, medical advice, and legal advice.

ii) VICTIM PREVENTION - This will be education based.

c. To provide quality services to Canadian Forces women whose lives have been affected by sexual misconduct and education geared towards the prevention of sexual misconduct within the Canadian Forces."

d. To establish a rape-crises center for Canadian Forces women.

e. To collect statistics on sexual misconduct within the Canadian Forces.

f. To provide education to Commanding Officers on how to handle reported cases of sexual misconduct.

g. To provide support to Canadian Forces Padres in the handling of victims.

h. To provide leadership within the Department of National Defence that results in a coordinated and victim-centered response to cases of sexual misconduct within the Canadian Forces."

Acknowledgements

A special thank you to all those who have reviewed my book for me and made it more readable. In addition, a special heartfelt thank you goes out to Madame Deschamps for her courage in accurately exposing the Canadian Force's sexual misconduct towards their women soldiers.

Heroes: GI Joe (Colonel J. Stevens), Mike Proctor, Celine Herieux-Payette, Mike Dadson, Major F. Pinkney

Reviewers: Jacquie, Lori, Karen

Editor:

APPENDIX A: Canadian Forces Rank Structure

NCM Ranks

JUNIOR NCMs
Master-Corporal (MCpl)
Corporal (Cpl)
Private (Pte)

SENIOR NCMS
Chief Warrant Officer (CWO)
Master Warrant Officer (MWO)
Warrant Officer (WO)
Sergeant (Sgt)

Officer Ranks

Officer Cadet (OCdt)

JUNIOR OFFICERS
Captain (Capt)
Lieutenant (Lt)
2nd Lieutenant (2Lt)

SENIOR OFFICERS
Colonel (Col)
Lieutenant Colonel (LCol)
Major (Maj)

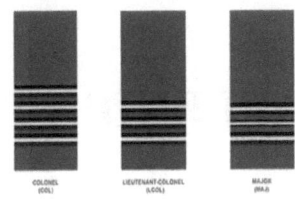

THE GENERALS
General General (Gen)
Lieutenant General (LGen)
Major General (MGen)
Brigadier General (BGen)

APPENDIX B: Acronym & Word List

AC&W	Air Control & Warning
Anik E	Communications Satellite launched by Telesat Canada
AOCS	Attitude & Orbit Control Subsystem
C&E Branch	Communications & Electronics Branch
CELE	Communications and ELectrical Engineering
CF	Canadian Forces
CFB	Canadian Forces Base
CFS	Canadian Forces Station
CFSCE	Canadian Forces School of Communications & Electronics
CSA	Canadian Space Agency
DEEM	Directorate of Electronics & Engineering Maintenance
DND	Department of National Defence
DS	Directing Staff (an A Sqn Instructor)
EMDR	Eye Movement Desensitization and Reprocessing
Epar	Rape spelt backwards
FOSC	Forces Ottawa Ski Club
FRP	Force Reduction Plan
IR	Infra-Red
JAG	Judge Advocate General
LCWB	Last Class With Balls
NCM	Non-Commission Member
NDHQ	National Defence Headquarters

Panic Attack	Panic attacks are periods of intense fear. A sudden onset accompanied by heart palpitations, dizziness, shortness of breath, or feelings of unreality. Panic attacks usually begin abruptly and may reach a peak within 10 to 20 minutes but the effects may continue for hours.
PMQ	Personnel Married Quarters - houses on base for military personnel with families.
POET	Performance Orientated Electronics Training
PTSD	Post-Traumatic Stress Disorder
Rad	Radio
RCC	Rape Crises Center
Rdr	Radar
RMC	Royal Military College
SATCOM	Satellite Communications
SGT	Satellite Ground Terminal
Sqn	Squadron
TD	Temporary Duty (travel assignments)
Tech	Technician
TQ	Training Qualification
Trg	Training
USPTO	United States Patent and Trademark Office
UTPM	University Training Plan Men
UV	Ultra-Violet
VAC	Veteran's Affairs Canada
VTN	Veteran's Transition Network
VTP	Veteran's Transition Program
WCT	The West Coast Trail (on Vancouver Island)